SEARCH AFTER METHOD

Methodology and History in Anthropology

Series Editors:
David Parkin, Fellow of All Souls College, University of Oxford
David Gellner, Fellow of All Souls College, University of Oxford
Nayanika Mathur, Fellow of Wolfson College, University of Oxford

Recent volumes:

Volume 40
Search After Method: Sensing, Moving, and Imagining in Anthropological Fieldwork
Edited by Julie Laplante, Ari Gandsman, and Willow Scobie

Volume 39
After Society: Anthropological Trajectories out of Oxford
Edited by João Pina-Cabral and Glenn Bowman

Volume 38
Total Atheism: Secular Activism and Politics of Difference in South India
Stefan Binder

Volume 37
Crossing Histories and Ethnographies: Following Colonial Historicities in Timor-Leste
Edited by Ricardo Roque and Elizabeth G. Traube

Volume 36
Engaging Evil: A Moral Anthropology
Edited by William C. Olsen and Thomas J. Csordas

Volume 35
Medicinal Rule: A Historical Anthropology of Kingship in East and Central Africa
Koen Stroeken

Volume 34
Who Are "We?" Reimagining Alterity and Affinity in Anthropology
Edited by Liana Chua and Nayanika Mathur

Volume 33
Expeditionary Anthropology: Teamwork, Travel and the "Science of Man"
Edited by Martin Thomas and Amanda Harris

Volume 32
Returning Life: Language, Life Force and History in Kilimanjaro
Knut Christian Myhre

Volume 31
The Ethics of Knowledge Creation: Transactions, Relations, and Persons
Edited by Lisette Josephides and Anne Sigfrid Grønseth

For a full volume listing, please see the series page on our website:
http://berghahnbooks.com/series/methodology-and-history-in-anthropology

SEARCH AFTER METHOD

Sensing, Moving, and Imagining in Anthropological Fieldwork

Edited by
Julie Laplante, Ari Gandsman, and Willow Scobie

berghahn
NEW YORK • OXFORD
www.berghahnbooks.com

First published in 2020 by

Berghahn Books

www.berghahnbooks.com

Library of Congress Cataloging-in-Publication Data

Names: Laplante, Julie, editor. | Gandsman, Ari, editor. | Scobie, Willow, editor.
Title: Search after method : sensing, moving, and imagining in anthropological fieldwork / edited by Julie Laplante, Ari Gandsman, and Willow Scobie.
Description: First edition. | New York : Berghahn Books, 2020. | Series: Methodology & history in anthropology; vol 40 | Includes bibliographical references and index.
Identifiers: LCCN 2020017991 (print) | LCCN 2020017992 (ebook) | ISBN 9781789208832 (hardback) | ISBN 9781789209389 (paperback) | ISBN 9781789208849 (ebook)
Subjects: LCSH: Anthropology—Fieldwork. | Ethnology—Fieldwork.
Classification: LCC GN34.3.F53 S425 2020 (print) | LCC GN34.3.F53 (ebook) | DDC 301.072/3—dc23
LC record available at https://lccn.loc.gov/2020017991
LC ebook record available at https://lccn.loc.gov/2020017992

British Library Cataloguing in Publication Data

A catalogue record for this book is available from the British Library

ISBN 978-1-78920-883-2 hardback
ISBN 978-1-78920-938-9 paperback
ISBN 978-1-78920-884-9 ebook

To Angela

CONTENTS

FIGURES

FOREWORD

Tim Ingold

Can there be research after method? The two words, "method" and "research," seem so closely implicated that the idea of one without the other is barely conceivable. Perhaps, at root, they even mean the same thing. If method is "the way beyond" (a contraction from classical Greek *meta*, meaning "beyond," and *hodos*, meaning "way"), research is the act of "searching again," a second search that doubles up on a quest previously enacted. Like repeatedly walking the same path, every search is an original movement that invites a double in its turn. Thus, method and research combine into the form of a riddle: what continually overtakes itself, in a movement that retraces ground already traveled while heading into the unknown? The answer, of course, is life. Literally, then, research is a method of leading life. As such, it is participatory, observant, attentive, generous, and open-ended. In the volume you hold in your hands, Julie Laplante and her colleagues show us how the conduct of research, as a life practice, can also be a practice of study. This is a practice that goes along with other lives, listening to them, waiting upon them, learning from them, and responding in kind. The name for this life study, in the contributions assembled here, is "anthropology."

"After method?" The title is craftily ambiguous. Is method in front of you or behind, something you seek, or something you have already overtaken? Perhaps it is both at once, for at the limits of conceptualization, where things are not yet or no longer quite within our grasp, past and future, memory and imagination tend to fuse. Method, in this regard, resembles habit. Of habits, too, we can ask: are they before us or behind? Do we form habits or do habits form us? And again, the answer entails a doubling up by which, in fashioning the future, we continually loop back to resume the custom of the past. Moved by our own movement, we become whom we were, having been whom we become. In a word, we *re-search*. Who, then, is researching whom? Perhaps researchers are like detectives, pitting their wits against criminal minds always one step ahead in the game. "I have my methods," explained Sherlock Holmes to the trusty Watson, but the arch-villain Moriarty had his methods too. One party's methods are, for the other, clues to follow. Methods, in other words, study each other. They are both ways of study and ways studied, and research lies in their entwining.

There is no a priori reason, however, why this entwining should be limited to human lifeways. In a more-than-human world, the *anthropos* in "anthropology" sounds increasingly anachronistic. Animals of all sorts, as well as plants and fungi, have their habits, which attend precisely to the habits of others. They, too, search and search again in the continuation of their lives. They follow their methods, studying others that follow theirs. There is sensing, movement, and imagination in the cat's study of the mouse, laced with predatory intent, but equally so in the mouse's study of the cat, in crafting its tactics of evasion. Plants, too, are not only deeply attentive to the movements of the sun and winds, and of creatures that come to feed or to pollinate; they also communicate their experience among themselves. And in a research grant application addressed to peer reviewers of its kind, an apocryphal fungus is alleged to have proposed the following: "I shall employ the technique of *mycelial proliferation* to establish a mesh of rhizomatic affiliations in my selected research site, and will disseminate my results using established mechanisms of *spore discharge*." No doubt the applicant's fungal reviewers doffed their caps in approval; what their colleague was describing, after all, was no more, and no less, than what every fungus does.

In this latter example, allegorical though it may be, the fungi have the last laugh. For the joke is on us humans—or at least, on those of us with academic pretensions—in holding up to ridicule our penchant for dressing up a habitual way of living in the garb of professional expertise. This is what fungi would say if they spoke as we do. We speak like this when methods are appropriated as insignia of professional qualification, ways of leading life as steps to building a career. In command of the techniques of mycelial proliferation and spore discharge, our fungus is already on his way to the top! And he is out not to learn from his fellow fungi but, through his mycelial affiliations, to gather data on them. We humans, of course, can spread our net far and wide, as fungi can. But to describe this, in the "methods" section of a research proposal, as the selection of interviewees by a "snowball technique," is no less preposterous. What drives us thus, to varnish method with fake objectivity? Why can we not simply admit that by engaging with people we happen to come across—maybe even with animals, plants, and fungi—we might actually learn from them?

The reasons lie in the subordination of research and its methods to the demands of the global knowledge industry. With this industrial model, research is not about going along with a world in formation, but about dredging the precipitate of a world already formed. It is about the mining of raw material, in the form of data, and its processing, through purification and analysis, into marketable knowledge products, otherwise known as "findings." With research on human subjects, data-mining entails methods of elicitation. The rules are as follows: do not listen to what people say, or take it at face value. Never be swayed by it. Always regard it as the outward expression of something deeper—of beliefs, attitudes, states of mind, or culturally shaped dispositions. In other words, treat what people say as ethnographic evidence, for what it says about them. By all means offer the hand of friendship to your so-called informants, but be sure to conceal your real intentions, which are to extract what information you can. Oh, and before you do, remember to have them sign a consent form, to ensure it is all ethically above board. Dissimulation and hypocrisy are fine so long as your interlocutors have unwittingly agreed to be taken in by them!

It is not uncommon to find ourselves having to present our research in this vein, as schemes for the production of "anthropological knowledge." It is a condition of funding. Yet in our hearts, we know it is a sham. We know, for example, that our most treasured method, of participant observation, is far from a systematic means of data collection, but rather a way of improvising a form of life through observing others who, at the same time, are showing us how to observe. As many chapters of this book will illustrate, it is a way littered with failures, which are always more instructive than success. You learn nothing from getting things right. We know, too, that fieldnotes are not the repositories of data we pretend them to be, in order to justify their collection to external agencies, but reminiscences set down in such detail and density that to read them, often years later, allows us to loop back and reflect on past moments as if they were underway in the here and now. Indeed, it is thanks to our fieldnotes that we can undertake the "second search" that research demands. We know all this, and yet continue to connive—and survive—in a discursive climate best described as one of tolerated mendacity.

"After Method" is a plea to put an end to this mendacity. It is time to expose the pretense that research in anthropology is about the extraction, collection, and analysis of data. It is not. It is about opening up to things and joining with the movements of their formation. It is about unblocking passages rather than fabricating conclusions, exploring the possibilities of being rather than foreclosing them. More fundamentally, it is a quest for truth. This is not some kind of truth that we can ever finally master. Wherever we may be, it is always beyond the limits of our present powers of conceptualization. That is why we need "a way beyond," literally a *method*, to seek it. But this is not a technique to be applied. To get back on track we need to put behind us, once and for all, the idea of method as an "off the shelf" instrument of data handling, just as we must finally relinquish the definition of research as the production of new knowledge. In the market model of knowledge production, only what is new sells. In life, however, novelty is not the point. What matters is that we should honor the truth of things. This book brings us nearer to doing so.

Tim Ingold
Aberdeen, July 2019

Tim Ingold is Professor Emeritus of Social Anthropology at the University of Aberdeen. He has carried out fieldwork among Saami and Finnish people in Lapland, and has written on environment, technology, and social organization in the circumpolar North, on animals in human society, and on human ecology and evolutionary theory. His more recent work explores environmental perception and skilled practice. Ingold's current interests lie on the interface between anthropology, archaeology, art, and architecture. His recent books include *The Perception of the Environment* (2000), *Lines* (2007), *Being Alive* (2011), *Making* (2013), *The Life of Lines* (2015), *Anthropology and/as Education* (2018), and *Anthropology: Why It Matters* (2018).

ACKNOWLEDGMENTS

Willow Scobie and I co-organized an inaugural event of the first "green building" on the campus of the University of Ottawa in April 2013 and invited Tim Ingold as the keynote speaker. It was truly amazing to feel students' excitement at the prospect of his speech *Dreaming of Dragons: On the Imagination of Real Life*. Meant as a single evening event, it turned into three days of *Living Research*, as baptized by Nicolas Rasiulis. Upon describing Tim's work, I remember hearing Nicolas whispering in my ear "it's like breath of fresh air!" The event involved reading Tim's work upstream as part of the graduate program in anthropology, and it turned into a vibrant student event, including a *nuit blanche* bringing the building to life with research materials, canoes, sound clouds, and scents of fieldwork. It also involved the launch of Ingold's book *Making* (2013), a Round Table discussion implicating many of our colleagues, and numerous students contributing to this volume. Following his keynote lecture, I asked if we should teach "methods" as a separate step in anthropology, to which he amusingly said "no." The intensity and vibrancy of this event continued to resonate in our hallways, with two other subsequent *Living Research* days occurring in 2014 and 2015. It is however this question of the dissolution of methods that lingered and has taken a life of its own now in the shape of this manuscript. We thank Tim Ingold for opening this route, as well as for honoring us with a Foreword. I thank all the other contributors of the book, many who have been involved in this project since its inception, for their genuine contributions showing how fieldwork is in continuous negotiation. From teaching fieldwork to undergraduate students for seven years exploring this opening, I thank them both for their resilience, as it can be disorienting, and for their enthusiasm in taking it upon themselves to do really rich and meaningful research. Finally, I thank Elisabeth Hsu for her suggestion to submit the manuscript to this wonderful *Methodology and History in Anthropology* Series at Berghahn Books. I also thank the editors David Parkin, David Gellner, and Nayanika Mathur, publisher and editor-in-chief Marion Berghahn, as well as anonymous peer reviewers for trusting, even pushing further, our perhaps daring although modest potential contribution to anthropology. I would also like to acknowledge the entire Berghahn production team for their diligence in preparing the manuscript amidst the turbulences of the COVID-19 pandemic. As such our call for doing anthropological research corresponding with how the world is unfolding in efforts to compose foreseeable futures might resonate.

INTRODUCTION

LINES OF FLIGHT

Julie Laplante, Willow Scobie, and Ari Gandsman

> Methods are the guarantors of objectivity, put in place to ensure that research results should not be contaminated by too close or affective an involvement of researchers with those they study. For anthropology, however, such involvement is of the essence.
>
> —Tim Ingold, *Anthropology*

As the opening quote indicates, methods are inherently paradoxical to the contemporary practice of anthropology. Nonetheless, the inherent contradictions of methods that distance and objectify even as anthropology rejected this conception of their field of study continue to haunt the discipline. Anthropology departments replicate stock approaches to teaching found in other disciplines, offering discrete *Methods* courses that are taught separately from "theory." Graduate student training is comparable to other disciplines and remains unchanged from previous decades in which a separate "methods" section is integral to any thesis or grant proposal or academic article. While anthropologists have moved away from seeing their work as a process of sorting or ordering according to codes, structural grids, or templates for revealing underlying structures, *Methods* continue to carry the baggage of this legacy. They direct us to think about our research in terms of applying or discovering a hidden order. The kind of anthropology that *Methods* produces may no longer be viable for most anthropologists, but *Methods* are still very much alive and with us. The purpose of this volume, therefore, is to help reorient the process of anthropological inquiry away from *Methods* and toward engagement with open-ended, creative ways of co-responding with the world.

Research approaches premised on the idea of "guarantors of objectivity" come from a reified idea of method. Even where objectivity is not presumed to be a relevant factor, *Methods* are understood to be systematic procedures that predetermine a research journey. *Methods* become prescriptive, a worrisome trend in ethnography, in particular when taken up by other disciplines. Where scholars undertake "ethnography" as though it is a matter of procedure, they are proceeding as though ethnography and anthropology are two separate moments in research (Ingold 2014, 2017): one of extracting data from the world in the former while analyzing it in the latter. This distinction posits ethnography as anthropological method—as adopted by other disciplines, presented in qualitative methods texts/courses, as an approach to interviewing, and so on. Although some scholars propose replacing ethnography with either "praxiography" (Mol 2002) or "phenomenography" (Piette 2011), the problem of *Methods* persists under new etiquettes.

Rather than shifting the terminology, this volume engages with the possibilities that anthropology opens up by following the distinction proposed by Tim Ingold (2014, 2017): ethnography seeks to document the world by reflection backward, while anthropology moves forward in order to learn from the world to know it. It is important to note that the distinction outlined here is not intended to be teleological—anthropologists may refer to "ethnography" or the qualifier "ethnographic" (as is the case in some of the chapters in this volume) without invoking a procedural aspect of the discipline. Instead, the emphasis is on using an approach to anthropology that moves forward and collapses the distinction between method and theory.

An example of this tradition can be found in Maurice Merleau-Ponty's ([1945] 2002) phenomenology of perception. Merleau-Ponty invites us to follow in the steps of a world in the process of being made rather than as something to document, classify, typologize, and compare; the level of abstraction given to the thinking mind as preceding action is dissolved to become a single interlacing of "eye and mind" (Merleau-Ponty 1964). Ingold further leads us to understand knowledge—and culture—as the ability to engage in the world in a way that is always in a process of renewal. Knowledge thus becomes not the result of measurable data analysis subject to replication, rather it is an ability to engage effectively within these processes; understood as "knowing from the inside" (Ingold 2013)—an idea also alluded to by the great poet but lesser known botanist Johann Wolfgang von Goethe ([1791] 2009) who describes a form of delicate empiricism. Research appears in a looping movement—one that is generative, relational, temporal, and continuously improvised (Ingold and Hallam 2007), in which we learn from becoming human and more-than-human in skilled ways, yet we also move beyond what is currently imagined or imaginable.

The movements inherent in the process of doing anthropology are also reminiscent of Gilles Deleuze and Félix Guattari's (1987) concept of lines of flight. Lines of flight are the third of three types of lines: the first is a solid molar line of hard segmentarity, the second a soft molecular line slightly bending the first yet easily returning to it, and the third is the line of flight. Translated from the French word *fuite*, it refers not only to escape, elude, or flee from others but also to let something flow, leak, disappear in the distance, and to ward off hardened standards. Lines of flight are creative becomings, bringing new levels of complexity by virtue of new knowledge or meaning. The three lines continuously intermingle, offering endless vital lines to draw and to draw from, as well as to embark on: "if the line of flight is like a train in motion, it is because one jumps linearly on it" (Deleuze and Guattari 1987: 198).

In this volume, the authors (both graduate students and professors alike—some rendering their first fieldwork experience while others reflect on as much as fifty years of research) offer multiple lines readers can pull, bend, or take by the middle in order to trace new ways forward. In *Search after Method*, we thus activate a sense of research that emerges beneath, during, or after a journey; it calls attention to letting the journey occur before we close in on it, even leaving the way open as elements continue to emerge through recording, editing (see also Boudreault-Fournier 2017), writing, and eventually to reading, if we have succeeded in breathing life into text. Stretching an understanding of fieldwork and writing as similarly lively processes, the contributions in this collection bring particular attention to these aspects of anthropology, as they are paradoxically the most important and least often addressed (Taussig 2015: 1–2).

Anthropology is a vibrant science in continuous flux and transformation as it connects to, delves into, and moves between human and nonhuman worlds. Its reliance on lived experiences "to know" remains relatively stable, even as the epistemological, phenomenological, and ontological grounds of what constitutes knowledge and how we know what we know has multiplied in the last few decades. Drawing insights from both classical and more recent cutting-edge propositions in anthropology, the chapters in this volume describe variously the processes of research, of being in the middle of things, of feeling unsettled, or balancing on the point of becoming something else: all common threads through the proceeding contributions.

Echoes

In *Decolonizing Methodologies*, Linda Tuhiwai Smith invokes a sense of method or methodology as process ([1999] 2008: 128-9). Along this line, Athena McLean and Annette Leibing's *The Shadow Side of Fieldwork* (2007) sheds light on some of the opacity in-between life and anthropological research, doing so throughout the situated studies. In their *Ethnographic Fieldwork: An Anthropological Reader*, Antonius Robben and Jeffrey Sluka (2012) also explicitly express what it feels like to do research through situated studies rather than discuss research techniques per se. Sarah Pink's *Doing Sensory Ethnography* (2015) pries open some of the boundaries of methodological dictates across the disciplines, for instance by pushing beyond an anthropology of the senses (which has fallen into an agenda of making maps and orchestrations of the senses by taking the cultural model as a starting point) toward exploring through more sensorial ways of doing research. Pursuing this idea, *A Different Kind of Ethnography: Imaginative Practices and Creative Methods* edited by Denielle Elliott and Dara Culhane (2017) similarly points toward co-creative, artistic, and collaborative approaches in anthropology. The latter two works respectively qualify "ethnography" as sensorial and imaginative, and as such do not fully problematize the critique of "ethnography" understood as a method preceding anthropology, even explicitly aiming to foster "ethnographic methodologies" (Elliott and Culhane 2017: 3). Both works also sustain a claim of "representation"—of either multisensory experiences, situations, or places—from which this volume distances itself. While our book differs on these last two points, we move in a similar direction toward ways of doing anthropology as an improvisatory joining in with formative processes.

Within the anthropological classic texts, there are elements of approaches with which contemporary anthropologists may still contend. Bronislaw Malinowski's famous work *Argonauts of the Western Pacific* (1922), for instance, served to systematize methods for fieldwork in anthropology for generations that followed. Franz Boas's *Ethnology of the Kwakiutl* (1921) meant to salvage a culture, rather paradoxically partook in depleting it of life: first by presenting it as something that was already dissolving, and second by turning it into data. Claude Lévi-Strauss's *La pensée sauvage* (The savage mind), stresses at length that there are two distinct modes of scientific thought. "These are certainly not a function of different states of development of the human mind but rather of two strategic levels at which nature is accessible to scientific enquiry: one roughly adapted to that of perception and the imagination: the other at a remove from it" ([1962] 1966: 15). That is to say that making sense of the world can "be arrived at by two different routes, one very close to, and the other more remote from, sensible intuition" (Lévi-Strauss [1962] 1966: 15). While all three of these anthropologists pursued a remote route of knowledge as a result of their absence or distance in these studies, there is also evidence that they relied on (sensible) intuition. Sensible intuition, at least in Henri Bergson's version of intuition as a relaxation of intelligence, is one that is steeped in duration (lived time) (in During 2008: 399–400).

Further, Marcel Mauss's (1923–24) oceanic metaphor, as highlighted by Tim Ingold (2015: 11), infers that we inhabit a fluid reality in continuous motion and through which we interweave in an ever-extending meshwork. Relatedly, Gregory Bateson merges scientific with artistic methods to bring attention to "tone" in cultural life ([1936] 1958: 2). Furthermore, it is only after surrendering to the context, which Bateson rightfully states should be the first step in all anthropological study, that it must be decided which tool, concept, or kind of analysis is relevant. He argued that concepts (i.e., ethos) that emerged in-between a study with the Iatmul and himself "offers no proof that it can be useful in other hands or for the analysis of other cultures" (Bateson 1972: 107). In his research in Bali emerged a new notion of schismogenesis, since they rather privilege interactions through a continuing plateau of intensity, by continual non-progressive change. This required adjusting attention to very different dimensions; in this case toward balance and motion to maintain this balance. As such neither "method" nor "theory" is necessarily transposable across contexts, both needing to adjust and emerge through, along, and from them as ways of composing and improvising affective worlds.

As for concepts, "method" can be an afterthought or a process abstracted after-the-fact, in this way maximizing attention to what is going on in everyday life during research. Gregory Bateson and Margaret Mead's (1942) pioneering work in visual anthropology explained that their anthropological research was "not about Balinese or Javanese 'custom,' yet more directly about the way in which they, as living persons, moving, standing, eating, sleeping, dancing, and going into trance, embody that abstraction which (after we have abstracted it) we technically call culture" (Bateson and Mead 1942: xii). As with "culture," "method" is not a beginning point, yet something we technically call that after we have abstracted it from the way we found to correspond within living contexts. As such, practices may point to a realm beyond the reach of method such as Jeanne Favret-Saada's (1977) "getting caught" or to become affected and to affect, as discussed at length by Bernhard Leistle in the closing chapter of this volume.

More recently, John Law's (2004) *After Method: Mess in Social Science Research* points to the elusive, ephemeral, and fluid realities that mostly escape current research methods. He thus suggests that we need "to live more in and through slow method, or vulnerable method, or quiet method. Multiple method. Modest method. Uncertain method. Diverse method" (2004: 11). Law hopes to see these versions of method grow in and beyond the social sciences, moving transversally across the natural and social sciences, as also suggested by Latour (2004: 215) and evident in the work of numerous anthropologists (i.e., Ingold and Palsson 2013; Tsing 2015). Law seeks to make method fractal and multiple by taking from science, and technology studies (STS) and sociology, suggesting that we need to imagine different forms of presence, and manifest absence, as part of research. In this description, however, the researcher's presence or absence is mostly left implicit. Coming from anthropology, our collection contributes to Law's work by explicitly discussing ways of becoming more or less (co)present or (co)absent, offering to understand "mess" as what makes the world alive. We also explore anthropology as a process needing to remain in flux through written accounts, as well as based on the potential of developing certain skills of improvisation, flexibility, and openness. The difficulty of making such supple and subtle ways of doing research legitimate comes from the hardening of methods as fixed pre-designed research models to execute.

Even though experience and experiment are derived from the same Latin term and were often used interchangeably through the Middle Ages, the development of the modern laboratory contributed to their separation to the point where an experiment is only deemed successful if it can be demonstrated independent of experience (the domain of human causation and human error). These endeavors are still experiences, however, and attempts to erase our (necessary) presence in experiments (paradoxically) creates a double bias—we are still present yet pretending that we are not. The cleavage between the experimental and the experiential persists to the present day. From Claude Bernard's "control experiment" outlined in his *Introduction à l'étude de la médecine expérimentale* (Introduction to the study of experimental medicine) (1865) and familiar to generations of scientists (Pickstone 2000: 13), the experiment has become the highest mode of investigating life in positivist science. "Controls" facilitate staging an experiment to observe the operation or mechanism of interest as well as work as a means of gaining control over living processes (2000: 144). In this "operationalist view of science the ability to control was the measure of knowledge" (Pauly 1987 in Pickstone 2000: 145). This ability to control through the demonstration of a pre-designed procedure is still the measure of knowledge in empirical practices, as is evident in randomized double-blind control trials (RCT)—the sciences' current gold standard. Imported into the social sciences, it becomes a means of establishing "controls" to collect data from the world, usually verbatim, in order to provide a representation of the world through analysis. As Law makes clear, however, "method is not . . . a more or less successful set of procedures for reporting on a given reality. Rather it is performative" (2004: 143); it produces realities. Law further specifies that it is not that standard research methods are straightforwardly wrong, as they can offer insights into causal relations, however they are "badly adapted to the study of the ephemeral, the indefinite and the irregular" (2004: 4).

An extension of the critique of a standardizing ethnography as method prior to research is evident in Law's delineation of a "method assemblage" (2004: 104). Law takes up the notion of "assemblage" (*agencement*) from Deleuze and Guattari (1987) and uses it to qualify what he means by "method." Deleuze and Guattari's concept of assemblage refers to "an increase in the dimensions of a multiplicity that necessarily changes in nature as it expands its connections" (1987: 8). It also owes a debt to the anthropologist Gregory Bateson who proposed it to map the relationship between stasis and change. While Law is aware of what is lost in translating assemblage from the more fluid French term *agencement* (a term more easily used as both noun and verb, 2004: 41–42), he sometimes fixes the continuous work of assembling as if "method" could be of a particular "nature" and thus no longer alive to its connections. At the very least it should be "methodological assemblage," thus nuancing a particular assemblage rather than nuancing method, which is thus left intact. This in turn may explain how he simultaneously states that "there can be no fixed formula or general rules for determining good and bad bundles" (Law 2004: 42) while leading us, for the purpose of illustration, toward fixing such bundles with a reification of "Aboriginal method assemblage" on one side and a "Euro-American method assemblage" (2004: 133) on the other.

To avoid that end, we look to lines of flight, which are forever in the process of being drawn. Lines of flight are immanent to social fields, according to Deleuze and Guattari (1987), animated by all sorts of decoding and de-territorializing movements affecting "masses," following speeds and differing allures; "the earth asserts its own powers of deterritorialization, its lines of flight, its smooth spaces that live and blaze their way for a new earth" (Deleuze and Guattari 1987: 423). They are not contradictions, but potentials to create new forms and to proliferate life. Science has its own lines of flight, making them act and create, or turn into a line of destruction or failure, this being a line of flight as well. Hence while Law suggests (2004: 10) method is not just a set of techniques but a way of being, this volume explores "method" more specifically as a way of becoming something else, as per the (trans)(de)(re)formative powers of learning from experience, and thus moving beyond "method."

In her summary of contemporary methodological possibilities, Annemarie Mol (2002: 152–57) describes three genres or general ways of attending to methods in research; the legislative kind (clinical trials, for instance), the critical kind (proposing new legislation), and the mingling kind (leading to new methods that might be taken up by the critical kind). These three genres are standard methods or methods that aim "to faithfully represent some object *as it is*" (Mol 2002: 158, emphasis in original). Mol opens up a fourth way of attending to method, one that seeks "worthwhile ways of *living with* the real" (2002: 158, emphasis in original). She adds, "we need to abandon the methods section of the library and move to the shelves that tell about the politics of academic work" (2002: 158–59).

Mol's (2002) example of scholarship that emphasizes the way things are written points to George Clifford and James Marcus's (1986) *Writing Culture*, namely the core text that highlights the reflexive literary turn marking the crisis of representation in anthropology. This text was swiftly critiqued and rebuked in Ruth Behar and Deborah Gordon's (1995) *Women Writing Culture* on the basis that women were not represented and it therefore fell right back into the crisis from which it aimed to emerge. While this volume is not explicitly engaged in the politics of academic work, it emerges from these debates. The research described here "is not about writing other lives, but about joining with them in the common task of finding ways to live" (Ingold 2018: 14); engaging with people and things in search of livable worlds. Hence while debates about "methods" are not new, the originality in these chapters involves showing ways of inhabiting research, and perhaps more broadly, science and academia.

Motions

The book is organized through the overlapping motions or three folds of knowing processes: (1) sensing as a vital process (similar to breathing or growth) that one can practice, hone, or train; (2) moving as physical mobility through space and time yet also as moving and being moved affectively by our own movements; and (3) imagining as giving form to the ephemeral or elusive, both virtual and actual. Each section is composed of four chapters throughout which are interspersed seven vignettes, or fieldwork encounters, by other anthropologists whose work resonates with the content of the chapter. The afterword, also composed with a vignette, reverberates with all three motions in an effort to rejuvenate the discipline, to keep it alive. The book itself is rhizomatic rather than linear. It is a triptych on many levels and the sections, chapters, and vignettes are designed to resonate with each other in the hope of creating a living sense of searching after method in anthropology.

While all of the chapters engage in some way with the ideas of sensing, moving, and imagining as knowing affectively, they do so in different ways. Nowhere is sensing defined physiologically, nor does it refer to psychological introspection, rather it suggests a vital process similar to procreation, breathing, or growth (Merleau-Ponty [1945] 2002: 10). Particularly in the first section of the book, sensing is discussed as event—as verb more than noun. It is thus to the subtle, almost imperceptible aspects of experience to which it brings attention. Within this section we see that beginning as an apprentice anthropologist, healer, martial artist, drummer, or falconer from a position of not knowing can be a way to become more aware, able to correspond with what is going on. The seven anthropologists involved in this section offer ways of expressing sensing as it stems from research done with people, plants, animals, and elements in Java, Colombia, Canada, Iran, Cameroon, Serbia, and Italy, thus taking us into everyday practices occurring in Europe, America, Africa, and Asia.

Chapter 1 unfolds in three ways. It opens with a vignette by Daniel Alberto Restrepo Hernández who poses questions about our presence as researchers and some of the sensitivities that are required therein. In his case, an attempted entry into a plant-milieu to work with indigenous healers in Colombia seemed to illicit an inhospitable response, yet also provoked reflection which clarified a previous calling. The main text by Julie Laplante pulls this thread through to explain an answer to a recent calling presented to her by a Bantu healer in Cameroon. Focusing on events that linger, stir, and transform in healing and research across people, plants, and elements, she reveals telling moments through the course of more than twenty years of fieldwork as processes of opening and increasing possibilities of attunement. Drawing from the healer's explanation that his practice is one of instilling joy, she connects these words with Spinoza's *Ethics of Joy*. This further leads her to address sensing through a Deleuzian notion of sense as event, having neither a physical nor a mental existence. She explores sensation as a wave that passes through us, an insistent feeling that is the way the healer both works and heals, more precisely by creating sonorous sensations, something anthropologists can also do. The chapter ends with a vignette by Boyan Atzev set in the context of mindful meditation in a classroom setting in Montreal, Canada. The vignette suggests that solace or healing occurs only once we exceed the bounds of organic and mental activity or let something leak. What weaves these three texts together is the idea that doing anthropology is a process of opening rather than closing.

The second chapter by Jaida Kim Samudra brings us into the "thickness of sensing," into the continuous micro-adjustments needed to sense "feeling" as per the extensive *pesilat* (martial artist) training she has been undergoing for the past thirty-five years. She explains that in Persatuan Gerak Badan (PGB, Body Movement Unification, based in Bogor, Indonesia) terms, "awareness" means sensing external stimuli from beyond your skin, mostly by using sight and hearing; however, being aware of your surroundings (and possible threats) also includes noticing sensations such as vibrations through the floor through your feet or movements of air or temperature changes on your skin that would indicate someone is approaching. She explains that unlike body movements labeled "feeling," the sensations and deployment of "feeling" cannot be observed; such subtle somatic phenomena can only be grasped through direct experience in the fieldworker's own body. Subtle sensing or the salience of "feeling," sensation, sense, or "rasa" (as per Sanskrit evoked in Javanese and Indonesian martial arts), also include an aspect of "adhering to something" we might understand as reaching common ground or air.

Chapters 3 and 4 draw attention to sound and wind as sensing, respectively, through drumming and weathering. Nima Jangouk's chapter explains that his research involved learning new drumming rhythms in order to join zar practitioners in their healing on Qeshm Island in Southern Iran. The "taming wind or affliction" of the zar practitioners "unsettled" affected people. Taking us through his own process of appreciation of the ritual through the lens of phenomenological approaches in anthropology, he locates his experience in a context of (academic) institutional resistance. Angeline Antonakos Boswell's vignette is embedded within this chapter, describing how a "back-to-the roots" movement in Serbia was unexpectedly therapeutic. Together they show the importance of knowing and embracing our tendencies to join people, rhythms, and tempos. Chapter 4 by Sarah Asu Schroer extends this argument, showing the need to open up an earthbound perspective of conventionally "grounded" fieldwork to consider the aerial world of birds of prey, where weather and air currents play a crucial role. Through stories and drawings presented in collaboration with artist Aina Azevedo, she brings attention to the textuality of air as it emerges between falconer, bird, and weather environment in a relation of trust and a sense of companionship; falconers need to develop "a feeling for birds of prey." She describes developing a sensitivity to the forces and intensities of the wind, a common thread passing through many of the contributions in this volume.

Overall the contributions in this section thus point us forward, illustrating how doing anthropology brings into being new compositions and seeks to reach common ground or air (such as ways of breathing together). Where the first section focuses on attunements, the next section—Moving—offers a counterpoint. In the second part of this volume, political structures are resisted or are used to produce new possibilities. Reflections on attunement are still present, but in terms of broader adjustments that we make as we travel/move along space and time, de-re-territorialize pasts, presents, and futures, (re)mapping grounds and skies. Knowing as movement applies to vital bodily processes across and in-between leaky bodies (as discussed above), yet it also applies to going along virtual and actual routes or paths as we (web) surf, walk, migrate, map, or haul water. The authors in this fold take us to Northern Canada, Mongolia, South Africa, Singapore, and China, yet also beyond those borders as worlds intermingle through cyberspace as well as through dreams, spiritual forces, and ecologies.

The opening chapter by Willow Scobie describes traveling through layers of time, landscapes, media, and Inuitness across the Inuit homeland. The contemporary tactics that Inuit use to "story themselves into being" (Jackson 2006) create new opportunities for anthropologists (and sociologists) to explore the ways nomadic subjectivities illuminate the coexistence of pasts, presents, and futures in layered strands. Being attentive to the ways Inuit youth contend with colonial logics involves mobilizing an indigenous epistemology that opens lines of flight where everything is always possible. Scobie's chapter includes a vignette by Meg Stalcup who writes of untimeliness, or a need to stay in time with one's fieldwork, notwithstanding the speed of the internet. Moving and being moved with and through internet techniques involves finding a relationship to the present unaffected by reigning norms, opinion, or academic fads. A second vignette by Carly Dokis explains how by both thinking with water and hauling it, she learns its importance for the Dene community in Behdzi Ahda First Nation. Maintaining their relationship with water, and by extension their relations with each other, was prized above adopting a water treatment facility. Together, this triptych shows the importance of attending to smooth space, or maximizing its creation with an understanding of how space and time are striated or could be striated otherwise.

In the sixth chapter, Giovanni Spissu draws inspiration from South African writer Alex La Guma's 1962 novel *A Walk in the Night and Other Stories* in which he describes District Six in Cape Town during the apartheid era. Spissu applies a similar approach to observe resignification processes of the urban territory by walking with its residents in post-apartheid Cape Town. He argues that La Guma's work can be conceived as a particular form of a literary sensorial map, giving meaning to the city's urban space as an empathic territory alive with the inhabitants' memories and imaginings for their futures. In this there are endless possibilities of re-territorialization. In chapter 7 we follow Nicolas Rasiulis becoming an anthropologist as he cohabitates with the Dukhas, nomadic reindeer herders in the alpine tundra and boreal forests on the Mongolian side of its borderland with the Russian Republic of Tuva. He describes the struggles and successes of learning everyday life as he joins migratory movements between West and East Taigas, as well as how one's presence is both affected by and affecting place, people and spirits. The core of his chapter takes us into deeply transformative manifold processes of (re)turning and (re)knotting, and most crucially of moving through and across ontologies and shaman-ish practices through continuous micro-adjustments and improvisations.

Bringing some order yet also showing how things stretch and bend, chapter 8 by Elisabeth Hsu and Chee Han Lim compares two styles of martial arts training that the authors learned in different places: Singapore and Kunming, Yunnan province, People's Republic of China. One style is the Hong Fist (*hongguan* 洪拳) version of the *Yijin jing*, the other was taught as a form of *qigong* 氣功. Together, they reflect on how comparative auto-ethnographic practices can enrich the repertoire of ethnographic field methods. In particular, they find that the intentionality underlying both *Yijin jing* styles of expanding the self into the universe predispose the ethnographer to recognize the importance of this trope in other cultural modalities, for example, in historiographic texts or healing rituals. Moving or stillness are discussed in minute detail, such as the requirement to remaining unmoved, learning "to let go and be a pine tree," and understanding how the pine tree stands for the pinnacle of martial excellence—"remaining unmoved is the tree's way of striking back." Moving thus co-exists with unmoving (minor, rounded, bodily, martial or suitable, pulling, pushing, naming, opening, doing; sometimes choreographed, administered individually, taught, enskilled, enacted, aligned, performed, reproduced, involved, long, and drawn out). Moving can also be a rationale or a string of movements flowing into each other, as illustrated in this chapter's phenomenology of the movements learned.

The Moving section thus offers endless possibilities of expressing or being un/re/moved through both space and time, yet also through extending and stretching space and time via bodily adjustments of human and more-than-human worlds. This can be understood through *qi* as "thing-y," tangible, resistance-offering, and even sentient, like winds that can be tamed or attuned to (sensing). Along this line, the Imagining section pays closer attention to the ways these winds and words, violence, loss, failure, and silence can be brought into writing. They do so based on research performed in Australia, Sri Lanka, Bosnia, Western Canada, the United States, and in literature.

It begins with a final triptych that considers the interview and the archive not as static and closed artifacts circumscribed by preexisting questions or material documents but as living and breathing processes. Ari Gandsman's text takes us into the difficulties encountered in persuading ethics boards to understand how the interview is fieldwork, underlining how often the most telling aspects are what spill out unexpectedly or remain unsaid. Taking us through the interview component of a study on "right to die" activism in Melbourne, Australia, we get a sense of the anxiety leading up to, and during the interview process, and how this is intensified by the recording machine (and lessened once it is off). This encounter ends with a line that disappears into the distance, a vanishing point that leads us to imagine so much more than the interview. Embedded within this chapter, the vignette by Larisa Kurtović also reflects on the interview process, offering insight into the possibility of disappointment when we expect certain answers. Situating us in the context of her doctoral fieldwork on a grassroots activist initiative in postwar Bosnia-Herzegovina, she explains that it was only much later on after the interview was done that she fully grasped the strength of a corporeal and affective response, while she had at the time wished for a more political or discursive one. She thus points to the importance of listening for the unexpected. Adding complexity to the classical methodological approach of archival research, Thushara Hewage's vignette takes his study of the Sri Lankan political to show how it leads to reconsidering the distinction between ethnography as method and anthropology as theory. Once the archive is no longer considered factual in the postcolony, it becomes useful to apply an idea of the discursive archive in Foucauldian terms, namely as an immanent system of dynamic relations in which we need to position ourselves critically. Leading us through three key moments of its constitution, he shows us its movement and its depth, or how an embedded concept of ethnicity performs through time in the archive.

Chapter 10 by Bradley Dunseith takes failure as a starting point, asking what it means to learn in the field. He describes how failing to learn to shoot a gun during the course of his fieldwork in the state of Georgia in the United States offers imaginative and creative ways to think more broadly about the environments people inhabit and what it means to inhabit them. More specifically, by juxtaposing learning to shoot a gun with learning how to do anthropology, he suggests that disproportionate attention to learning skills as a straightforward process and repetitive technique can also shed light on how un-tuning ourselves and awkwardness can be revealing, opening up space for one's imagination to unfurl. Next, the chapter by Kristen Anne Walsh brings us to the tops of the Rocky Mountain range in order to learn with alpine lookout observers. She explores the wonder involved in the deep probing of the sky and of the wind, such as in differentiating a "spook" or false plume from a real one. Her chapter evokes a heightened imagination to what is out there, a broadened awareness in sensing winds laterally and through the skin. She tells her process of becoming both an anthropologist and a lookout observer as she turns to drawing, walking, and listening in order to write from the movements at the mountain tops.

Chapter 12 by Bernhard Leistle brings forth that which is often elusive within the grasp of *Methods* (as well as teaching *Methods*), what he describes as "getting caught," and how this constitutes a sophisticated aesthetic-artistic maneuver. By leading us through a classic work by Jeanne Favret-Saada, he invites us to think of anthropology as bewitchment, a realm beyond method. More poignantly, he calls our attention to the way things are written and how they can "get to us" affectively, highlighting an aspect that is not only "after method," but eludes the grasp of method. It can be understood as a marriage of form and content close to artistic creation—exploring the aesthetic-artistic dimensions of ethnographic writing by moving beyond understandings of "neutral objectivity." The afterword takes up the idea that writing produces (rather than describes) experience as it explores the relation between silence and method. Anchoring his thoughts in more than ten years of fieldwork in and across novel ecologies, David Jaclin takes us on the road and brings the road home as he grasps the liveliness and open-endedness of meta-odos. This enables him to problematize "data," as well as reflect on double mechanical modes of the inscription of fieldwork (writing/reading/multimedia recordings) with some of the organic ones often less considered (moving/inferring/transducing/becoming more-than-one). Composed in dialogue with a vignette by Everett Kehew, together they propose an infra-linguistic argument to rejuvenate the practice of anthropology, a semiotic consciousness for working the field. Jaclin does this from the perspective of a loss, while Kehew draws from yoga as well as from Georges Bataille's invitation to embrace writing as productive and not descriptive of experience. This interestingly brings him to discuss inner experience of both ethnographic yoga and writing as a means of breathing life into the practice of anthropology. A brief epilogue pulls out some of the threads that move through the manuscript, not as prescriptive models but rather as invitations.

Julie Laplante is Professor in Anthropology at the University of Ottawa. She works in phenomenological approaches in anthropology with interests in indigenous and humanitarian medicine, attuning to bodily, clinical, sensorial, and sonorous abilities in healing with plants or molecules. Her fieldwork in the Brazilian Amazon and at two edges of the Indian Ocean (South Africa, Java Indonesia) has more recently moved to Cameroon. She produced the anthropological film *Jamu Stories* (2015) and is the author of *Pouvoir guérir* (2004) and *Healing Roots* (2015, 2018).

Willow Scobie is an Assistant Professor in the School of Sociological and Anthropological Studies at the University of Ottawa. She began working with Inuit youth in 2007 on projects related to YouTube, Twitter, Facebook, and Isuma.tv. She is currently working with youth and young adults in Inuit communities documenting their responses to mining projects operating in the Inuit Nunangat. Her most recent publication, "Diversions, Distraction, and Privileges: Consultation and the Governance of Mining in Nunavut," with Kathleen Rodgers, was published in *Studies in Political Economy* 100 (3): 232–51.

Ari Gandsman is a cultural and medical anthropologist and associate professor at the University of Ottawa in the School of Anthropological and Sociological Studies. His research examines the intersection of new technologies and rights-based claims. He has conducted fieldwork in Argentina, Australia, and Canada, working on long-term research projects on medical aid-in-dying and post-dictatorship human rights movements. His work has been published in a wide range of anthropological and interdisciplinary journals including *Death Studies*, *Anthropologie et Sociétés*, *The International Journal of Transitional Justice*, *Anthropologica*, *The Journal of Latin American and Caribbean Anthropology*, and *Ethos*.

References

Bateson, Gregory. 1972. *Steps to an Ecology of Mind: A Revolutionary Approach to Man's Understanding of Himself*. New York: Ballantine Books.

———. [1936] 1958. *Naven: A Survey of the Problems Suggested by a Composite Picture of the Culture of a New Guinea Tribe Drawn from Three Points of View*. Stanford, CA: Stanford University Press.

Bateson, Gregory, and Margaret Mead. 1942. *Balinese Character: A Photographic Analysis*. New York: Academy of Sciences.

Behar, Ruth, and Deborah A. Gordon, eds. 1995. *Women Writing Culture*. Berkeley: University of California Press.

Bernard, Claude. 1865. *Introduction à l'étude de la médecine expérimentale*. Paris: Garnier-Flammarion.

Boas, Franz 1921. *Ethnology of the Kwakiutl*. Washington, DC: Government Printing Office.

Boudreault-Fournier, Alexandrine. 2017. "Recording and Editing." In *A Different Kind of Ethnography: Imaginative Practices and Creative Methodologies*, ed. Denielle Elliott and Dara Culhane, 69–90. North York: University of Toronto Press.

Deleuze, Gilles, and Félix Guattari. 1987. *A Thousand Plateaus*, trans. by Brian Massumi. London: University of Minnesota Press.

During, Elie. 2008. "Trois lettres 'inédites' de Henri Bergson à Gilles Deleuze." *Critique* 732: 398–409.

Elliott, Denielle, and Dara Culhane, eds. 2017. *A Different Kind of Ethnography: Imaginative Practices and Creative Methodologies*. North York: University of Toronto Press.

Favret-Saada, Jeanne. 1977. *Les mots, la mort, les sorts*. Paris: Gallimard.

Goethe, Johann Wolfgang von. [1791] 2009. *The Metamorphosis of Plants*. Cambridge, MA: The MIT Press.

Ingold, Tim. 2013. *Making: Anthropology, Archaeology, Art and Architecture*. London: Routledge.

———. 2014. "That's Enough about Ethnography!" *HAU: Journal of Ethnographic Theory* 4(1): 383–95.

———. 2015 *The Life of Lines*. Oxford: Routledge.

———. 2017. "Anthropology Contra Ethnography." *HAU: Journal of Ethnographic Theory* 7(1): 21–26.

———. 2018. *Anthropology: Why It Matters*. Cambridge: Polity Press.
Ingold, Tim, and Elisabeth Hallam. 2007. "Creativity and Cultural Improvisation: An Introduction." In *Creativity and Cultural Improvisation*, ed. Elisabeth Hallam and Tim Ingold, 1–41. New York: Berg.
Ingold, Tim, and Gisli Palsson, eds. 2013. *Biosocial Becomings: Integrating Social and Biological Anthropology*. New York: Cambridge University Press.
Jackson, Michael. 2006. *The Politics of Storytelling: Violence, Transgression and Intersubjectivity*. Copenhagen: Museum Tusculanum Press.
Latour, Bruno. 2004. "How to Talk About the Body? The Normative Dimension of Science Studies." *Body & Society* 10(2–3): 205–29.
Law, John. 2004. *After Method: Mess in Social Science Research*. London: Routledge.
Lévi-Strauss, Claude. [1962] 1966. *The Savage Mind (La Pensée Sauvage)*. trans. by Weidenfeld and Nicolson Ltd. The Garden City Press: Letchworth, Hertfordshire.
Malinowski, Bronislaw. [1922] 2005. *Argonauts of the Western Pacific: An Account of Native Enterprise and Adventure in the Archipelagoes of Melanesian New Guinea*. London: Routledge.
Mauss, Marcel. 1923–24. "Essai sur le don: forme et raison de l'échange dans les sociétés archaïques." *L'Année sociologique* 1: 30–186.
McLean, Athena, and Annette Leibing. 2007. *The Shadow Side of Fieldwork: Exploring the Blurred Borders between Ethnography and Life*. Malden: Blackwell Publishing.
Merleau-Ponty, Maurice. [1945] 2002. *La phénoménologie de la perception*. Paris: Éditions Gallimard.
———. 1964. *L'œil et l'esprit*. Paris: Éditions Gallimard.
Mol, Annemarie. 2002. *The Body Multiple: Ontology in Medical Practice*. Durham, NC: Duke University Press.
Pauly, Phillip J. 1987. *Controlling Life: Jacques Loeb and the Engineering Ideal in Biology*. New York: Oxford University Press.
Piette, Albert. 2011. *Fondements à une anthropologie des hommes*. Paris: Hermann Éditeurs.
Pickstone, John V. 2000. *Ways of Knowing: A New History of Science Technology and Medicine*. Manchester: Manchester University Press.
Pink, Sarah. 2015. *Doing Sensory Ethnography*. Los Angeles, CA: Sage.
Robben, Antonius C. G. M., and Jeffrey A. Sluka, eds. 2012. *Ethnographic Fieldwork: An Anthropological Reader*. West Sussex: John Wiley & Sons Ltd.
Smith, Linda Tuhiwai. [1999] 2008. *Decolonizing Methodologies: Research and Indigenous Peoples*. New York: Zed Books.
Taussig, Michael. 2015. *The Corn Wolf*. Chicago and London: The University of Chicago Press.
Tsing, Anna Lowenhaupt. 2015. *The Mushroom at the End of the World: On the Possibility of Life in Capitalist Ruins*. Princeton, NJ: Princeton University Press.

PART I

Sensing

Chapter 1

SONOROUS SENSATIONS

PLANT, PEOPLE, AND ELEMENTAL STIRS IN HEALING

Julie Laplante

> Vocation: calling, calling with, called by, calling as if the world mattered, calling out, going too far, going visiting.
>
> —Donna Haraway, *A Curious Practice*

This chapter is composed of three texts resonating with each other as they all share interests in healing exceeding the bounds of organic activity. Woven together they argue doing anthropology is a process of opening rather than closing. It begins with a vignette by Daniel Alberto Restrepo Hernández expressing how an (in)hospitable attempt to do fieldwork in one human-plant milieu evoked the hospitalities of another milieu in the form of an "ancestral calling." My main text delves into a recent answer to such a hospitable calling. I then move through prior fieldwork experiences that enabled opening ontological categories and develop sensorial affectivities corresponding with what was going on. Boyan Atzev's vignette echoes a similar process occurring in research done through mindfulness meditation in a classroom setting, expressing how a constricted atmosphere only provides solace or healing if one manages to pry things open.

Vignette 1
Plant Milieus: (In)Hospitalities
Daniel Alberto Restrepo Hernández

> A perfect definition applies only to a *completed* reality: now vital properties are never entirely realized, though always on the way to become so; they are not so much *states* as *tendencies*.
>
> —Henri Bergson, *Creative Evolution*

Upstream from read, traveled, and navigated cartographies, whether it be the inscriptions of a map, a book, or the landscape through which we find a path—wandering lines of ink or pixels, grass snakes, waterways, or pathways carved by machetes through the imbricated densities of equatorial biomes—my story of *taitas*[1] and sacred vines begins with a certainty that emphasizes the relevance of following open portals rather than trying to open closed ones that have never insinuated an invitation to open them. This certainty, immediately raising the question of the (in) hospitality of those worlds, came to me as I was hundreds of kilometers away from the Amazonian basin, near Colombia's Northern geographical edge in Nabusimake, the spiritual and political heart of Arhuaco indigenous people.

A contextual anchoring is necessary beforehand: located in a small altiplano incrusted in the foothills of the Sierra Nevada Santa Marta, the village, built on platforms of enormous stones polished and rounded by thousands of years of elementary and civilizational f(r)ictions, gives the impression of being a living archaeological place, mineralized and assembled in its own cosmogonic durations and reconfiguring the perception of time otherwise. The site may well have been inhabited since time immemorial by thousands of successive generations of Arhuacos and the associated biota. A stone wall and a belt of tobacco, banana, and corn plants surround it, giving it an oval shape.

I had gone to the village to ask for a residence permit from the Nabusimake Native *Comisario* (commissioner), so that I could immerse myself, as a sound anthropologist, in the bioacoustic world(s) of their sacred plant, the *ayu* or *hayu*, the coca plant. Two *mamos* (the spiritual authorities of the people) would probably introduce me to the knowledge of the *anuge*, the soul of the plant, with the collaboration and translation of my ethnolinguistic mentor, an ex-Catholic missionary priest known by the mamos, called Javier Rodríguez Moreno. Nevertheless, according to the *mamos*, it was necessary that the *Comisario*, the political leader of their community, approve my presence in "the land where the sun is born" so that they can all willingly welcome me.

Figure 1.1. Nabusimake, 2017. Photo by Daniel Alberto Restrepo Hernández.

While my mentor explained to him in Arhuaco that I was a student of anthropology ("respectful of all traditions" and surely other pleasant descriptions) and that I was there to understand the local universe of the *ayu*, the *Comisario*, a native man dressed in the traditional white Arhuaco costume, scrutinized me with a hard, sharp look, like the crests of the surrounding mountains. He had his *poporo*[2] in his hand and a ball of coca leaves swelled his right cheek. He kept silent for two endless minutes, piercing me with his implacable gaze. Finally, he pronounced in perfect Spanish: "We do not like anthropologists. You have up to two days to leave." He then explained in an austere and calm voice: "They take more than they give. They appropriate what does not belong to them. An anthropologist who had been welcomed here wrote in a book what he should not reveal. Then, *huaqueros*[3] came to ransack sacred places."

By the hermetism that he expressed, I had the impression that our exchange ended there, ipso facto. I replied that I would leave within the time limit he gave me. Javier silently offered him a bag of *ayu* leaves, and we prepared to leave the village within two days.

Despite the fact that my mentor looked disconcerted, I had the clear conviction that it was not the tragic conclusion of my fieldwork nor the opportunity to run ink to speak about ethnographic failure. On the contrary, it was a sign inviting a certain critical reflexivity in relation to my condition as an anthropologist. The act of unilaterally presenting oneself in a place, as well as the how and why of this presence, which is that of the "anthropologist," potentially creates conditions of possibilities, but can, nevertheless, prevent certain possibilities from becoming actualized, as it went for my hypothetical exploration of what I vaguely understood as a "bioacoustic and cosmogonic ec(h)ology of the *ayu* plant in the Sierra Nevada of Santa Marta." In the meantime, and downstream of these reflections involving plants, *mamos*, undesired anthropologists, *huaqueros*, and relics buried in these wild escarpments, my certainty of an encounter with the culturo-bioacoustic universe of a plant began to sketch itself otherwise.

In this respect, instead of searching for local hospitalities in order to continue with a methodology corresponding to a preconceived epistemic universe, I instead had to follow the (in)hospitalities that from the beginning opened portals, or conditions of possibilities, toward the relational and qualitative dynamics of a probable and unfolding "fieldwork." Along these archaeological walls and walking over these platforms of antediluvian stones, I was convinced that this inhospitable denial had offered me the invaluable opportunity to learn that I had to answer the hospitable call of plants and shamans rather than attempt to orbit around constellations composed of plants and shamans without having received their calling beforehand. Yet, this premise is particularly tied to my interest in delving into "sacred" human-plant relationships and their sensorial, expressive, and transformative potential, knowing that this denial paradoxically involves a rich and a fertile soil to conceptualize about anthropological failures, epistemic or ontological collisions, or even about the political and colonial tensions tied to the coca plant in the Sierra Nevada de Santa Marta.

The sun hid behind a towering and bluish mountainside (Sokaklrua, the mountain of the father of *poporo*). At that precise moment, I remembered a plant that had manifested itself several times in my life in the form of an invitation to follow its promises and permissions. It was *yajé* or the ayahuasca vine, and all the baroque and composite milieu surrounding this mysterious Amazonian plant.

* * *

Entering the "field" hence requires certain sensitivities both to our own presence and to its welcoming. It has less to do with our imagined "state" of being an anthropologist, and more to do with the vital and relational tendencies of how we intend to become one; in this case, this became clear by going in another direction, reaffirming a path that was already there that reasserted itself. This tendency further corresponds to both a people, in occurrence the *taitas*, yet also to their ally plant; *yajé* and its particular vitalities engaging me with more certainty than *ayu* at that particular remote village.[4]

Moreover, since in these human-plant *milieus* or mediums (*ayu* and *yajé* worlds) we are dealing with life processes, tendencies and lines or vectors of "hospitality" toward qualitative transformation and relational instances of becoming-other-than-ourselves (allopoiesis), the "ancestral calling" of plants and its more-than-human specialists constitutes a journey in which the researcher becomes part of an entire and affective "ecology of selves" (Kohn 2007). Becoming intimately transformed by plants and their ecologic, cosmogonic, and affective contexts entails an open immersion into a changing and moving fieldwork. In such encounters, human and plants potentially subjugate, absorb, or reject themselves, transforming through their mutual f(r)ictions, affects, and inner experiences into something that grows, expands, and flourishes beyond the human-plant involution. Consequently, the task was one of following the paths opened by such ancient entanglements of lively realms, while attuning oneself to the hospitalities offered by that "ancestral calling" encrypted, contained, or sensed in the plural modes of existence of plant lives. This affective and sensorial immersion cannot be done without a sense of diplomacy and, curiously, without a sense of reverence.

The invitation had come in the name of the Association pour la recherche en anthropologie de médecine traditionnelle (ARAM, Association for research in the anthropology of traditional medicine) through a Cameroonian historian working on Fulani (Foulbé) medicine (Mengue Me Ndongo 2014) whom we had invited to a conference in Canada in 2017, the year before my visit. A gesture of hospitality returning a previous one, the invitation felt genuine, kind, generous, and fit neatly with the kind of research I had been doing for the last two decades. While it was difficult to fully grasp what was waiting ahead, something attracted my attention enough to imagine it and eventually accept the invitation "to go visiting," a sort of politeness which "does the energetic work of holding open the possibility that surprises are in store, that something *interesting* is about to happen" (emphasis in original).[5]

It is only when I arrived around the fireplace in the middle of the night, somewhere on the outskirts of Yaounde, Cameroon, that I realized I had been invited by a Bantu healer.[6] More than thirty people, including the healer, had been awaiting our arrival. It would soon enough strike me that I had just stepped into the very heart of ancestral and contemporary African healing practices and would be living in the midst of them for the next month. Sharing a house with the healer who lived upstairs, we were given a room on the first floor near the living room where long philosophical discussions to discern health issues occurred on a daily basis. A kitchen on a ground floor with an adjacent massage and divination room was in a separate building in front of our house. To our left was another small building that served to store fresh or dried plants, barks, and seeds, all organized and numbered so as to find them quickly when needed, with a small fireplace in the back to prepare them into medicine when cooking was required. Between these two buildings and a bit lower down the property was a square hut with the main fireplace surrounded by benches where people could both wait and be treated in the open air surrounded by all the other people, plants, animals (often roosters) present at the moment when the healer felt the timing was right. Plants grew semi-wild, strategically scattered for easy access in different areas on the property. Some minerals or other temporarily "animate" objects (still partaking in healing) were sometimes in odd places on the property, which we had to avoid displacing. The place was continuously buzzing with these synergies, enlivened through a continuous flow of people arriving with small gifts, usually fresh banana, wild mushrooms, bottled water, or palm wine, in exchange for healing. It felt as if I had entered what Gregory Bateson calls a plateau: "a region of continued intensities, vibrating on itself, without a particular orientation towards a culminating point or other exterior finality" (1972: 113). A steady state in which all was alive (plants, minerals, elements, sounds, people, and more) prevailed and made to resonate with each other in a noncompetitive manner; nothing reified, the healer worked barefoot and alert among and in-between plants, elements, those to be healed, and everything else currently ongoing. It was a sort of "dream" fieldwork setting culminating practices I had encountered before yet never all resonating at once in the same setting where I was also living. While I had previously done research across multiple sites, ARAM's invitation offered something new: a possibility of moving along with the healer through different sites to both sense as well as enhance his lively forms of medicine in ways that could be transduced and taken seriously across milieus of practice, in this case in anthropology yet with prospects to reach broader health practices as well.

What I had (un)done with prior fieldwork however came in handy. One crucial thing I had learned is that while it takes a lot of work to make objects and subjects according to dominant scientific approaches, it takes as much work to undo them to learn from the world in flux and to pay attention to lifeways at the interstice, which is riskier but closer to the way the world is unfolding. Upon considering that the air we breathe is "the very medium in which our lives are mixed and stirred" (Ingold 2015: 149), our attention turns toward finding ways to correspond laterally, to create affects, to disconcert life, as is done by music. I learned how to know plants by encountering their scents as I walked through them, by having them in my pocket, or by tasting, mashing, rolling them to extract their juices, yet also from cringing as they passed through a blender or a machine to make them into animal feed and as they choked in a pot, or from indifference to them as they lay in neat cultivated rows, dried or tested through gloved hands in laboratory worlds. I have in all of these ways let them transform my imagination in meaningful ways, eventually moving towards rhizomic and poetic theoretical approaches in my own discipline. It is useful here to go back through this process of learning before moving forward into the Cameroonian context and making sense of it.

Upstream

My anthropological journey following healers, scientists, pills, and plants as they come together to discern ways of healing or keeping people healthy has been a process of opening ontological categories to be able to sense what is going on. Although I have always been interested in ways of healing, I involved myself more intensively through anthropology when I set out to do my doctoral fieldwork in the Brazilian Amazon in the late 1990s. I entered difficult to access indigenous areas as a volunteer working for the Dutch section of Médecins Sans Frontières (MSF, Doctors Without Borders), following human/plant/biopharmaceutical entanglements along this humanitarian line as well as extending my stay to learn more from indigenous shamans' healing practices (Laplante 2004). I had previously done my master's research in the area, in a medicinal plant shop (Casa das Plantas Medicinais da Amazonia) in Belém de Pará, at the time tentatively calling myself an "ethnobotanist" with ideas to map out how indigenous people in the Brazilian Amazon identify, classify, and use plants. From working in this shop where indigenous people arrived on a daily basis with fresh plant material, I had already noticed how lively this kind of knowledge was yet it is upon living in indigenous villages during my doctoral studies that I fully grasped how it was something to continuously work at. The idea of documenting the use of plants was thus entirely missing the point, as well as potentially harmful to the livelihood of their practices.[7] Furthermore, while people knew where to find plants they need for specific uses, it had little to do with species or isolate botanical entities, and much more to do with the kinds of life plants shared with them in the milieu. Plants were on the same plane of immanence as humans,[8] some that could share cosmological wisdom if we learned how to open up to them.

To heal with plants implied learning to sense their expressions, something I mostly failed to do the at the time. Similarly, I could hear the answers to my questions, but it seemed my questions were out of place; I was even told they caused "headaches." Perhaps I was trying too hard to extract information from people, as if they were containers of "data" I thought I needed to complete my PhD. Doing interviews with health professionals from MSF worked to a certain extent but trying to do so with indigenous people deep in the Amazonian forest always turned into a fiasco. It was impossible to isolate one person to have a discussion, moreover it was painful; it created obstructions as it stopped things in time and took them out of context. It was better to learn through circumstances and events, adjusting to things as they emerge in their own time. I learned much more from how plants partake in healing when I returned to the villages a year later as a mother who had to keep her six-month-old son alive and well. Women would guide me toward certain plants, and it involved maintaining good relations with them as well as with people. Still, it was only a decade later, around 2007, that I understood how signing, humming, and dancing were central in healing, giving access to other vital lifeways, including plants, but not only.

This, I learned from a Xhosa *isangoma* (healer) during postdoctoral studies[9] following how an indigenous medicine called *umhlonyane* (Artemisia afra) entered a preclinical trial, one conducted by The International Center for Indigenous Therapy Studies (TICIPS, pronounced tea-sips) at the University of Western Cape in Cape Town, South Africa (Laplante 2015b). As I became more interested in what did not enter the laboratory and came to know this *isangoma*, at some point I asked him, "How does *umhlonyane* work?" It was a good clinical question, yet a very bad anthropological one. He seemed to roll his eyes in discouragement and decided to answer nevertheless, yet by pointing toward drums and inviting me to a drumming healing session the following Sunday. Plants did not "work" in themselves, nor were they objects containing molecules that would heal: rather they were sentient mediums through which to communicate, in this case with ancestors. This implied opening up to "sense" with plants by experiencing lengthy hours of drumming and dancing. In *ngoma*, what Victor Turner (1968) called the drums of affliction, repetitive drum rhythms are indicated as the first thing an *isangoma* (healer) needs to sense to be able to heal another; this means that she needs to "open up" to feel vibrations to become a healer. Sensing these temporal rhythms are in turn what enables one to heal with plants as they open pathways to connect with ancestors, *umhlonyane* enables purifying dreams when placed under the bed sheets the night before a healing session. Hence, a plant or a sound in itself are not what heal, nor are they what enables healing or becoming a healer; it is rather that, as illustrated beautifully in Jeanne Favret-Saada's classic (1977), that we can learn to affect and be affected through these mediums, namely through vegetal lives, although not exclusively. Partaking in the three-hour drumming session, I had to discern the event as sense.

While this fieldwork in South Africa enabled me to unpack an idea of a plant as a commodity, botanical entity, bioresource, or as a species, it took other fieldwork events in Java to learn how to unpack an idea of the human as an isolate individual subject[10] or as a universal biological body as per biomedical thinking. *Jamu* is the form of medicine practiced on a daily basis and thriving in Yogyakarta (Jogja) on the Island of Java, Indonesia, where I conducted my research (Laplante 2017). It consists of fresh liquid plant preparations made into beverages to maintain good health, mainly attending to vitalities. It is only in this more recent study that I entered directly through sound, visuals, and movement, making a film of these practices (Laplante 2015a). In this audiovisual work, I let the city and its peripheries delimit the research, and more precisely following how *jamu* surfaced in practice, whether prepared in homes and carried out by women walking barefoot, as part of the agritourist industry, clinics, women's spas, farms, streets, and so on. Javanese healing practices, as those practiced by shamans in Amazonia and by healers in South Africa, are not using plants as commodities toward health, nor are they attending to human bodies as bounded entities; bodies are rather perceived as fluid and leaky. Preparing *jamu* is done through particular movements of leaning into the plants barehanded and leaning backwards; speeds and slowness are repetitively done to reach the desired textures and intensities, a lengthy process involving the whole body. At some point, I noticed how these bodily movements were similar to those in *Pencak Silat*, a popular martial art in Java;[11] in particular, the hand movements pushing forward and leaning backward, synchronizing breath and motion and producing energy.

In its healing aspect, *Pencak Silat* can enable one to transfer and mobilize life-forces. Achieving inner power and attuning *rasa* (sensing) can augment the possibility of making and preparing the right *jamu* for the right problem at the right moment. It is in this way that *jamu* beverages can be understood as tailored vegetal flows that can enable, restore, or clarify fluid human bodies, which are understood as neither isolated nor subjects or objects. In *Pencak Silat*, producing energy is to correspond breath with movement in kicks, yet also through firm movements of the arms, and it is this action—corresponding breathing with upper body motions—that was done repetitively in preparing *jamu*. The added value in the case of *jamu*, in contrast with *Pencak Silat*, is that it is human energy entangling with plant-lives, the latter also in motion and producing energy. *Jamu* makers both gain as well as put energies in their beverages through corresponding motions, making the beverages that much more powerful and connected to the customer they have in mind as they prepare the drink. The idea of life-forces that one can hone to mobilize an increased ability to sense, including with other kinds of life, is invested in doing *jamu* that treats a fluid body of flows and winds, using "a variety of medicines and medical practices to organize and bring about smooth flows and circulations" (Ferzacca 2001: 118). It is by doing this research through film with a focus on people-plant sound and movements in *jamu* that these intricate philosophies made sense, as well as transformed my own thoughts and practices with plants, creating openings that can be understood as listening, adjusting, or corresponding. It is with this loosened attention that I arrived in the Cameroonian intensities and was able to make sense within them.

Joy

For the past twenty years or so, I have thus been looking for ways to express how vital these kinds of medicine are, literally and on their own terms, and I was now experimenting with methods in or through sound—essentially an approach of disorientation or open to what is yet to come. When I received ARAM's invitation to attend an Open House conference event, I offered to come a month ahead of time to do a small project on their healing practices through sound. I had recently followed a four-day Sonic Triptych workshop with Carlo A. Cubero, Pablo D. Herrera, and Brandon Labelle (2018), and the idea was to pay attention to intensities and pauses, speeds and slowness, temporal rhythms, tempos and tonalities often very sophisticated in these kinds of practices and expressing the strength of this sort of healing. More specifically, and without knowing what to expect or how I would proceed, I suggested I could accompany them in their everyday practices and in their expeditions to the ancestral forest where they obtain fresh medicine. About a sixty miles east of Yaoundé, just north of the road toward Douala, the association has an Antenna (base) where, having obtained the support of the Ministry of Forestry, they have replanted twenty-four hectares of forest with some of its original medicinal plants in ways to let the forest regenerate itself.

They have also secured access to the adjacent Sacred Forest of Bassinglègè[12] where healers replenish themselves regularly with fresh healing materialities; this sacred forest is known for its gaiety and as the best place both to collect remedies and to pass by the palaver tree (called *Yap djég*) that discerns if people are guilty (or not) of committing non-conforming acts (Kañaa 2018: 108). It is also known as

Figure 1.2. Entry into the replanted forest through the cocoa plants, ARAM Antenna Lamal-Pouguè, Cameroon 2018. Photo by Julie Laplante.

one of the best forests within numerous others born from humans to hide truth and to modify history (Kañaa 2018: 110), insinuating its sentience and power to act in, through, and across human entanglements. Since communication was difficult from afar due to bad and expensive internet connection, we decided that the rest would be decided spontaneously when I arrived. It is this spontaneity, or working on the cusp of things, that was the most fortuitous, for the very reason that it was precisely how this healer worked and healed people, namely through skilled improvisation, light touches yet with profound sensorial awareness to ongoing everyday processes.

More importantly, it is through his flexible attuned ability to correspond laterally with other kinds of life, human and other-than-human, that he worked to augment the potentials of life in-between people and other lifeways. As we wandered through the ancestral forest to seek medicine for specific healing issues, we followed the healer in all sorts of directions as he was apparently attracted by certain plants. He explained that as he was sensing the health problem of the person he was healing; plants attracted his attention, making themselves visible, expressing or reminding him that they could do something in this situation, often in combination with other plants, sometimes in a specific order, one plant leading to another plant. There is no desire or necessity to have a name for these plants beforehand, nor for having used or tested them in another situation, since the healing consists in finding the beneficial correspondence in this particular case, moment, and time. While numerous plants and mixtures are already known, there is still room for new ones to take part in a quest to augment someone's effort to persevere in existence, and it all passes through sensing carefully what is yet to come with the intent of creating affects, ideally joy. The lively synergies in the ancestral forest served to maximize the benefits of his practice, and we were made to be part of it all by our own presence from abroad, passing by the palaver tree to confirm our integrity as well as our welcome.[13] Equipped to record, it is the healer who provided us with a video camera, as we decided to simultaneously work on a film; one that is currently in production and that he insists we entitle *La joie de Bassinglègè* (Joy of Bassinglègè).

At first, I was surprised by and a little bit hesitant about the word "joy," not grasping fully how I could make sense of it anthropologically. When I googled the word, I was surprised a second time when the philosophers I was currently thinking with appeared; namely, Baruch Spinoza and Friedrich Nietzsche. Since I was more familiar with the former, I returned to his work. Spinoza ([1849] 2002) developed an ethics of joy, defining it as the passage from a lesser to a greater perfection, as an augmentation of the capacities to act linked to the realization of our desires and effort (*conatus*) to persevere in existence (Deleuze 1988: 48). In this ethics, Spinoza makes a distinction between "affection," how bodies mix and leave traces of each other in one another, and "affectus" (passions or affects) of bodies that augment (joy) or diminish (sadness), favor or hinder one's power to act (Spinoza [1849] 2002: 82). Gilles Deleuze refers to the latter as the body's longitude, while its latitude would be its affective capacity—its power to act and be acted upon by other bodies and the affections of which it is subsequently capable. "In this sense, one affective power flows through the other: *affectio*—how a body is affected by its relational encounters with other bodies—shapes and is shaped by *affectus*—the body's continuous variation in its power to affect and be affected" (Thompson 2017: 47, emphasis in original). The kind of body Spinoza refers to is a non-anthropocentric one composed of many individual bodies and bodies are distinguished from one another in respect to motion and rest, quickness and slowness, and not by reason of substance ([1849] 2002: 75). This is what Gilles Deleuze and Félix Guattari (1980), following Antonin Artaud (1934), call the body without organs (BwO), or one that is not defined by organism, all notions that correspond with how the bantu healer seemed to be working: leading energies across bodies, sideways,[14] creating sonorous sensations, thus making the non-sonorous of virtual force (such as duration or intensity) sonorous or affective. "The tightening and dilation of the body can be understood in terms of sad and joyful affects—a sound that tightens (distresses) negatively affects us and a sound that dilates (rejoices) positively affects us, though the outcome of such affects remains to be seen" (Deleuze: 1988 as discussed in Simpson 2009: 2568). The stirs, affects, or sonorous sensations occur between BwOs.

From this perspective a body is not defined by abstract notions of genus or species and moves across a plane of immanence. In this way a body can be heterogenous: "even a sound wave can be conceived of as a body, in that it is composed of dynamic relations of motion and rest (i.e., the movement of the air particles or another medium in a particular pattern) and has a certain capacity for modification (by, for example, other sounds and vibrations)" (Thompson 2017: 48). With Spinoza and Deleuze, affect is thus an entire, vital, and modulating field of myriad becomings across human and nonhuman, a plane the healer excelled at moving across. It is upon adhering to this idea of affect that Deleuze (2004) opposes power (one priests, psychoanalysts, judges, physicians might possess as per their status) since it hinders and divides, thus always goes against the effort (*conatus*) to persevere in existence, diminishing another's power to act. In other words, they need to sadden life to exercise their power over someone's actions; for instance, the priest or the physician will do so by instilling guilt or fear. In contrast, the Bantu healer explicitly seeks to add to someone's capacity to act, sometimes by distracting or entertaining them with ludic performances, moving carefully in-between or laterally with other kinds of life, loosening them lightly to enhance correspondences beneficially. As described by Jaida Kim Samudra with relation to the martial arts (this volume: 71), he 'feels' "to read other people's intentions and anticipate their next moves" yet he also does so to read the intentions of other lifeways, making minute and indivisible adjustments to their bodies before they have physically committed themselves, realigning them through touch or other inter alia at hand. Roger Amos Kañaa does so through intimate copresence, heightened flexibility, attunement, and improvisation within the context at hand as it unfolds, attending life through its flux, enriching and steering it to do his healing work, even when the people being healed have returned to their homes. His work subsists, lingers, doing something akin to what Deleuze and Guattari (1980) and Pierre Boulez (1971) have called sonorous sensation or the duration of an experienced event that continues to grow meaningfully beyond its occurrence.

Sense

In this approach and practice, sense or sensing is an event; something that arises as an event of sense. Sense is thus not something that exists outside of the event, nor is it situated in an organ, and it especially does not have a "role" in an event yet is the event. A tree or a person do not "have senses" yet it can be said that a "tree greens or arborifies" and that a "person shines or humans," for example. Therefore, "we cannot say that sense exists, but rather that it inheres/insists or subsists" (Deleuze 1969: 33). Learning from experience in anthropology can in this way be directly understood as sensing in more or less intense or telling ways, getting caught or affected or becoming toward through more or less successful, subsisting, and insisting correspondences, as in the instances of embracing hospitalities evoked above. We can thus be more or less present or absent during research, as well as more or less able to sense what is going on depending on our attentive and responsive posture or ability to attain "corhythmy" through copresence, permeability, resonance, and opening (Motta 2013: 115). Sensation is when common ground (or air, breath) is found, creating a rhythmic unity of the senses that is not cerebral, rational, or representational yet rather similar to a wave passing through us, exceeding the bounds of organic activity.

Upon reflecting on the way the works of the painters Cézanne and Francis Bacon make visible a kind of original unity of the senses, Deleuze suggests sensation appeals to a unity of the senses when a vital power exceeds every domain and traverses them all: "this power is rhythm, which is more profound than vision, hearing, etc." (Deleuze [1981] 2003: 43). "Sensation is vibration" (Deleuze [1981] 2003: 45). When two sensations, each with their own level or zone, confront each other and make their respective levels communicate, "we are no longer in the domain of simple vibration, but that of resonance" (Deleuze [1981] 2003: 55). At play, and foreshadowing Samudra's notion of "polypirous" in the following chapter explaining that "feeling" is multi-experienced; is an idea that every sensation implies different levels (of order, of domain) not accounted for by phenomenological unity; in short, "sensation develops through the fall, by falling from one level to another" (Deleuze [1981] 2003: 67). The fall is precisely the active rhythm, tension is experienced in a fall; or in other words, "the fall is what is most alive in the sensation, that through which the sensation is experienced as living" (Deleuze [1981] 2003: 68). The intensive reality of the sensation is a descent in depth yet it can also coincide with a rise, or in other words, it can coincide with a diminution or an augmentation, with a dilatation or with a contraction. In his empirical study of Bacon's triptychs (paintings of three Figures), Deleuze suggests they constitute three fundamental rhythms (active, passive, and attendant). The simple sensation (vibration) and the coupling of sensation (resonance) still merged together with the melodic lines, the points and counterpoints, of a coupled Figure. "With the triptych, finally, rhythm takes on an extraordinary amplitude in a *forced movement* that gives it an autonomy and produces in us the impression of Time" (Deleuze [1981] 2003: 60–61, emphasis in original). In this triad, the limits of sensation are broken yet at the same time a phenomenon of (re)composition or redistribution is produced, the rhythm itself becoming sensation.

To make sense of this with relation to anthropological practice, we can think of immersion in the field as a descent into the ordinary alluding to its violence (Das 2007), however we might also sense a fall as a rise into cosmological or aerial space. This sensation might further couple with another, for example, it can resonate with a prior sensation, wrestle with it, and let it merge into a different rhythm. Finally, it can take on its own autonomy, reach a new plateau, if we return to this term as evoked at the beginning of this piece. This can offer a way to explain how we can become attuned to events in ways that transform both thought and practice all at once, yet also take us elsewhere. Together these rhythms indicate actions of different forces and offer not a narrative or a story yet a living sense of knowing. Method in this case is not something designed in advance to execute once in the field in a contrived manner; rather it is a practice of dilation or sensing through the skin, one akin to listening: "to listen is to stand in wait for the event; for the voice that may come; it is a preparation for common recognition, for confronting what may be so familiar or what may stand in contrast to myself . . . listening is never stable or certain; sound is a type of pressure upon the skin, onto the bones, and sent directly to the heart, to tremble us" (Labelle 2013: 5).

Upon entering new milieus to learn how people (dis)entangle with plants in healing in this case requires preparing to surrender to the ways the world is continuously emerging anew when we are welcome to do so. It is thus quite the opposite of being prepared with an arsenal of questions, strategies, or techniques with objectives to extract data from a context or people whether they like it or not. This latter idea supposes that the world is already "out there" to document or pass through a grid, while the former idea attends to what is yet to come. "To pay attention to things—to watch for their movements and listen to their sounds—is to catch the world in the act, like riding the cusp of a wave ever on the point of breaking" (Ingold 2018: 22). It is to be there, present and alert, to let events, people, plants, elements . . . pass through us, affect us as well become ready to affect them with interests in what occurs and can occur in between. Listening, like breathing, is not always something we are taught directly, nor is it here understood as strictly related to the physical ear, since we hear/sense/feel vibrations through our skin or on the skin of things. Pauline Oliveros suggests "deep listening" is a practice or a kind of meditation, "learning to expand perception of sounds to include the whole space/time continuum of sound—encountering the vastness and complexities as much as possible" (2005: xxiii). Animals are "deep listeners" since sensing someone's presence is survival, yet so are plants, who sense sound vibrations to detect water, for instance. Listening in these receptive ways enriches research, and it implies certain kinds of discretion.

The etymology of the word "listen" is "pay attention to," yet how we are paying attention can differ. We can listen to identify isolated sounds or bits of information or we can listen meaningfully to tone, speed and slowness, rhythms in transformative manners; one way has an interest in form, while the second pays attention to the wellspring of formless "stuff."[15] In the first way we want to count, name with objectives of controlling, abstracting, or measuring a situation, while in the second case we surrender, let ourselves be disoriented, and inhabit a situation to get a sense of what it (un)does. While both paths of listening require attention, it is not the same kind of attention, and what we learn will differ. Victor Stoichita and Bernd Brabec de Mori (2017) discuss different listening postures; they distinguish indexical listening (which relates the sounds to their physical cause), structural listening (which searches them for abstract patterns), and enchanted listening (which can form an autonomous realm). While these authors claim an ontology of sonic percepts, or that these three ways of listening are universal across humans, it here suffices to say that I have brought the first two ways of listening together since they both assume a preexisting "physical world out-there" and reflect a corresponding desire to make abstractions of these sounds out of context as per a certain idea of science, while the third way involves the actual and the virtual, as well as a capacity to let formless stuff transform as well as grow in the imagination. This, in turn, is what I mean by "surrender," or when lives can mix and stir.

More precisely, it is surrender to the flux or in what Deleuze and Guattari (1980) describe as smooth space in contrast with attention turned toward striated space according to desires to control, count, name, or measure. In any case, as soon as we attempt to measure a moment, it escapes; we measure an immobile, a complete line, while time is mobile and incomplete, accelerates or slows down. Henri Bergson differentiates between mathematical time, which measures the distance, the degree, a cut and poses an objectifying and analytical perspective, and pure time, which constitutes duration, the irreducible flux of becoming, affective, creative, an irreversible and unpredictable process ([1938] 2013: 3, [1941] 2009: 9–10). It is in duration that we can correspond with other lives, listening or attuning attention toward open-endedness and flux in the milieu. It is thus missing the point to pay attention only to measured, cadenced rhythms since they are always overflowed by rhythms without measure. Cadenced rhythm relates to the coursing of a river between its banks and to what Deleuze and Guattari call the form of striated space: "but there is also a rhythm without measure, which relates to the upswell of a flow, in other words, to the manner in which a fluid occupies a smooth space. . . . smooth space is occupied by intensities, wind and noise, forces, and sonorous and tactile qualities, as in the desert, steppe, or ice" (1987: 364, 479). Smooth space arises from striation of space, which can help understand how predesigned methods always produce further indeterminacies. In this situation, we can choose to further striate, or we can join in the flux of these indeterminacies to learn along with them, even steer them. Method as a recipe or steps to follow is "the striated space of the *cogitatio universalis* and draws a path that must be followed from one point to another. But the form of exteriority situates thought in a smooth space that it must occupy without counting, and for which there is no possible method, no conceivable reproduction, but only relays, intermezzos, resurgences" (Deleuze and Guattari 1987: 377). This is "after method," sonorous sensation, or what we can call more simply "telling moments" in anthropology, events that profoundly stir or affect the researcher, approach, and method all at once. "The sonorous bloc is the *intermezzo*" (Deleuze and Guattari 1987: 297), sense, or event.

Attending to what is yet to come is attending to smooth space; it implies stepping out of Euclidean space and to experience in the midst of things. It is the French composer/conductor Pierre Boulez who first brought a distinction between two kinds of space-time in music: in striated space, the measure can be irregular or regular, but it is always assignable; in smooth space, the partition, or break, "can be effected at will" (1971: 85).[16] Taken up by Deleuze and Guattari, they express the distinction as one between sedentary or Royal science in which "space is counted in order to be occupied" while in what they call "nomad or minor science," toward which they lean, "space is occupied without being counted" (1987: 362). A current overemphasis on interests in striated space, a space with straight lines and isolated objects, should give way to attending to the open air in which we live. This is where anthropology is at its best and is consistent with its claim to learn from experience. Its strength is in pushing smooth space through striated space rather than weakly attempting to striate further. Smooth space is where life can proliferate, and it seems opportune to both make and occupy this space in meaningful ways, as the Bantu healer readily does.

In my own research, this further offers ways to learn from, with, and through vegetal worlds, perhaps the kinds of life occupying smooth space most successfully in the sense that plants stretch out and couple with wind, sound, air, water, animals, humans . . . in complete surrender as a means to proliferate and to stay alive. "The wisdom of plants: even when they have roots, there is always an outside where they form a rhizome with something else" (Deleuze and Guattari 1987: 11). Occupying smooth space is after method or paying attention to what emerges in between. It can also be called becoming-plant (Houle 2011; Houle and Querrien 2012; Laplante 2016, 2017), not in the literal sense of becoming a plant, but in the sense of letting something new emerge in encounters with the vegetal. It is by occupying the space in-between that we can con-spire with plants, as an act of breathing together (Choy 2011, 2016; Myers 2015, 2018). This is very different from encountering plants with desires to domesticate, control, or turn into commodities, all gestures that hinder learning from plants, obliterating possibilities for listening, sensing, and for improvisation and affective transformation to occur. In all the contexts where I did fieldwork, healers follow vegetal rhythms in healing, preferring plants that thrive in the medium as opposed to plants cultivated in rows on a farm who are considered to have lost their life or efficacy (Laplante 2015), precisely because it is someone else taking over their capacity to persevere in existence, thus diminishing their own effort to live. It is however this potency of life that is prized and cherished as a way to augment lives laterally.

Stirs

Sonorous sensation is what is attended to in Java, actually mixing and stirring human, elemental, and vegetal lives in the practice of *jamu* medicine in attempts to add vitality by making fluids smooth, adjusting their speeds or slowness, and unblocking passages in a plane of immanence. Xhosa healers in the Cape maximize potentials to discern and attend to the lives of people who are unwell by using skilled drumming and dancing to resonate with and across the vegetal, as was also done by shamans in the Amazon through song and humming, all in highly orchestrated fashion. It is also such an approach that enables understanding of how the Bantu healer in Cameroon heals or maximizes life's potentials laterally, or in between, something we can excel at in doing anthropology. How might this begin by breaking through rigid ideas of method or classrooms walls, perhaps as plants resist objectification or burst through concrete sidewalks?

Vignette 2
Breath of Fresh Air

Boyan Atzev

Session 1

The clinic has a quiet, businesslike ambiance: empty rooms, modern minimal lighting, hardwood floors, and bare white walls. We are sitting on chairs arranged in a circle. There is little small talk or eye contact, smile, chit-chat; we are mostly looking at the teacher as we await instructions. In the round of introductions, no one volunteers more than their first name. I am the only one who mentions depression or anxiety as reasons for taking the course. Others hint at reasons, but nothing is shared. Most say they want to reduce stress and feelings of dissatisfaction and disconnection from their body, or issues of absent-mindedness due to going through routine. People leave immediately after the class, making businesslike small talk. The atmosphere is of formal reservation.

Session 2

I want to be lighter and freer; to not ask too many questions and see too many inconsistencies; to let go and just "be." But the uneasy feeling grows in me. A red light is flashing in the murky insides of my being. For now, I am caught between the inkling of the intuition and half-formed thought.

Session 6

I face my partner in the exercise. Since no emotions are to be displayed, I settle at expressing empathy only through my eyes. The story he tells me is a heavy one, much heavier than other stories shared in the course so far. It involves the acceptance of the death of a close person. He was tearing up. In the midst of it, he shares that he realized he cried for himself, as he had been sad but had repressed it. He had been bottling up this feeling until he was encouraged to feel it. The story moved me: I have experienced the same feeling in different circumstances. I feel an urge to reassure, to show empathy, but I hold back as per the instructions.

After, I decide to share with him my desire to show empathy. I tell him a bit about my personal experience with the exercise. He shares a bit of his. He says that he had wanted to show empathy toward my story as well. It is hard to know exactly the feeling of my partner but I could say that feelings of joy, ease, freedom, hope, gratitude, and care are all present. The encounter was unplanned, unexpected, and interrupted with the end of the exercise. Yet it lingered.

When later on we made eye contact, he smiled. I would say something of it stayed with each of us.

Session 8

People took to expressing their definitions of the word anger with gusto. They got up from their chairs or cushions. The structure of the course was interrupted now. They disagreed and questioned. Discussing examples of anger, students told stories based on situations either from home or from work. The stories were about conflict and dealing with temperamental bosses, incompetent employees, clients, and family members. This was the last session and the first-time people shared stories; they shared things that had shaken them up. In their tones of voice and expressions on their face, one could see frustration, anger, sadness, and depression. People empathized with themes of abusive bosses, the impotence of being in a hierarchical structure, the financial dependency on a job, job insecurity.

The affect charge triggered a change in me. The pent-up resentment that I had half-consciously been holding against this course was released. I felt less alienated by the attempts of my classmates to achieve serenity. I thought less in terms of them versus me, rather I saw all classmates as other human beings that now I was more willing to engage with. I was more open to trust and to let go, at least a little, of the cynical attitude of my over-vigilant mind.

* * *

These sketches of experiences come from a Mindfulness-Based Stress Reduction (MBSR) course I followed as part of my master's research in anthropology on the Mindfulness movement in the medicine and wellness industry.[17] The weekly two-month course is recommended for stress management, anxiety, and depression. Mindfulness is a Buddhist meditation method for achieving greater awareness of one's body and the world. One of the key techniques is attuning to one's breathing by focusing on the flow of breath during inhalation and exhalation. This awareness is then extended to every act of life.

Mindfulness does not posit that there is a particular rhythm of breathing ideal to sync to. The instructor did however notice that most "people today breathe in unnatural disconnected manners." The reconnection is done not by controlling the breath but by becoming aware of it, following it, relaxing into it, or sinking into it.

During the class in MBSR, I noticed I often held my breath, a small but important insight not only in personal regard but also for my research. The fact that I held my breath revealed a personal state of tension and a tendency to constrict or hold back, making my connection to my body disrupted and the world beyond distorted. That most people in the class expressed their breath as being shallow might reflect a familiar a state of being in a hurry, skimming over the waters of life.

Buddhism postulates that there is no self as essence, but just accumulation of all parts that make up an individual on many levels. What we experience is a false self. Buddhism teaches to realize one's true nature through meditation. In the practice, rather than selves, we begin to see ourselves as processes that unfold. Similarly, Tim Ingold's (2012) perception of *atmosphere*, being both the ethereal space but also the atmospheric space of moods and forces that affect breath shows the connection between the body and the entire world. The air in our lungs and the air of the whole world cycle with its involved conversion of various gases and processes and players are one and the same. One's breathing also reflects how one is affected. In this sense to study meditation is to meditate. To study the social phenomena is to immerse into mindfulness lessons, in its atmosphere, dynamic, healing, or realignment.

This particular course however was not Deleuze and Guattari's (1987) *smooth space* (the fluid space in which the process of life takes place), it was striated space: a sterile, restrictive environment with emphasis on relaxation. Most material was being taught verbally and things explained, with little meditation done and charged affects suppressed.

A key attitude in mindfulness is that of non-judgment. The meditator is instructed to practice not judging and controlling one's emotions and thoughts. Similarly, the anthropologist is better off moving away from a controlled type of a study and go into the opposite approach of complete immersion, suspending judgment, becoming one with the field. In the given atmosphere, and having decided against formal interviews, insights came from paying attention to affective events. I came to believe that what Mindfulness contributes to psychology (and in this case to anthropology) is a renewed engagement with experience of life, which must include piercing the "the happy-place bubble" by shaking and prying things open. Only then can attunement, therapy, and healing begin.

Julie Laplante is Professor in Anthropology at the University of Ottawa. She works in phenomenological approaches in anthropology with interests in indigenous and humanitarian medicine, attuning to bodily, clinical, sensorial, and sonorous abilities in healing with plants or molecules. Her fieldwork in the Brazilian Amazon and at two edges of the Indian Ocean (South Africa, Java Indonesia) has more recently moved to Cameroon. She produced the anthropological film *Jamu Stories* (2015) and is the author of *Pouvoir guérir* (2004) and *Healing Roots* (2015, 2018).

Daniel Alberto Restrepo Hernández is a postgraduate student in anthropology from the University of Ottawa. He specializes in developing a phenomenological, philosophical, and aesthetic approach to understand the relationship between humans and plants (from *yajé* to cannabis) beyond all anthropocentrism or plant reification. Understanding plants as living, active, and intelligent powers, he now lives in Colombia where he is carrying out projects for the co-creation of biodiversity nodes, and where he continues to delve into plants as generators of worlds, knowledge, and lively transformations.

Boyan Atzev has studied and practiced Tibetan Buddhism, Yoga, and participated in psycho-therapy and political activism. His very intimate auto-ethnographic MA thesis in Anthropology examines phenomena of Mindfulness-Based Therapy and its social implications. Raised in Bulgaria, Boyan has lived in number intentional communities and written articles about the phenomena in independent Canadian media. Attempting to bring back the art of the public intellectual, he weaves these topics of psychology, spirituality, and social movements and analyzing through the lens of critical phenomenology both in academic realms, as well as in freelance articles and public talks.

Notes

Epigraph: Haraway 2015: 5. Epigraph in Vignette 1: Bergson ([1911] 2014: 17–18), emphasis in original.

1. The *yajé* or *ayahuasca* shamans, as they are called in Colombia. The word literally means "father" in Quechua.
2. An endemic squash in which is placed a powder of sea shells tinged with a yellow flower. The device has a hole in the upper part in which he introduces a wooden stick wet with his saliva, and then mixes this powder with a ball of *ayu* leaves he has in his mouth. It is a practice with cosmogonic connotations.
3. They are the seekers and looters of *huacas* or *pagamentos* (funeral or ritual offerings), which are usually underground, often placed centuries or millennia ago.
4. See Daniel Alberto Restrepo Hernández (2018).
5. As Donna Haraway (2015: 6) describes Vincianne Despret's philosophical and scientific work, also evoked in the opening quote to this chapter. "To go visiting" is an expression borrowed from Hannah Arendt (1982: 43) who suggests we need to train our imagination to think with an enlarged mentality. For Despret, and in my own work, it implies training not only the imagination, yet opening our whole being or affective body laterally.
6. The Bantu healer, Roger Amos Kañaa, is in fact the founder and president of ARAM, which is entirely self-funded and maintained by a thoroughly involved and present team of followers, all thankful for his healing either

of themselves or of family members. Their mother tongue is Basaa (a Bantu language) yet they are all fully proficient in French (my mother tongue), working and writing in French. The healer launched his first book describing his healing practices a few months after my departure (Kañaa 2018). I had been invited to give a conference at their annual Open House event at the Solomon TANDENG MUNA Foundation in Yaoundé.

7. One of the first things I was asked to do as an MSF volunteer when I arrived in Brazil in the fall of 1998 was to fly to São Paulo to attend the Sixth Meeting on Medicinal Plants in Public Health on the themes of Biodiversity, Intellectual Property, and Biopiracy. As an anthropologist, I was asked to represent MSF at this conference to reaffirm that neither the organization nor I will be providing information on plant use that could risk being "stolen" by pharmaceutical companies.
8. See A. Irving Hallowell (1960) and Gaetano Mangiameli (2013) for illustrations of such ontologies, respectfully with relation to Ojibwa in Canada and with Kasena people in Ghana.
9. As a senior research fellow of the Biomedicine in Africa group at the Max Planck Institute für ethnologische forshung in Halle/Saale, Germany.
10. Gregory Bateson (1972: 489), who did fieldwork in the neighboring island of Bali, similarly came to find the idea of the self or the "I" as separate from others, and against nature, as the greatest epistemological fallacy of Western thought, even referring to it as the "pathology" of contemporary subjectivities and subsequent ecological crisis (see also Shaw 2015).
11. See chapter 2 by Jaida Kim Samudra on another form of martial arts in Indonesia, as well as chapter 8 by Elisabeth Hsu and Chee Han Lim on such practices in China.
12. In Basaa, *Bassinglègè* means "training of wise (wo)men or warriors" or "the wisdom and combat left by our ancestors." The prefix "Bassing" signified "school of wisdom and combat" and the suffix "lègè," to delegate. When one would say "I am going to Bassinglègè," it would mean "I am going to the replenishment of my capacities/to the secret reunion." Teachings from the forest are often received without one knowing, through the manifestation of its magnetic forces or through the diverse encounters of "gift and receiving" of the healers and the spokespersons called Bambombog by the Basaa of Cameroon (Kañaa 2018: 107).
13. "We" refers to my nineteen-year-old son and to my seventeen-year-old daughter who joined me on this trip, largely because of the enthusiasm manifested by ARAM when I asked if this were a possibility. Their presence, in turn, multiplied the insights and angles, as they joined in to film, record, ask questions and underwent quite a few spontaneous healing events. They have become true allies in the field, both of them having partaken in all the other fieldwork I mention in this chapter, with the exception of my daughter not yet born during my work in the Amazon. I also learned once I arrived in Cameroon that it was the healer who was

particularly enchanted to have more people join me to learn from his practice, seeing this as a possibility to enhance his own practice and more generally ancestral African medicine, particularly in terms of increasing its legitimacy within the Ministry of Health of Cameroon yet also beyond it to interest the youth both in Cameroon and abroad.

14. This "transverse, oblique" or "sideways" approach can also be understood as "transduction," a term introduced by Gilbert Simondon to break through the individual-milieu dyad, expressing how a *being* "can pass out of phase with itself, it can—in any area—break its own bounds in relation to its *center*." ([1964] 1992: 311). Stefan Helmreich suggests the term "transduction" would solely be useful to assess "technoscientific mediations—and even electric, electronic, and electromagnetic—infrastructural instantiations" (2015: 228), however the healer in question here is working explicitly through these very fields as per his own explanations.
15. According to a distinction given by Gaston Bachelard (1942: 10) to indicate two forms of imagination and more specifically as taken up by Ivan Illich (1985: 6).
16. See also Michael Gallope (2008) for further discussion on sonorous sensation in the works of both Deleuze and Boulez.
17. See Boyan Atzev (2017).

References

Arendt, Hannah. 1982. *Lectures on Kant's Political Philosophy*. Brighton: Harvester.

Artaud, Antonin. 1934. *Héliogabale ou l'anarchiste couronné*. Paris: Denoel et Steele.

Atzev, Boyan. 2017. "Mindful of Mindfulness-Based Therapy." M.A. thesis. Ottawa: University of Ottawa.

Bachelard, Gaston. 1942. *L'Eau et les Rêves*. Paris: Corti.

Bateson, Gregory. 1972. *Steps to an Ecology of Mind*. New York: Balantine Books.

Bergson, Henri. [1911] 2014. *Creative Evolution*. New York: Henry Holt and Company. Ebook Edition.

———. [1938] 2013. *La pensée et le mouvant*. Paris: PUF.

———. [1941] 2009. *L'évolution créatrice*. Paris: PUF.

Boulez, Pierre. 1971. *Boulez on Music Today*, trans. Susan Bradshaw and Richard Bennet. Cambridge, MA: Harvard University Press.

Choy, Timothy K. 2011. *Ecologies of Comparison*. Durham, NC: Duke University Press.

———. 2016. "Breathers Conspire—On Drawing Breath Together." Society for Social Studies of Science Annual Meeting, Barcelona, 3 September 2016. Spain: 4S/EASST.

Cubero, Carlo A., Pablo D. Herrera, and Brandon Labelle. 2018. "Sonic Triptych: A Sound Laboratory in Three Counterpoints." CASCA-CUBA annual meeting, Santiago de Cuba, 16–20 May 2018. Cuba: CASCA and SfAA.

Das, Veena. 2007. *Life and Words: Violence and the Descent into the Ordinary*. Berkeley: University of California Press.

Deleuze, Gilles. 1969. *Logique du sens*. Éditions de minuit: Paris.

———. [1981] 2003. *Francis Bacon: The Logic of Sensation*. New York: Continuum.

———. 1988. *Spinoza: Practical Philosophy*, trans. Robert Hurley. San Francisco: City Lights Books.

———. 2004. *L'abécédaire de Gilles Deleuze* [video], ed. Pierre-André Boutang, Michel Pamart, Claire Parnet, interview. Paris: Éditions Monparnasse.

Deleuze, Gilles, and Félix Guattari. 1980. *Mille plateaux*. Paris: Minuit.

———. 1987. *A Thousand Plateaus*, trans. Brian Massumi. London: University of Minnesota Press.

Favret-Saada, Jeanne. 1977. *Les mots, la mort, les sorts*. Paris: Gallimard.

Ferzacca, Steve. 2001. *Healing the Modern in a Central Javanese City*. Durham, NC: Carolina Academic Press.

Gallope, Michael. 2008. "Is There a Deleuzian Musical Work?" *Perspectives of New Music* 46(2): 93–129.

Hallowell, A. Irving. 1960. "Ojibwa Ontology, Behavior and World View." In *Culture in History: Essays in Honor of Paul Radin*, ed. Stanley Diamond, 19–49. New York: Columbia University Press.

Haraway, Donna. 2015 "A Curious Practice." *Angelaki: Journal of the Theoretical Humanities* 20(2): 5–14.

Helmreich, Stefan. 2015. "Transduction." In *Keywords in Sound*, ed. David Novak and Matt Sakakeeny, 222–231. Durham, NC: Duke University Press.

Houle, Karen. L. F. 2011. "Animal, Vegetable, Mineral: Ethics as Extension or Becoming? The Case of Becoming-Plant." *Journal for Critical Animal Studies* 9(1/2): 89–116.

Houle Karen L. F., and A. Querrien. 2012. "Devenir-plante." *Chimères* 1(76): 183–194.

Illich, Ivan. 1985. *H2O and the Waters of Forgetfulness: Reflections on the Historicity of "Stuff."* Dallas: Dallas Institute of Humanities and Culture.

Ingold, Tim. 2012. "The Atmosphere." *Chiasmi International* 14: 75–87.

———. 2015. *The Life of Lines*. London: Routledge.

———. 2018. *Anthropology: Why It Matters*. Cambridge: Polity Press.

Kañaa, Roger Amos. 2018. *Médecine traditionnelle et savoirs thérapeutiques endogènes*. Paris: L'Harmattan.

Kohn, Eduardo. 2007. "How Dogs Dream: Amazonian Natures and the Politics of Transspecies Engagement." *American Ethnologist* 34(1): 3–24.

Labelle, Brandon. 2013. "Dirty Ideas." In *Dirty Ear Report 1: Sound, Multiplicity, and Radical Listening*, ed. Zeynep Bulut et al., 4–7. Berlin: Errant Bodies Press.

Laplante, Julie. 2004. *Pouvoir guérir: Médecines humanitaires et autochtones.* PUL: Québec.
———. 2015a. *Jamu Stories.* Anthropological Film 104 minutes. Retrieved 16 December 2019 from https://www.youtube.com/watch?v=CMRZRw1z2Fw.
———. 2015b. *Healing Roots: Anthropology in Life and Medicine.* Oxford: Berghahn Books.
———. 2016. "Becoming-Plant: Jamu in Java, Indonesia" In *Plants & Health: New Perspectives on the Health-Environment-Plant Nexus*, ed. Elizabeth Anne Olson and John Richard Stepp, 17–65. Cham: Springer International Publishing.
———. 2017. "Devenir-plante: enlacements vivants en Océan Indien et en Amazonie." *Drogues, santé et société* 16(2): 36–54.
Mangiameli, Gaetano. 2013. "The Habits of Water: Marginality and the Sacralization of Non-humans in North-Eastern Ghana." In *Biosocial Becomings: Integrating Social and Biological Anthropology*, ed. Tim Ingold and Gisli Palsson, 145–161. Cambridge: Cambridge University Press.
Mengue Me Ndongo, Jean Paulin. 2014. *La médecine chez les Peuls du Cameroun Septentrional 1754–2013.* Paris: L'Harmattan.
Motta, Marco. 2013 "Jouer au théâtre. Le rythme de l'expression." In *A contrario Campus*, ed. dans: Groupe Anthropologie et Théâtre, 111–187. Bangkok: BSN Press.
Myers, Natasha. 2015. "Conversations on Plant Sensing: Notes from the Field." *NatureCulture* 3: 35–66.
———. 2018. "How to Grow Livable Worlds: Ten Not-So-Easy Steps." In *The World to Come*, ed. Kerry Oliver Smith, 53–63. Gainsville, FL: Harn Museum of Art.
Oliveros, Pauline. 2005. *Deep Listening: A Composer's Sound Practice.* Lincoln, NE: iUNIVERSE.
Restrepo Hernández, Daniel Alberto. 2018. "Milieugenèses du yajé, un tour de la jungle kofán pour la re-existence." M.A. thesis. Ottawa: University of Ottawa.
Simondon, Gilbert. [1964] 1992. "The Genesis of the Individual," trans. Mark Cohen and Sanford Kwinter. In *Incorporations*, ed. Jonathan Crary and Sanford Kwinter, 296–319. New York: Zone.
Shaw, Robert. 2015 "Bringing Deleuze and Guattari down to Earth through Gregory Bateson: Plateaus, Rhizomes and Ecosophical Subjectivity." *Theory, Culture & Society* 32(7–8): 151–171.
Simpson, Paul. 2009. "'Falling on Deaf Ears': A Postphenomenology of Sonorous Presence." *Environmental and Planning* 41: 2556–2575.
Spinoza, Baruch. [1849] 2002. *L'éthique*, trans. Saisset. Retrieved 3 April 2020 from http://palimpsestes.fr/textes_philo/spinoza/ethique.pdf.
Stoichita, Victor A., and Bernd Brabec de Mori 2017. "Postures of Listening: Ontology of Sonic Precepts from an Anthropological Perspective." *Terrain.* Retrieved 6 January 2020 from http://terrain.revues.org/16418.

Thompson, Mary. 2017. *Beyond Unwanted Sound: Noise, Affect and Aesthetic Moralism*. New York: Bloomsbury.
Turner, Victor W. 1968. *The Drums of Affliction: A Study of Religious Processes among the Ndembu of Zambia*. Ithaca, NY: Cornell University Press.

Chapter 2

SENSING "FEELING" IN INDONESIA'S PERSATUAN GERAK BADAN (BODY MOVEMENT UNIFICATION) SCHOOL

Jaida Kim Samudra

> Within many approaches to embodied practice there exists the potential to gradually elaborate or unfold a certain complexity or "thickness of sensing" that constitutes the living "world" of that practice. There is available—if one attends to it and opens one's awareness to it—an experience of "what it is like" to inhabit/sense/live within that specific "world."
>
> —Phillip Zarrilli, *Inner Movement*

Upon entering the field of Persatuan Gerak Badan (Body Movement Unification, PGB), an international Chinese-Indonesian *silat* (self-defense) school based in Java, even a neophyte anthropologist would soon recognize the salience of "feeling." Beginning with archival research, one would notice the word appearing in PGB texts written in the national language, Bahasa Indonesia. For example, it is the only English-derived word used for any of the names of the 108 standard short movements that constitute basic training in Silat Bangau Putih (White Crane Silat, WCS), PGB's signature movement system. While observing training sessions (*latihan*), one might hear *pelatih* (trainers) call out "Feeling" from a printed list and then see students perform a distinct movement. One would also hear *pelatih* tell students to "*latihan* [practice] *feeling*" or "do feeling." If one had surmised that "feeling" referred to a specific bodily form, one might then be surprised to observe students taking partners to practice several interactive exercises, only one of which resembled the short movement by that name. "Feeling" would then seem to constitute a category of movements, not just a single form.

You would uncover yet other uses of the term if you delved further into PGB archives and recorded discussions among advanced practitioners. "Feeling" is one of seven categories of assessment in the rubrics used for belt tests. "Feeling" is also invariably brought up by *pelatih* discussing basic training principles. For example, during a trainers' Q and A at an international retreat in Bali, an Indonesian German elder explained, "To understand the *tui cu* ["sparring" in Hokkien Chinese], you need: position, feeling, nerve, rhythm, control" (Q and A, 28 July 2000). PGB grandmaster Guru Gunawan Rahardja (henceforth Guru, "Teacher") then commented, "Feeling is the highest one." Similarly, a 2005 essay in PGB's online newsletter *Warta Bangau* (Crane News) listed five fundamental aspects of *tui cu* training: Position, Nerve, Application, Feeling, and Timing (my translations). The fourth was glossed, "*Feeling/Wirasa* (*Perasaan/tempelan*)." The Javanese *wirasa* and Indonesian *perasaan* (both from the Sanskrit root *rasa*, meaning "sense," "sensation," or "feeling") are straightforward translations; only *tempelan*, meaning "adhering to something," hints at one attribute or purpose of "feeling," that is, sustaining physical contact with a partner.

Even if you were a native Indonesian speaker, knowing this gloss would not enable you to understand what trainers mean when they caution students, *Pakai feeling!* (Use feeling!) or "More feeling!" while practicing *ambilan* (take-downs), since people only touch their partners briefly before throwing them to the floor. If you heard Guru advise sparring partners, "Be strong until you enter. After you enter, use your feeling" (fieldnotes, 17 March 2000), you also might be disconcerted when the students resumed sparring without adjusting their positions to match any of the forms in the Feeling category of movements, although you might observe them slowing a bit, moving into closer proximity, or touching each other a little more often.

By now in your field research, you would have realized from these various discursive and performative encounters that "feeling" was highly significant to PGB's culture of movement.[1] From overhearing *pesilat* (martial artists) critiquing each other in comments such as "that person has good feeling" or "his technique is good, but he has no feeling," you might surmise that some sort of hierarchy was implicated in "feeling" training just as for other forms of physiological abilities. You would eventually recognize its polysemy in simultaneously referencing a specific bodily form and class of interactive exercises, as well as a training principle and possibly a stylistic modification to movement or even a method or skill, although what the latter usages implied for self-defense training would remain in question. What are people actually doing when they "do feeling"? What are they attempting to add (or possibly subtract) to their practice following the injunction "more feeling"? And what are skilled practitioners expected to "use" when told to "use feeling"?

To grasp what "feeling" is, does, and how it is used in PGB's somatic culture, one would have to move beyond textual and observational research methods. I mean literally move beyond by engaging your body in new physical interactions in close proximity to other people's bodies in order to collect the kinds of sensory data that would enable you to answer such questions (Csordas 1993; Jackson 1983; Ram and Houston 2015). More than polysemous, "feeling" is "polypirous": it is multi-experienced in a variety of related somatic interactions, movements, and sensations.[2] Instructions such as *pakai feeling* or "more feeling" only make sense—become accessible to one's senses as well as conceptual understanding (Rudie 1994: 30)—in the context of somatic training, as when trainers physically maneuver students' bodies to give them the experience of "feeling." Comprehending such phenomenological complexity requires "deploying the body as tool of inquiry and vector of knowledge" (Wacquant 2004: viii). Engaging in "thick participation" (Samudra 2008), "radical participation," or "participant *sensation*" (Howes 2009:31, italics in original) generates unfamiliar sensory impressions in the field that then may be externalized as "textual data [i.e., fieldnotes] for purposes of analysis" (Samudra 2008: 667).

Thick participation in PGB as a field site would entail joining WCS classes. Indeed, PGB members might demand that you do so. I had practiced WCS in the United States for sixteen years before I began doctoral research on how people acquire inclusive social identities through shared bodily practices (Samudra 2006). Shortly after starting fieldwork in Indonesia, I decided to forego *latihan* to make more time for interviews. My consultants then objected that I could not do research in PGB without participating in training because "PGB is *latihan*!" They understood something I, in my new guise as anthropologist, did not: that knowledge inheres in "the skills of perception and capacities of judgment that develop in the course of direct, practical, and sensuous engagements" (Ingold 2013: 5). Bodily practices are not merely observable performances of culture, they are inherent to enculturation itself. Furthermore, the "recurring behaviors, habits, and comportments" learned during physical training "cause our bodies and nervous systems to adapt, to become more refined, and to accumulate change" (Downey 2015: 128). In short, undertaking "feeling" practices is essentially an inquiry into what Tim Ingold (2013: 4) calls the "conditions and potentials of human life," which in this case involves investigating what it means to "unify" body movement (as per the name of the school).

To appreciate PGB's movement culture, one would not have to undergo decades of training to become an advanced *pesilat*, however. You need only attune your attention to some of the unusual sensations of this embodied practice. Registering your own neurological adaptations to unfamiliar movements during *latihan* would minimally enable you to compare PGB's sensory modalities and concepts to other movement cultures.[3] You might then be able to discern the similarities between WCS's "Feeling" (capitalized when referencing specific movements) to the "pushing hands" and "sticky hands" exercises of other self-defense systems (Frantzis 1998: 339; Reid and Croucher 1983: 107, 110). You could also explore the differences between PGB's "feeling" (lower case when referencing sensations or skills) from "the central sense" of *rasa* or "inner feeling" developed in other movement arts (de Grave 2011: 124; Wilson 2015). For example, for South Indian *kathak* dancers, *rasa* is "most often translated as mood or aesthetic enjoyment" (Dalidowicz 2015:90). Indonesians at *silat* schools other than PGB use *rasa* to refer variously to "all that can be perceived and felt within the body: combining sensations of the skin and proprioception as well as the "emotions and feelings" (de Grave 2011: 124) or to "an intuitive understanding of the inner, spiritual reality (Mulder 1998) . . . kinaesthetic awareness . . . [and] sensitivity to one's opponent" (Wilson 2015:59). While PGB's *pelatih* sometimes gloss "feeling" as synonymous with *rasa*, emotions and aesthetics do not enter into their "feeling" training. Only by practicing "feeling" yourself would you begin to understand that it primarily involves increasing refinement of a sensorial complex.

To illustrate, I next describe learning "Feeling" and the sensations of "feeling" from the perspective of a beginning *silat* student. Although I did not inquire into "feeling" as an analytic subject until after I became an anthropologist, my translations of these movements and sensations into (inevitably inadequate and incomplete) words are based on over thirty-five years of observing interactions between other *pelatih* and students and modulating my own and other people's bodies to generate the "feeling" experience.

Doing Feeling

Figure 2.1. Doing "Feeling" at 2016 Belt Test, Santa Cruz, California. Photo courtesy of David Gilbert.

Students are introduced to "Feeling" only after learning fundamental stances, hits, parries, kicks, and how to fall down safely. *Pelatih* first model "Feeling" for students to emulate, then correct their form before partnering with them. To start, stand straight with your heels together, arms bent and elbows back at chest height, with wrists hyper-extended so your palms face forward with fingertips pointing toward the ceiling. Slide one foot forward while simultaneously pushing the arm on the same (*yang*) side straight out. At the completion of the forward step/ push, move your opposite (*yin*) hand across your chest to just under your upper *yang* arm; your *yin* palm now faces out to your side. Now slide your forward foot backward while pulling back the *yang* arm to your armpit. After your upper *yang* arm clears your lower *yin* wrist, sweep your *yin* hand back across your chest in an outward parry, ending in the same position from which you began the movement. Repeat on the other side.

Pelatih usually leave students practicing this back and forth step/ push and parry movement for five or ten minutes or until they have established a relaxed rhythm. A *pelatih* then initiates partnered "Feeling" by standing facing you just as you are stepping and pushing forward. The trainer deflects your outstretched arm slightly outward with a parry so your hand does not touch their chest. Maintaining contact at the wrist, the *pelatih* then steps and pushes forward, forcing you to move back and parry the trainer's incoming hit to your own chest (Figure 2.1). This reciprocal interaction continues for several minutes until students are told to change partners. Students go on to practice "Feeling" with everyone in the class so they can experience the minor variations in speed and positioning (i.e., angles of trajectory and deflection, length of stance, points of contact along the arm) occurring from partner to partner.

Merely observing "Feeling" partners would probably not enable you to discern the immediate goal of the exercise, which is not to try to hit each other, but to remain in physical contact while continually moving. Trainers make this goal known to students by subtly manipulating their bodies throughout the exercise. As a beginner, you would probably experience a trainer curling a finger or two around your wrist to pull your palm closer toward their chest as you step toward them and then putting a little more force into their open palm hits as they step toward you. You might feel a slight tugging or pushing on your arms, although in the moment you might not notice these sensations or that the trainer has deliberately altered your experience of the movement.

Once you are able to sustain the movement with a partner, trainers make it more difficult for you to remain in physical contact. They adjust the speed and depth of their steps, the force and angle of their hits, and where their hands touch your arms during the parries. As the interaction becomes more intense and complex, your heart rate increases, your breathing becomes shallower and more rapid, and you begin to sweat and flush as your body temperature rises. Most beginners also react to a perception of increased danger from these faster, heavier hits by forgetting the "Feeling" form. Your footwork will get sloppy and you will probably add force to your parries, knocking your partner's arms aside instead of deflecting them gently. Or you might tighten the muscles in your forearm and keep it angled across your torso to prevent your partner's hand from touching your chest. You will likely begin anticipating incoming hits by stepping back and pulling your arm back faster than your partner is stepping toward you, while swinging your parrying hand outward well before the approaching palm has come close to your torso.

If you start reacting like this, the trainer will suddenly slow down or even halt their forward movement, allowing you to continue pulling back and lose contact with their arm. Many students do not immediately notice that the trainer is no longer touching them and they continue retreating all the way back. Other students, disconcerted by the sudden change in rhythm and loss of touch sensation, hesitate mid-stride. The trainer then either moves forward to re-establish contact and continues the movement at a slower pace or resets to the original position and nods to the student to start over. Then, as soon as a steady rhythm has been achieved, it happens again. The trainer stops moving and lets you lose contact, then restarts the exercise. This awkward interchange is repeated until you learn to adjust your speed to match theirs without either resisting or anticipating, but still effectively parrying, their hits while remaining in continual motion and physical contact. You have now begun to do "Feeling."

This pedagogical interaction teaches students that doing "Feeling" correctly depends on the sense of touch. Discursive data would likely support that conclusion. As Guru once commented, "Awareness is outside your arm. Feeling is touching your skin" (Q and A, 28 July 2000).[4] In distinguishing "awareness" of distant stimuli (such as those that might be sensed through the eyes or ears) from closer stimuli (sensed at the skin), *pelatih* recognize touch as "an especial modality of perception in that it blurs subject and object, bringing them together" (Skinner 2013: 112). However, touch is only one of the sensory modalities deployed in PGB's "feeling" practice. By attending closely to your sensations while doing "Feeling" and related improvisational exercises, you would discover that "feeling" involves the even more intimate mechanoreceptions of balance, kinaesthesis, proprioception, acceleration, and possibly others (Howes 2009: 24). Some of the sensations involved in tracking variations in position, speed, trajectory, and force within your own body, while simultaneously sensing your partner's structural microadjustments, are described next.

Sensing Feeling

Figure 2.2. Blindfolded sparring partners, PGB WCS Bay Area Regional Retreat 2015, Santa Cruz, California. Photo courtesy of Bessma Khalaf.

Pelatih occasionally refer to the basic "Feeling" exercise as a *yin-yang* movement because people alternate between *yin* receptivity as they back up and allow their partners to enter their physical space and *yang* activity as they move forward with some force toward their partners.[5] Each phase is accompanied by distinct sensations. You might experience the *yang* phase as tightening, hardening, tingling, or trembling in your muscles, heat in your hands and feet, rigidity through the legs, waist, and shoulders, and heavy, fatiguing, even painful pressure on your arms, especially if your partners resist being pushed backward. The *yin* phase might be experienced as softening, cooling, or opening sensations as your muscles and tendons relax through your arms and shoulders; your spine and your hip, knee, and ankle joints may feel smooth, as if oiled; your palms and the soles of your feet might feel cool or empty and you would probably feel light, brushing sensations at your wrists, forearms, or the sides or backs of your hands.

The more attentive you become to such minute stimuli and the more ably you adjust your movements in response to them, the more adept you are becoming at what some trainers call "harmonizing" with others, which is another purpose of practicing "Feeling." Some expert *pesilat* move so precisely in tandem with their partners that they become imperceptible to the sense of touch. This occurs when they move backward at exactly the same speed as you step forward, without tightening their arm muscles or resisting your pushing hand in the slightest. If they constantly recalibrate the tension in their arms to match yours, you will cease to register sensation at any point of contact, even when you can see with your eyes that you are still touching each other. I recall being amazed thirty years ago by an assistant trainer who had this capacity to completely disappear from sensation in my hands during "Feeling."

Besides formal "Feeling" exercises, *pelatih* set up less structured, playful activities to further train "feeling" sensitivity. Sometimes they pair people up, designating one partner the "leader" and the other the "follower." Each leader holds their arms out about chest height, palms flat and facing down; the follower holds their own arms out in parallel and slightly above the leader's arms and drops one or two fingers of each of their hands to rest lightly on the back of each of the leader's hands. The leader then improvises a series of slow movements, which the partner attempts to follow without lifting their fingers from the leader's hands. The goal for the leader is to guide the follower into a position of imbalance from which they cannot recover unless they release contact.

As a beginner, you would probably tense your muscles and put pressure on the leader's hands as you followed them into increasingly complex twisting, crossing, or extended positions. You might stumble and begin sweating as you attempted to remain upright. As you reached a position of instability, you would probably stop moving and lock up at the joints. You might feel a slight jolt or nausea at the moment you lose balance. More experienced followers put their attention in the soles of their feet: they glide across the floor and flow through the gestures without freezing and their limbs extend and contract into various positions while their center of gravity remains stable. Meanwhile, experienced leaders feel their followers shift into imbalance through minute changes in the pressure on the tops of their hands. I also sometimes register my partners nearing imbalance as a slight internal kick within my gut or as a nudge from within my hip or shoulder. Whether in the following or leading role, I experience stability as a contained liquid or force rolling or surging around belly or hip height.

In another variant of this "following" exercise, the follower grips the leader's wrists instead of lightly touching the tops of their hands. The goal for the leader in this case is not to make the follower lose contact, but to draw their partner into such an unbalanced position that they fall over. One of the ways a skilled leader achieves this is by adjusting the relative pressures in their own limbs, say by leaving about 10–20 percent of muscular tension in one stationary arm, while putting 80–90 percent tension in the other moving arm or hand.[6] If you were the follower, you would likely tighten your grip and adjust your position in response to the leader's subjectively heavier and more dynamic arm, while ignoring or even forgetting about their unmoving, more relaxed arm. Once the leader feels that you are becoming unbalanced, they will switch the tension, relaxing the moving arm and suddenly hardening the stationary one. Moving their fingers, wrist, elbow, or shoulder in the formerly relaxed arm by as little as an inch will then be sufficient to throw you completely off balance and topple you to the floor.

I and other PGB trainers sometimes blindfold our students and have them spar slowly to teach them to anticipate their partner's next gestures and positions in the tension in their muscles and joints and in the acceleration and deceleration of different parts of their body. By touching their partners with various parts of their body (minimally a finger, shoulder, hip, knee, or foot), students learn to sense within their own bodies the moment their partner is going off balance.[7] They then sweep their feet to throw their partner down. The ability to feel the subtle sensations of someone going off balance just by touching them and thus maneuver them into falling is so surprising when blindfolded that both partners often burst out laughing when it occurs (see the two people on the right in Figure 2.2).

One of the strangest aspects of these more goal-oriented "feeling" practices is that they are most effective when people offer the most resistance. It is easier to throw someone who holds rigid positions or grips tightly than someone with a light touch who smoothly adjusts their positions as you change yours. By the same token, highly skilled *pesilat* seem to exert hardly any force on their partners as they execute their movements. Once when I was sparring vigorously with Guru, I ended up on the floor with no idea how I had gotten there. I knew he must have used his hands to guide me into losing my balance and then knocked my feet out from under me, but there was no residual sensation of touch contact anywhere in my skin. Instead, I felt within my chest and back as if I had been caught by a sudden wave while bodysurfing, as if my entire body had been buoyed up from below, then overturned and slammed into the ground.

Not only do students sometimes lose the subjective sensation of being touched by their partners while sparring or doing "Feeling," they may even cease to remain aware of their own limbs. Guru once advised me to practice sensing where both my hands were positioned at all times.[8] He commented, "People forget where the other hand is. This [hand] is closer [to the incoming hit], but they try to block [the hit] with the other. Why? Because they aren't feeling where their hands are. It's a waste of time" (fieldnotes, 11 June 2000). Such somatic experiences of momentary losses of touch sensation and even seeming to "forget" your own spatial positioning provide you with further clues as to how skilled *pesilat* might use "feeling" in PGB.

Using Feeling

Having the sensory experiences described above would enable an anthropologist to grasp that "feeling" is not only a category or style of movement, but a set of sensory skills. In pushing *pesilat* past ordinary limits of perception, "feeling" practices are similar to other sensory trainings in taste (as for vintners) or smell (as for perfumers). Like the most delicate surgical training, "feeling" refines the sense of touch, but that is not the only sense involved. "Feeling" also develops balance as a sensory system for noticing another person's center of gravity and how it shifts in dynamic motion. Kinesthesia and proprioception also constitute "feeling," as *pesilat* endeavor to remain conscious of the position of every part of their bodies as they move, regardless of how much sensation they are receiving from their partners at any point of skin contact. "Feeling" practices thus seem intended to develop a number of sensory "hyper-capacities" among PGB's *pesilat* who, like other martial artists, undergo extensive training to "operate at a level of efficacy beyond what is normally possible" (Downey 2015: 114).

Pesilat do not usually articulate their development of these sensory capacities, but one European American assistant trainer noticed that "feeling" training was enabling her to read other people's internal structures:

> I like doing "Feeling" and *tui cu* with people because you can feel what's going on inside their body. It's really interesting to feel that, "Oh, someone's got a really strong base, but they feel hollow somehow." What is that? How can I feel that? . . . Or somebody's got posture problems, it's like their spine is slipping in a couple places . . . It's very interesting to feel the core of someone's body. (Interview, 20 June 1999)

She used "feeling" to assess students' musculo-skeletal limitations so she could modify how she trained them and improve their *silat* movements.

Heightened kinaesthetic, proprioceptive, balance, touch, and possibly other sensitivities are also deployed for specific self-defense purposes in PGB. Just as *pesilat* gauge when they might effectively throw someone by feeling their partners' tiny physical adjustments as they strive to maintain their balance, *pesilat* use "feeling" sensitivity to read other people's intentions and anticipate their next moves before their partners have physically committed themselves. For example, a slight tensing of a sparring partner's bicep may signal that your partner is about to hit you before they have taken any visible action. Registering minute changes in someone's body as they ready for attack gives you time to maneuver into a more advantageous position and block the attack. Some *pesilat* can also deploy "feeling" as kinesthetic hyper-capacity so as not to communicate their own intentions to their partners. Able to feel and thus control their muscles and tendons relaxing or activating in isolation from the whole, they only move a limb or increase the speed or force of a gesture at the precise moment necessary, without tensing up any other part of their body. It is extraordinarily difficult to anticipate and block such skilled practitioners.

The most advanced *pesilat* are not only able to anticipate and respond to other people's movements, they use their hyper-sensitivities to control other people's sense systems and nerve reactions. This aspect of "feeling" was hinted at in the descriptions above of "forgetting" your limbs or places where you are being touched. Such moments of subjective absence of sensation occur because of a peculiarity of all human sensory systems, which is to be activated by change at the neurological level and go more or less dormant as they become habituated to regular, repetitive, steady, and thus seemingly nonthreatening stimuli, even in the very short term. Ordinarily, one's sensory attention is caught by potential sources of danger. People become focused on objects (including fists) they see suddenly coming toward them or on parts of their bodies where they sense increasing weight or acceleration. People's attention is also captured more by light but intermittent sensations (such as from arrhythmic finger tapping) than by heavier but sustained and steady sensations (such as from a stranger's hip pressed against theirs on a bus). The fact that change engages more attention than a steady state is that aspect of human neurobiology that makes it possible for the sensory skill of "feeling" to be used most effectively in sparring. Guru instructs PGB trainers to use "feeling" strategically by capturing and retaining their partners' attention at the part of their body where they are being held or pushed with some force so as to distract them from noticing that they are also being lightly touched at another part of their body. Their partners can then be manipulated by the predictability of their reactions to the perceived danger at the more obvious point of contact into shifting into a compromised position. The trainer then transfers pressure from one side or limb to another, which makes their partners switch their attention to the new point, while again "forgetting" they are still being touched at the other point. As they continue to react to changing stimuli, they will increasingly move out of balance. Eventually they can be made to fall down, apparently without the trainer having pushed them or swept their feet out from under them. *Pesilat* who can use their "feeling" to distract other people's sensory attention and manipulate their physical reactions cannot be beaten, even by larger, heavier, and more technically skilled opponents. Their ability to throw people while barely touching them may seem like magic to inexperienced observers.

Indeed, my ongoing attention to the sensations of "feeling" practice and the effortless effectiveness of the most advanced *pesilat* are related to my intellectual interests in medical and martial art conceptualizations of energy, *qi*, or *tenaga dalam* (internal energy) that some Indonesians (including practitioners from other *silat* schools) view as a kind of magic. That is, I am partly motivated to investigate sensory hyper-capacities so as to grapple with older anthropologies of "magic" and newer anthropologies of "energy," as well as interpretations of extraordinary experiences that have often been classified as "spiritual" or "religious" precisely because they could not be explained based on the relatively narrow physiological experiences of most anthropologists. Regardless of where "attending to, learning from, ever more elaborated and subtle sensory experiences" leads you, by willingly undergoing a transformation of your own nervous system during the course of fieldwork, you will enter "into a different cultural world" (Ingold 2013: 2–4), the core of what it means to be an anthropologist.

Dr. Jaida Kim Samudra is a medical anthropologist working in northern California as an independent researcher and editor. Most of her scholarship focuses on Oceanic and East and Southeast Asian cultures. Current interests revolve around bioethics, conceptualizations of "energy" in complementary and alternative medicine and martial arts, neurological hyper-capacities, and methods for conducting ethnographic research on somatic experiences. She is also Managing Editor of the archaeology journal *Asian Perspectives* and runs writing and publishing workshops for social scientists.

Notes

1. The term is so ubiquitous throughout PGB worldwide that many non-English-speaking members remain unaware of its English derivation and assume it is unique to the school (North American Chief Trainer Sutrisno Samudra, pers. comm., 11 August 2018).
2. I coined the terms "polypiry" and "polypirous" from the Greek *poly* (many) combined with *peira (*try, attempt), the root for "experience."
3. Experiencing for yourself the sensations of "feeling" might also enable you to better address questions of who gets to teach and who does not and what kinds of abilities render respect and status to certain people over others in PGB compared to other movement cultures.
4. In PGB terms, "awareness" means sensing external stimuli from beyond your skin, mostly by using sight and hearing; however, being aware of your surroundings (and possible threats) also includes noticing sensations such as vibrations through the floor felt through your feet or movements of air or temperature changes on your skin that would indicate someone is approaching.
5. In PGB, *yin-yang* is shorthand for various dichotomous gestures and sensations, including opposite/same side, receptivity/activity, emptiness/fullness, and so on. An advanced Chinese American practitioner explained that "the movements and forms do somehow calibrate both yin-yang, feeling-reflexes, intellect-emotion, soft-hard" (email, 23 February 2004).
6. A variety of exercises are used to teach advanced *pesilat* to isolate and control the movements and pressures independently exerted by each part of their body. Some *pelatih* also tell students to "split" their "energy" between one arm and another, letting one hand become "empty" (soft, relaxed, light) while the other remains "full" (hard, tense, heavy), and then switch. Advanced practitioners also dynamically isolate and switch movement intensities between shoulders, knees, hips, and so on.
7. Inexperienced *pesilat* seldom register when their partners have become unstable or overextended and tend to react by going off balance themselves. Adjusting to stabilize themselves then allows their partners to regain stability, so they miss the opportunity to take them down. Beginners who cannot throw their partners through "feeling" alone also resort to force to compensate.
8. Concentrating on such subtle sensations while moving one's body with feeling in contact with another person's moving body for extended periods (as long as three hours at a stretch) generates its own peculiar sensations. At a retreat in 2016, Guru introduced to international *pelatih* a new training system that relies highly on "feeling" sensitivity. Many subsequently reported unusual sensations in their heads. They said they felt "spacey," lightheaded, dizzy, or as if they were entering an "altered" state. After a few hours of such advanced "feeling" practice, I feel as if

champagne bubbles are effervescing in my head. I also find it difficult to speak intelligibly, sometimes remaining inarticulate for an hour or so afterward. Such reactions may be difficult to explain in biomedical terms, but *pelatih* attribute them to trying to concentrate on very subtle and unusual stimuli for protracted periods of time.

References

Csordas, Thomas J. 1993. "Somatic Modes of Attention." *Cultural Anthropology* 8: 135–56.

Dalidowicz, Monica. 2015. "Being 'Sita': Physical Affects in the North Indian Dance of *Kathak*." In *Phenomenology in Anthropology: A Sense of Perspective*, ed. Kalpana Ram and Christopher Houston, 90–113. Bloomington: Indiana University Press.

de Grave, Jean-Marc. 2011. "The Training of Perception in Javanese Martial Arts." In *Martial Arts as Embodied Knowledge: Asian Traditions in a Transnational World*, ed. D. S. Farrer and John Whalen-Bridge, 123–43. Albany: State University of New York Press.

Downey, Greg. 2015. "Beneath the Horizon: The Organic Body's Role in Athletic Experience." In *Phenomenology in Anthropology: A Sense of Perspective*, ed. Kalpana Ram and Christopher Houston, 114–37. Bloomington: Indiana University Press.

Frantzis, Bruce K. 1998. *The Power of Internal Martial Arts: Combat Secrets of Ba Gua, Tai Chi, and Hsing-I*. Berkeley, CA: North Atlantic Books.

Howes, David. 2009. "Introduction: The Revolving Sensorium." In *The Sixth Sense Reader*, ed. David Howes, 1–52. Oxford: Berg.

Ingold, Tim. 2013. *Making: Anthropology, Archaeology, Art and Architecture*. London: Routledge.

Jackson, Michael. 1983. "Knowledge of the Body." *Man* 18: 327–45.

Mulder, Niels. 1998. *Mysticism in Java: Ideology in Indonesia*. Amsterdam: The Pepin Press.

Ram, Kalpana, and Christopher Houston. 2015. "Introduction: Phenomenology's Methodological Invitation." In *Phenomenology in Anthropology: A Sense of Perspective*, ed. Kalpana Ram and Christopher Houston, 1–25. Bloomington: Indiana University Press.

Reid, Howard, and Michael Croucher. 1983. *The Way of the Warrior: The Paradox of the Martial Arts*. London: Leopard Books.

Rudie, Ingrid. 1994. "Making Sense of New Experience." In *Social Experience and Anthropological Knowledge*, ed. Kirsten Hastrup and Peter Hervik, 28–44. London: Routledge.

Samudra, Jaida Kim. 2006. "Body and Belonging in a Transnational Indonesian Silat Community." Ph.D. dissertation. Honolulu: University of Hawai'i at Mānoa.

———. 2008. "Memory in Our Body: Thick Participation and the Translation of Kinesthetic Experience." *American Ethnologist* 35(4): 665–81.

Skinner, Jonathon. 2013. "Leading Questions and Body Memories: A Case of Phenomenology and Physical Ethnography in the Dance Interview." In *The Ethnographic Self as Resource: Writing Memory and Experience into Ethnography*, ed. Peter Collins and Anselma Gallinat, 111–28. New York: Berghahn Books.

Wacquant, Loïc. 2004. *Body and Soul: Notebooks of an Apprentice Boxer*. Oxford: Oxford University Press.

Wilson, Lee. 2015. *Martial Arts and the Body Politic in Indonesia*. Leiden: Brill.

Zarrilli, Phillip B. 2016. "'Inner Movement' between Practices of Meditation, Martial Arts, and Acting: A Focused Examination of Affect, Feeling, Sensing, and Sensory Attunement." In *Ritual, Performance and the Senses*, ed. Michael Bull and Jon P. Mitchell, 121–36. London: Bloomsbury Academic.

Chapter 3

DRUMMING WITH WINDS

LEARNING FROM ZAR PRACTITIONERS IN QESHM ISLAND, IRAN

Nima Jangouk

> We do not belong to those who have ideas only among books, when stimulated by books. It is our habit to think outdoors—walking, leaping, climbing, dancing, preferably on lonely mountains or near the sea where even the trails become thoughtful.
>
> —Nietzsche, *The Gay Science*

> I ask the wind to bring me the Beloved's smell, the wind starts playing harp and singing a song.
>
> —Rumi, *Gozideye Ghazaliyate Shams*

This chapter is composed of two texts that resonate with one another as they both share interests in exploring human beings' intertwined-ness with the world, healing practices, and moving as well as being moved when doing anthropological fieldwork. My main text concerns the study of zar healing rituals as practices during which life processes created by human, nonhuman living beings, and things' moving bodies, are interwoven with fluxes of media in the world. Angeline Antonakos Boswell's vignette expresses how human beings are interconnected to the world and suggests that we should embrace rather than discard the tendencies we lean toward when we do research, namely joining the tempos and rhythms of the medium.

Midnight Drumming: The Possession

My first encounter with zar[1] happened when, as an adolescent bookworm, I started reading a short story collection titled *Tars O Larz* (Fear and trembling).[2] All of the collection's stories—which take place in an unknown small village in southern Iran—extensively describe people's confrontations with suffering and sickness, exotic events, possession, alien creatures (*jinns*[3]), and the rage of natural elements, such as the cruelty of the sea or the winds. The collection also describes their experiences of life, drumming, (sacred) healing, and more. Reading the stories connected me to a previous experience of participating in an evocation session,[4] but did not make me sympathetic to zar healing practices at the time. As a seventeen-year-old son of an academic musician raised in an artistic/intellectual environment, I was following the author's approach in seeing zar practitioners as primitive, ignorant, horrified, passive, and superstitious people who were lost and had failed.

Ten years later, my father was invited to an outdoor music festival and shared his tickets with me. I decided to attend a nightly zar performance by Gholam Margiri (*Ḡolam Mārgiri*),[5] a healer who was from a small village in Hormozgan Province, Iran. I still clearly remember when the wrinkled face of the old healer—his long white hair and beard and his white turban and cloak making him look like an ancient sorcerer—walked onto the scene. He started drumming and singing with his unbelievably impressive treble voice, gracefully beating his drum and imploringly calling God's prophet to help him tame the devil winds: "Shir ellāh yā seyyed Ahmad, shir ellāh yā shir ellāh!"[6] Immersed in his songs, I was completely bewitched by his performance. I felt caught, distracted, and unable to stop shuddering even for a few minutes after he had finished singing and drumming. I asked myself: "If this man is ignorant, if this music is primitive, how could it have such a strong impression on me; a master's candidate of sociology who has been following a quite intellectualist approach throughout his academic undertaking?" I have probably been affected by one or some of his winds since that night.

Blowing with Winds

As my initial encounter with zar occurred while reading Gholam-Hossein Saedi's *Tars O Larz* (Fear and trembling) (1966), my first path to study the ritual began with fear and trembling, too. Upon first undertaking my study of the ritual, however, I used an approach that was closer to Saedi's views about zar:

> Coastal regions of southern Iran are fertile lands for madness and mental disorders. Living in such coastal regions is unwillingly associated with failure, frustration, fear and anxiety. Fighting with the sea, being afraid of starvation, thirst, disease and death, as well as hard work and monotonous life have made people to slip towards zar ritual . . . Higher levels of panic and stress lead to more confrontations with devil winds. Whenever people are poorer and more unemployed, the winds get more powerful. (Saedi 1966: 22–23 [my translation])

In *Deadly Words: Witchcraft in the Bocage*, Jeanne Favret-Saada (1977: 3) mentions the "folklorists'" tendency to regard witchcraft as an untruthful belief of credulous and backward people, with roots in the healer's charlatanism. This idea still influences social scientists, including anthropologists, in contemporary Iran.[7] When I started to study zar, I did not feel brave (or even knowledgeable) enough to risk my social or academic status by working on a "misleading," "deceptive," and "superstitious" ceremony that was banned by the government on the one side and disdained by the proponents of modernization policies on the other.[8] Therefore, following common approaches to studying zar ceremonies in Iran, I started to define a superficial project that could be accomplished by applying banal anthropological research methods such as interviewing and observation. My objective was the study of zar performances as primitive medical practices that could be described by applying evolutionist and diffusionist approaches of medical anthropology as well as anthropology of religion and anthropology of the body. It took a couple of years to find out that I was definitely on the wrong track: as a matter of fact, this type of anthropological research—relying on inattentive application of adapted theories and research methods to study a specific ceremony that stems from (and also recreates) its own locality and temporality—has already led to considerable misunderstandings of zar.[9] For instance, in accordance with the hegemonic anthropological discourses of the twentieth century, zar participants' bodies have been studied as the "universalized natural body" (Haraway 1990: 146), which is "a fixed, material entity subject to the empirical rules of biological science, existing prior to the mutability and flux of cultural change and diversity and characterized by unchangeable inner necessities" (Csordas 2003: 1).[10] In addition, following the protocols of normal science by which being-in-the-world is incessantly sundered from knowing the world (Ingold 2013: 18), zar practices have been considered symbolic activities empty of, or at best detached from, the environment.[11] The world of nonhuman living beings and things, all of the winds, sounds, seawaters, drums, aromatic herbs, flaming embers, moon, sea monsters, and sandy hills and valleys that are primary actors of the ceremony, are routinely dismissed from anthropological studies of zar to the benefit of a kind of knowledge that tends to engineer a material world that consists of natural, discrete, and finished objects (Ingold 2010: 9).

I began my doctoral studies with this problematic approach of "seeing" zar as a monotonous and predictable "surgery procedure" done by "traditional" healers on the "isolated" body of the "motionless patient" through the employment of "medical" tools to change conditions from chaotic to well-ordered ones. My understanding shifted when I began to read Maurice Merleau-Ponty and Tim Ingold, and more importantly when I became involved with the movements of zar and learned how to move with the winds. While these philosophical and anthropological manuscripts may appear too far from Iran's sociopolitical situation, the approach they propose is much more amenable to understanding its zar. Zar is all about blowing, about moving, and studying zar was moving me, too.

Anthropology of Being-in-the-World as a Path to Studying Life

Beginning a doctorate and learning about phenomenology as another path of performing anthropological research led me to consider my previous approach as a distorted type of knowledge. The former approach had prevented me from seeing/hearing/sensing the interconnectedness of moving bodies within the flows of wind and sound on the one side and with other human and nonhuman living beings and things on the other (through which the possession-healing process was improvised).

Constructing more appropriate paths to study zar requires applying new approaches that embrace all of these elements. Moreover, such paths welcome different types of knowledge about the world, body, and medicine, specifically those non-Western ways of perceiving the world that are unceasingly prevalent among zar practitioners. Phenomenological anthropology provides a more profound knowledge of zar ceremonies. In fact, in the late 1980s and early 1990s, anthropologists started to shift their focus away from existing symbolic, interpretative, and practice-oriented approaches toward embodiment and life ecologies (Gieser 2008: 301). Such shifts were deeply rooted in the work of Martin Heidegger and his concept of Being-in-the-world

(Heidegger [1927] 2008) and Maurice Merleau-Ponty's approach to studying perception and embodiment (Merleau-Ponty [1945] 2012). Both works created solid foundations for phenomenological anthropology (Csordas 1990, 2003; Ingold 2000, 2007, 2012). Briefly, Heidegger mentions "Dasein," which is his "label for the distinctive mode of Being realized by human beings" (Wheeler 2018) as Being-in-the-world. Two further explanations are required here: first, Dasein should be understood neither as the individual nor as the biological human being (Heidegger [1927] 2008). Rather, Dasein could be defined as "a way of life shared by the members of some community" (Haugeland 2005: 423). Also, Being-in-the-world as an indispensable feature of Dasein is profoundly intertwined with three other a priori conditions of being (Heidegger [1927] 2008): being-with, being-in, and being there. It is only through within-ness or through relationships with the world that we "are" (Gieser 2008: 301; Wheeler 2018). Occasionally, the term "dwelling" has been applied by Heidegger to describe our way of being in the world (Heidegger 2013: 145–61).

Inspired by Heidegger's philosophy, Merleau-Ponty suggests similar ways to explore the connectedness of perception and the world, but along a unique path that includes the body as well. As Merleau-Ponty suggests, our consciousness emerges from our bodily experiences in the world:

> Consciousness is being-towards-the-thing through the intermediary of the body. A movement is learned when the body has understood it, that is, when it has incorporated it into its "world," and to move one's body is to aim at things through it; it is to allow oneself to respond to their call, which is made upon it independently of any representation. ([1945] 2012: 138–39)

More specifically, Merleau-Ponty suggests that, to perceive, one has to move in the world and perception only grows from experiencing the world tangibly. Being-in-the-world is thus in connection with our movements. A phenomenological approach to "Being-in-the-world of lived experience" (Gieser 2008: 302) facilitates an anthropological undertaking that is more suitable for the study of moving bodies and their intertwinements with human and nonhuman living beings and things; and this also implies letting myself be moved.

The phenomenological anthropologies of Thomas J. Csordas (1990, 2003) (who borrows from Merleau-Ponty and Pierre Bourdieu) and Tim Ingold (2000, 2007, 2012) (who at different times takes from Heidegger and from Merleau-Ponty) have been the main sources of inspiration in my own approach to studying zar. Initially, Csordas's theory of embodiment reformulates the body "as much a cultural phenomenon as it is a biological entity" (2003: 4); it is the existential ground of culture, an experiencing agent that should be at the center of our anthropological meditations on self, experience, and culture (2003: 3–6). Furthermore, Ingold's ecology of life introduces human and nonhuman living beings and things as "active materials that compose the lifeworld" (2012: 427) in an unfinished open world that "everything may be something, but being something is always on the way to becoming something else" (2012: 435). The world is therefore not prepared for us beforehand, but is rather ceaselessly coming into being around us (Ingold 2007: S24). Moreover, to inhabit the open world "is to be immersed in the fluxes of the medium: in sunshine, rain, and wind. This immersion, in turn, underwrites our capacities—respectively—to see, hear, and touch" (2007: S30). And finally, humans as living organisms in the environment not only move but are their movements (2007: 437).

From here my approach to anthropology focuses on studying life processes created by humans' moving bodies, as well as other agents (nonhuman beings and things) that are interwoven with fluxes of media in the world. Before entering into zar through this more open-ended and conciliatory approach to understand its potential benefits in the medium, a vignette written by a colleague anthropologist similarly expresses how we should embrace rather than discard the tendencies we lean toward when we do research, namely joining the tempos and rhythms of the medium.

Vignette 3
Ethnography through Anxiety
Angeline Antonakos Boswell

I lived primarily on a permaculture farm during the summer of 2018 while researching the motivations people had for leaving urban centers and seeking a life "closer to nature" in Serbia. The owners of the farm, Mimi and Titi, were motivated to make this urban-to-rural shift to experience a spiritual closeness to nature and to thus live more meaningful and fulfilled lives. Since we are beings intertwined with nature "in a big web" and yet are not allowed to experience this interconnection, they insisted, this has destructive effects on our happiness, health, and souls. Recognizing the role of my own anxiety in the ethnographic process deepened my understanding of this nature-bound holistic health as an undercurrent throughout my research and informed my pursuit of alternative medicines and healing practices to heal my own anxiety. The fundamental question of what anxiety is came to the fore. To those I was staying with, there was no division between mental, physical, and even spiritual health. As Titi told me, "We try to disconnect them with these names, but they are not disconnected at all."

A couple of weeks into my fieldwork, I snuck my orange tube of anxiety pills into the farm's kitchen to gulp them down with a glass of water. Mimi happened to see me, even though I had been thus far careful to hide this necessity of mine like a shameful secret. It was a clash between two worlds: I was exemplifying the pragmatic biomedical approaches that were so often critiqued in these contexts. For my interlocutors, taking pills in order to get through every day is indicative of a "life you're not supposed to be living," thus blaming the soul-crushing urban environment for my anxious state rather than the brain chemistry of the isolated individual.

This act of bringing my secret out into the open was a pivotal moment in my research. Now, I was not only researching them, but they were helping me. "If only I lived in nature, I wouldn't need any pills" was the assumption, and the idea certain environments could foster different emotional states—a theme running parallel to the "meaningful lives" my interlocutors sought in changing their own environment—was tested out with urgency. Immediately after hearing about my need for anxiety pills, Mimi was on the phone with an herbal remedy healer I had interviewed a week before. In our interview, he had told me that in healing he allows God to move him toward whatever is necessary for the patient. The importance of openness for inspiration resurfaced often among those with whom I spoke—and "nature" was a space in which this inspiration was more readily encountered. This healer told me he prayed specifically for the people he was healing as he picked the herbs and as he made his tinctures and syrups. I had a delivery in the mail within a week with eight remedies and two teas combined particularly for me—a far leap from taking a homogenous pill. The healing properties of these remedies rested on so much more than just the simple fact of consumption: there were specifics of tempo, time, and context in which to take them. Its efficacy, much like our souls, was seen to flourish only in a specific affective space.

A crucial component of this quest for healing anxiety, and eventually a crucial component of my research as a whole, was the blurring of my self and my environment. Rather than imagine myself as an isolated brain impenetrable to the affective environment surrounding it, I was discovering, for example, how the daily ritual suggested by Mimi of standing on the top of the highest green hill in the morning before I do anything else, breathing in the dewy air, and focusing on excitement for the future instead of fear could entirely color the rest of my day. I was learning to blur the illusory boundary between my mental and physical self when Mimi suggested I take off my shoes and go barefoot if I felt stressed, letting my toes (and my thoughts) ground themselves in the grass and dirt. I did tangible, laborious farm work that gets you "outside of your mind" and into a sort of meditative flow; I spent my time nurturing children, animals, and plants, something I was told soothes the soul because it is what we are "meant to be doing." A life lived close to nature, tied within that affective web with everything else, is "what we expect," and so being under the guise that we can be broken off from it (such as in an isolating, paved-over city), all the while deeply craving it, would of course be seen as a source of anxiety.

Figure 3.1. *Approaches to Healing*, 2019. Drawing by Angeline Antonakos Boswell.

Looking back, I recall a conversation I had with a friend before I left for my fieldwork. I vented to her over coffee about feeling unprepared to leave. I could not stand to let myself "spoil" the fieldwork-to-come with my persistent worries. I was hoping to become a more stable, more emotionally-neutral researcher by the time the month of May came around, and yet, there it was around the next worrisome corner. "But there is no separate you and Serbia and anxiety," she said, "this experience has to be all three or else it isn't your experience." When we speak about being "explicitly present," as the introduction of this book suggests, this is what comes to mind: to be explicitly present is to recognize the emotional states we carry with us as we enter the field, and to readily accept that, in place of the impossible ideal of an emotionally blank and "objective" study, we may delve into our own embodied experiences as a source of richness in ethnography. My anxiety quickly became an important point of access in my fieldwork, as I was able to feel what the draw to nature might be and what the push away from the soul-constricting city might be in my own skin. My then-shameful secret of anxiety, which I sought to hide during the first half of fieldwork, ended up, once I allowed myself to recognize and embody its presence, touching the very core of my research question. Rather than hinder my fieldwork, then, delving into my own emotional context gifted it with an embodied knowledge that extended far beyond my notebook.

Drumming with Winds: Learning from Zar Practitioners

Embracing the tendencies I was leaning toward in my case played itself out on numerous levels, including the affective experiences evoked in the introduction, yet also shaping the way I would enter zar healing ceremonies in other ways, which also imply how zar practitioners embrace my own presence. My fieldwork constituted two different periods of two consecutive months: July and August 2015 and July and August 2016 in Salakh [*Salak̠*], a village on Qeshm Island, Iran (where the most prominent Baba [*Bābā*] in the Persian Gulf region, Bab Isa [*Bāb Isā*], and his community live). My initial fieldwork strategy was to perform an apprenticeship under the supervision of Bab Isa. After our first encounter, however, I quickly discovered that he was not willing to accept me as his apprentice. I therefore decided to adopt an alternative approach and start making connections with *dohol gap* players who were members of Bab Isa's band with the idea that I could probably accompany them in their future performances. Since childhood, I had been playing *tombak* (an Iranian drum somewhat close to *dohol gap*, the main drum that is played during zar ceremonies). This strategy was more successful: on the fourth night of my stay on the island, there was a recreational soirée planned, but one of the drummers who was supposed to play was feeling sick and could not participate. The band leader, who was also a zar drummer, asked me if I could accompany them by playing *darbuka*, a drum which is similar to a *tombak*. I jumped on this opportunity. After the performance, I was accepted as a drummer by some of the zar drummers and disciples of Bab Isa. In order to become a zar drummer, however, I had to change the instrument I was accustomed to playing, as apparently my own instrument, *tombak*, was not sacred enough to help me become a zar drummer. And so I started practicing *dohol gap* in order to learn more about zar.

Playing *dohol gap* under the supervision of zar drummers on Qeshm Island provided me with an opportunity to be accepted by the Salakh zar community. I had the chance to play and sing zar songs, participate in different gatherings held by Bab Isa's disciples, help them in their palm groves, get involved in the unique relationship they had with their camels, sail from Salakh to nearby islands, attend their wedding and funeral ceremonies, and take part in three different zar ceremonies held by Bab Isa. In other words, becoming a *dohol gap* apprentice/player helped me attune myself to the world of zar practi-

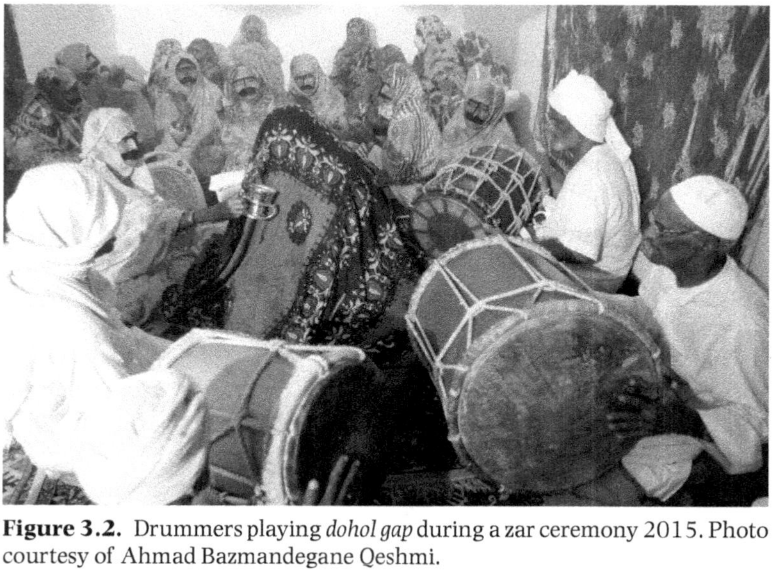

Figure 3.2. Drummers playing *dohol gap* during a zar ceremony 2015. Photo courtesy of Ahmad Bazmandegane Qeshmi.

tioners. It was only by entering their worlds of rhythm and songs that I started to understand their sensory worlds of living with plants and animals, their understanding of blowing winds and the dancing sea. It was only by drumming that I started to understand their worlds of sorrow, happiness, revelry, suffering, sickness, and healing; It was by learning to move with them, and in turn letting myself be moved by them, that I could know them meaningfully

"There are almost seventy-two winds," as Bab Isa told me, "which are eternally blowing in the sky, but might decide to pass through us, to possess us, at specific times and locations." They all have their own dwellings and dispositions around us, but a stranger wind that is lost at sea from other parts of the world could also possess us. Some of the most well-known and cruelest indigenous winds in southern Iran are: Matouri, Bibi, Dingamaro, Sheykh Shangar, Leyla, and Zar. Depending on the devil wind, getting caught means starting to experience pain, suffering, and problems such as feeling itchy all over the body, having nightmares, painful blisters on the body, long headaches, major weakness, frailty, depression, muscle contractions, an intolerable backache, foot and knee pain, chest and heart contraction issues, blindness, and more—issues that require that the afflicted ask a healer's help in taming the wind.

Little by little, drumming provided me the opportunity to learn from Bab Isa's healing practices. Generally, after a short visit by a patient, he gives his initial diagnosis of the issue, the type of wind, and what needs to be done in order to tame the wind. Depending on the hostility of the wind, an isolation period might be necessary. During the isolation period, Bab Isa takes care of the sufferer in his own home, talks to them to find out more about their issues, applies herbal medicine, gives massages, spreads anointment, and prays to help the afflicted feel better before the main ceremony. The primary stage of the zar healing ritual is led by him and held in the presence of his apprentices and musical band, as well as with formerly possessed people who are available and trustworthy enough to participate in the ceremony (Ahle hava [*Ahle havā*]). Every wind has a specific song, and so when all required things are provided, Bab Isa commences drumming. Usually he starts by playing some miscellaneous pieces. By listening to the songs of other winds, participants connected to those winds begin to lose their consciousness and dance with their winds. Little by little, Bab Isa approaches them while playing a more specific song. This drumming is played around the afflicted who sits in the middle of the circle, covered by a white cotton sheet. Other participants are also present, anointing them and burning aromatic herbs under their nose, all building to an ecstatic moment in which the afflicted gradually begins to sing and dance. At the peak moment of the ritual, identified by the healer, the wind comes down and is ready to talk. Thus Baba talks to the wind and asks about its motivations and expectations. Demands from the winds can consist of a variety of gifts (including golden rings, bamboo sticks, holding another ceremony or ceremonies in the forthcoming months, food, pastries, etc.) or orders (not to drink alcohol, to meet up with parents regularly, not to have same-sex intercourse, etc.). Bab Isa normally tries to negotiate with winds and reach a compromise on a fair gift. On the other side, the wind promises to stop making the afflicted suffer as long as they donate specified gifts and keep their promises. If the ceremony goes well, the devil wind is tamed and sufferers will no longer be afflicted.

By becoming a *dohol gap* apprentice I had the chance to participate in different zar ceremonies. Not long after I started drumming with Bab Isa's band of drummers most of the community (Ahle hava) started to see me differently. I also insisted on participating in their religious ceremonies, sailing, nightly musical gatherings, palm cultivating, camel breeding, fishing, selling their dates, repairing boats, and helping them (as much as I could) to finalize some financial calculations and reach a compromise on a disagreement about fishing shares. The effect of my collaboration with them seemed to be that they were persuaded I was not going to harm or label them as backward, superstitious infidels, as others had. After a couple of weeks, and at the end of one of my training sessions, Hammood Memar, prime drummer of Bab Isa's band, told me that I was "serious" and "trustworthy," and that Bab Isa had agreed to talk to me about zar. I could now pose questions and participate in ceremonies, but only as a "simple" participant who can "move and understand," but not as a drummer. Although I was not permitted to play during the ceremonies, I learned a lot from zar practitioners as well as their practices by having the chance to participate. I understood how zar rhythms were similar to the other rhythms of the inhabitants of the island. For instance, zar rhythms are surprisingly similar to the rhythms of sailors rowing, dhow makers nailing, and how local musicians play and sing in wedding ceremonies. While dancing during the ritual—as well as my first training session playing the *dohol gap*—I tried to immerse myself in the different rhythmic flows. It was tough, but I found out that moving within zar rhythms could feel like the experience of sailing on the sea in a boat or dhow: that as a drummer who had walked and driven cars for most of his life, I had to learn about a new rhythmic world that could, every now and then, challenge my existing knowledge of musical rhythms.

I tried to understand people's experiences of pain and suffering by listening to their stories, seeing dullness and frailty in their eyes, hearing their sighs; I tried to understand their movements to Bab Isa's songs: how they would change from frightening rapid crawling, to trembling, glossolalia,[12] shouting and crying as a first step in taming the wind.

I still recall the crescendo of one of the ceremonies in which, after more than three hours of drumming and dancing in a small, half-blurred room full of herbal aromas and smoke, Bab Isa caught the wind, stood up in front of the afflicted, and started to drum and sing in an unprecedented manner: "Vadoye valadoye zār yā varār, Yā varār rā vadoye kalandar, hoye zār yā varār."[13] I clearly remember having the impression that Bab Isa had transformed into Satan, a devil wind: violent, unconscious, and cruel. With a weird light in his eyes, he started to beat the afflicted woman with his bamboo stick. The wind inside her was crying loudly, begging the healer to stop the punishment, announcing that it agreed to temporarily stop her suffering.

This was the turning point: when the healer hugged the woman, caressed her hair and face in order to calm her down, she started to cry silently in his arms. The doors opened, the lights were turned on, and people started hugging each other. The healer's assistants entertained the community with herbal oils and odors, hookahs, and small cups of goat milk and black tea. The wind was tamed.

As I was learning about zar I was also learning that zar is not one specific healing ritual. Rather, there are different zar ceremonies all over the region. In Salakh, with less than three thousand inhabitants, there are two rival Babas with completely different approaches to the ritual: while Bab Isa follows a more flexible approach that entitles him to apply innovative healing ways during the ceremony[14] (such as letting people who are curious participate in the ceremony),[15] and to perform zar songs at different art festivals, Dellā Medu considers zar more conservatively. And although Dellā Medu respects Bab Isa's healing knowledge and sometimes assists him during the ceremonies, he believes that because of his more profound knowledge as well as his loyalty to zar traditions, he is the most prominent Baba. According to tradition, he believes Babas should be thoroughly careful about even the smallest rules of the ritual, should not permit "strangers" to participate in ceremonies, and should not perform zar songs at any event other than healing ceremonies.

Ways of zar are not limited to these two approaches. There are several communities throughout the region that "play" zar in their own ways. Nuban (*Nubān*) ceremonies, for instance, mainly follow zar practices, but at the same time attempt to be faithful to Islamic teachings, especially rules related to socializing, permissible/forbidden foods and drinks, and clean/unclean things and beings. Moreover, some musicians and movie/theater directors are applying zar practices to produce their own works of art. For example, *Macbeth Zar*, a musical comedy that blends zar with Shakespeare's *Macbeth*, has won the New Experience Section at the twenty-eighth Tehran International Theater Festival (2009) as well as the award for the best theater ensemble in Moscow Nights Theater Festival (2012). France's Avignon Festival and Armenia's HighFest Theater Festival also hosted the play (Sheikhi 2018).

Rowing across a Healing Ritual: The Gay Science

As a dynamic practice, zar has roots in ancient Mesopotamian as well as Iranian pre-Islamic medical knowledge. These ceremonies have blended with Islamic, Greek, African, and Hindi beliefs, as well as with biomedical healing paths up to the present day. Even now some practitioners try to connect their practices with contemporary spiritual and sacred healing forms such as energy healing. According to zar knowledge, people are intertwined with God, angels (*malā'eke*), Satan (*Šaytān*), *jinns*, good and evil winds, good and evil spirits, moon, sea, mountains and hills, desert, sun, stars, fire, palm trees and other plants, and camels and other animals. This intertwined-ness means that all of these beings/things live inseparably and without clear-cut borders. Such blurred boundaries enable them to influence each another, to permeate into one another, and to become each other. Such blurred borders enable them to move, and to be moved. Perceptions of zar ceremonies are also dynamic and in flux: an artist could consider zar a source of inspiration for artwork, an anthropologist could try to understand how moving within healing rhythms might help a sufferer feel better; a philosopher may find other forms of dealing with the problem of evil in zar; and practitioners themselves could participate in ceremonies to solve their family issues, entertain themselves, negotiate their financial difficulties, practice, play, and improvise music. Practitioners may also participate in ceremonies to immerse themselves in a world of pleasant aromas, tastes, songs, and dances to forget their affliction and sufferings and, through this, to feel relieved and healed. In the lifeworlds of zar, a sailor's wife could become a wind that lives in a well, a healer could become a crow that steals golden rings, a snake could become Satan, and a wind could become a dancing *jinn* that should be punished. These becomings, however, may seem unthinkable for "strangers" or distant observers. For practitioners themselves, zar is a way in which they drum and dance—a way in which they live. This way of life is endlessly moving with different beings and things, and is moving them, too. In terms of blending with other paths of medicine, livelihood, worshipping God, philosophizing, and religious and artistic performances, zar has been, and is, ceaselessly moving. Moreover, it moves people during the healing ceremonies in its different flows of drumming, singing, and dancing. It also moves people by changing their ways of experiencing suffering, sickness, and healing, as well as their manners, status, and identities. Finally, zar ceremonies can move researchers who want to study the ritual. My own experience involves moving from a sociology student who was going to study "about" zar practitioners from within his office to an apprentice who decided to learn how to drum with winds, to dance within the sensory world of the ritual, and to learn from and with zar practitioners.

Zar ceremonies are difficult for anthropologists to study. Initially, as the ritual is principally a form of sacred performance, an anthropologist cannot apply mainstream research methods such as documentary research, interviewing, or participant observation in order to interpret it. Rather, in order to understand zar, and in order to start learning from the devil winds, the anthropologist should first and foremost get caught by the winds. Moreover, zar practices are complex, embodied, essentially non-verbal, irregular, indefinite, and endless lines of flight in which the worlds of beings and things, music, senses, illness, and healing are ceaselessly redefined and reconstructed. Historically, hegemonic social science research methods have presumed a universal human body that could be separated from the world, viewed, recorded, decoded, and reported by observers. Such procedures may produce data, but not knowledge, about practices such as zar. Social sciences may presume a world of modern/traditional, science/superstitions, rational/sensory (intuitive), natural/supernatural, and mind/body dichotomies, but it prevents us from gaining profound knowledge about practices like zar. In *After Method: Mess in Social Science Research*, John Law describes the necessity of "slow, multiple, modest, uncertain, diverse" research methods that let us study the "impossible or barely possible, unthinkable or almost unthinkable, vague, unspecific, disordered, emotional, angelic, demonic, and intuitive" (2004: 11). In the same way, and in taking inspiration from Ingold's "knowing from the inside" (2013), I suggest that drumming as an anthropological research strategy lets us open ourselves to the world and attune ourselves to its different flows of senses, rhythms, and movements in order to learn from them. Along this line, the anthropologist is an apprentice who dances with the world to improvise his or her fieldwork. Moreover, anthropology—not limited to social science departments but alongside arts, philosophy, and religion—is a constantly moving path of apprenticeship in which the moving world unfolds.

Nima Jangouk is a PhD candidate in sociology at the University of Ottawa. His main research interest is how human and nonhuman living beings and things that are interwoven with fluxes of media in the world create life processes. Walking this path, he is studying zar healing practices in Iran as his thesis project. Sentient ecology, eco-phenomenological anthropology, music-moving-healing, and phenomenology are his other fields of interest.

Angeline Antonakos Boswell (under the supervision of Dr. Larisa Kurtović) conducted a research project on back-to-the-land urban-to-rural migrations in Serbia while an undergraduate student in Anthropology at the University of Ottawa. She became fascinated with the question of what makes a "meaningful life," and why so many people she was meeting through back-to-the-land movement networks in Serbia found this meaningful life to be one lived "in nature." This research has become pivotal in her own life, as she now pursues a career in the field of counseling, exploring holistic approaches to healing and wellness.

Notes

Epigraph: Nietzsche 1974: 322 and Rumi 2005: 71.

1. Zar [*zār*] rituals are time-honored and unendingly living healing ceremonies that are most prevalent in the Middle East and the Horn of Africa, mainly among inhabitants of Iran, United Arab Emirates, Kuwait, Qatar, Bahrain, Egypt, Israel, Oman, Sudan, Kenya, Somalia, and Ethiopia (Sabaye Moghaddam 2012; Edelstein 2002; Lewis et al. 1991). In Iran, zar practitioners are predominantly people who live in southern coastal regions of the country by the northern coastline of the Persian Gulf. Nowadays, zar ceremonies are primarily practiced in Hormozgan (*Hormozgān*) province and especially by the inhabitants of Qeshm (*Qešm*) Island (Dejgani 2014).

2. *Tars O Larz* (Fear and trembling) is composed by Iranian writer, folklorist, ethnographer, psychiatrist, and leftist political activist Gholam-Hossein Saedi (*Ǧolām-Hoseyn Sāedi*) (1968).
3. According to Islamic teachings, *jinns* are nonhuman living beings created from fire by Allah.
4. At my aunt's house in Bandar Abbas (*Bandar Abbās*), the capital of Hormozgan Province and a port city in southern Iran, which is my paternal grandfather's city of origin.
5. The transliteration used for Persian names in this chapter is the transliteration system suggested and applied by the Encyclopaedia Iranica (http://www.iranicaonline.org/pages/guidelines).
6. Please help us, the Lion of God, Prophet Muhammad, the Lion of God, please help us!
7. During the summer of 2015, I had a short talk about anthropological paths to studying zar in a research institute in Tehran, Iran. After presenting some parts of my work, a well-known researcher who teaches anthropology at the most prestigious Iranian university (the University of Tehran) condemned me for "forgetting my principal anthropological duty to train the backward superstitious people who believe in the ceremony, and for receiving money from Western states to keep Iranians ignorant by assigning truth to deceptive ideas such as zar."
8. As a consequence of modernization policies in contemporary Iran, zar practices have been labeled superstitions, therefore silenced and marginalized by the central governments for about a century. Furthermore, since the Islamic revolution in 1979, zar communities have been constantly suppressed as deviant, infidel, and even demonic cults, hence, the practitioners tend to preserve themselves from the probable harms of the outsiders and are thus inclined to conceal themselves from the inquiries of social science researchers.
9. When reviewing the existing Iranian anthropological literature on zar, one will frequently find such explanations: "Zar ritual should be seen as the product of mental disorders; 'unconscious' illusions and delusions that arise from the emotional deprivations and sufferings in a historical context" (Naghavi 2014: 163).
10. Gholam-Hossein Saedi (1966), Kaveh Safa (1988), and Hesam Naghavi (2014) are three examples of seeing zar practitioners' bodies as universal, fixed, and material entities that exist prior to the flux of cultural change and diversity.
11. Ali Bulookbashi (2002) and Manijeh Maghsudi (2013), for instance, are two works that consider zar practices symbolic activities detached from the environment.
12. Thomas Csordas (1993: 24–25) portrays glossolalia as a phenomenon of embodiment that appears as a form of "nonsense" or "gibberish" and describes how speakers consider the common language an incommensurate means of communication with the divine.

13. Two nights later, when I asked Bab Isa about the meaning of these words, he said: "They are songs in old Arabic and only God knows exactly what they mean."
14. Such as using new medicinal herbs or improvising new songs.
15. Researchers or musicians from different parts of the world, for instance.

References

Bulookbashi, Ali. 2002. "Hoviyatsaziye Ejtemaei az Rahe Badzodayi" [Social Identification through Taming the Winds]. *Anthropological Letter* 1(1): 33–43.

Csordas, Thomas J. 1990. "Embodiment as a Paradigm for Anthropology." *Ethos* 18(1): 5–47.

———. 1993. "Somatic Modes of Attention." *Cultural Anthropology* 8(2): 135–56.

———. 2003. *Embodiment and Experience: The Existential Ground of Self and Culture*, Cambridge: Cambridge University Press.

Dejgani, Fatemeh. 2014. *Jen Zadegan dar Jonube Iran* [Possessed people of southern Iran]. Rafsanjan: Nashre Soorme.

Edelstein, Monika D. 2002. "Lost Tribes and Coffee Ceremonies: Zar Spirit Possession and the Ethno-Religious Identity of Ethiopian Jews in Israel." *Journal of Refugee Studies* 15(2): 153–70.

Favret-Saada, Jeanne. 1977. *Deadly Words: Witchcraft in the Bocage.* Cambridge: Cambridge University Press.

Gieser, Thorsten. 2008. "Embodiment, Emotion, and Empathy: A Phenomenological Approach to Apprenticeship Learning." *Anthropological Theory* 8(3): 299–318.

Haraway, Donna. 1990. "Investment Strategies for the Evolving Portfolio of Primate Females." In *Body/Politics: Women and Discourses of Science*, ed. Mary Jacobus et al. New York: Routledge.

Haugeland, John. 2005. "Reading Brandom Reading Heidegger." *European Journal of Philosophy* 13(3): 421–28.

Heidegger, Martin. [1927] 2008. *Being and Time.* New York: Harper & Row.

———. 2013. *Poetry, Language, Thought.* Toronto: Harper Perennial Modern Thought.

Ingold, Tim. 2000. *The Perception of the Environment: Essays on Livelihood, Dwelling, and Skill.* London: Routledge.

———. 2007. "Earth, Sky, Wind and Weather." *Journal of the Royal Anthropological Institute* 13: S19–S38.

———. 2010. "Bringing Things to Life: Creative Entanglements in a World of Materials." Realities Working Paper, University of Manchester.

———. 2012. "Toward an Ecology of Materials." *The Annual Review of Anthropology* 41: 427–42.

———. 2013. *Making: Anthropology, Archaeology, Art and Architecture*. New York: Routledge.

Law, John. 2004. *After Method: Mess in Social Science Research*. New York: Routledge.

Lewis, Ioan M., Sayed Hamid Hurreiz, and Ahmed El Safi. 1991. *Women's Medicine: the Zar-Bori Cult in Africa and Beyond*. Edinburgh: Edinburgh University Press.

Maghsudi, Manijeh. 2013. "Badhaye Kafar va Dohole Se Sar Dar Khalije Fars: Maraseme Ayeeniye Darmane Zar" [Infidel winds and Dohol Gap in Zar healing ceremony in Persian Gulf]. *Iranian Anthropological Research* 2(2): 117–40.

Merleau-Ponty, Maurice. [1945] 2012. *Phenomenology of Perception*. New York: Routledge.

Nietzsche, Friedrich. [1882] 1974. *The Gay Science*. New York: Random House Inc.

Naghavi, Hesam. 2014. "Mo'allefe haye Bineshe Ostoore i dar Maraseme Zar" [The elements of mythical insights in zar ritual]. *Cultural Research Journal of Hormozgan* 6/7: 143–66.

Rumi, Jalaleddin Mohammad. 2005. *Gozideye Ghazaliyate Shams* [Selected Poems of Rumi]. Tehran: Nashre Elmi va Farhangi.

Sabaye Moghaddam, Maria. 2012. "Zar Beliefs and Practices in Bandar Abbas and Qeshm Island in Iran." *Anthropology of the Middle East* 7(2): 19–38.

Saedi, Gholam-Hossein. 1966. *Ahle Hava* [People of the air]. Tehran: Nashre Amir Kabir.

———. 1968. *Tars O Larz* [Fear and trembling]. Tehran: Nashre Amir Kabir.

Safa, Kaveh. 1988. "Reading Saedi's Ahl-e Have: Pattern and Significance in Spirit Possession Beliefs on the Southern Coasts of Iran." *Culture, Medicine and Psychiatry* 12: 85–111.

Sheikhi, Marjohn. 2018, "Moscow to Stage Iranian Play *Macbeth Zar* on World Theater Day." MEHR News Agency, 5 March. Retrieved 4 January 2020 from https://en.mehrnews.com/news/132616/Moscow-to-stage-Iranian-play-Macbeth-Zar-on-World-Theater-Day.

Wheeler, Michael. 2018. "Martin Heidegger." In *The Stanford Encyclopedia of Philosophy*, ed. Edward N. Zalta (Winter 2018 Edition). Retrieved 4 January 2020 from https://plato.stanford.edu/archives/win2018/entries/heidegger/.

Chapter 4

FIELDWORK ALOFT

EXPERIENCING WEATHER AND AIR IN FALCONRY

Sara Asu Schroer

In the essay "Hawks in Air," nature writer Richard Jefferies (1843) describes his observation of two birds of prey flying on motionless outstretched wings, rising higher and higher, seemingly defying the gravitational pull of the earth. It is easy to visualize him standing firmly on the ground, his head tipped back to better watch the two birds, observing them intently. He is fascinated by the apparent effortlessness of the flying birds and wonders how it might be possible, arguing about this problem at length without finding a satisfactory solution. Jefferies describes how the two birds started their flight above the treetops and while circling in broad spirals, without any visible exertions, rose higher and higher to disappear out of sight in the blue sky above. Without an understanding of what was going on in the airy spaces above, he was unable to interpret what was happening before his eyes—the rising air currents remained imperceptible to him.

Jefferies' observation and marvel at the birds' flight reminded me of my own, admittedly rather ignorant position, at the beginning of my fieldwork into the practice of falconry.[1] Like Jefferies, I was intrigued by the beauty and elegance of soaring birds but was not yet familiar with the complex movements of air currents and weather that constitute the environments of airborne creatures such as birds of prey. In this chapter I aim to show that working with falconers and their falcons, hawks, and eagles required an opening up of the earthbound perspective of conventionally "grounded" fieldwork, and I will consider the aerial world of birds of prey in which weather and air currents play a crucial role. This will be done through a combination of ethnographic stories and the inclusion of drawings complementing the text—both aiming at drawing attention to the texturality of air, revealed in the engagement between falconer, bird, and the weathering environment (see also Azevedo and Schroer 2016).[2]

Falconers gain an intricate knowledge of how birds of prey use the air and develop an intimate understanding of how air currents direct the flights of birds, prey species, and consequently their own movements on the ground. Falconry is a hunting practice in which humans and birds of prey learn to hunt in cooperation with each other. This hunting cooperation is formed through a variety of taming and training methods and techniques particular to falconry and depends on a fine balance of wildness and tameness, dependence and independence of the falconry bird (Schroer 2015). Falconers understand their relationship with birds of prey as being based upon trust and a sense of companionship rather than as coercive and utilitarian. In order to train a falcon for cooperation in hunting, the bird needs to be "lured" and "politely charmed" into a relationship with the falconer and cannot be forced or bullied into submission. In order to do so, it becomes central for falconers to develop "a feeling for birds of prey" and to learn to understand the world in relation to these airborne creatures, who in so many ways perceive and act upon the world differently from the earthbound falconers (Schroer 2018).

Soaring in Thermal Currents

During fieldwork in Italy in the hot summer months, I was sitting together with a falconer in the shadow of a tree sheltering from the heat of the midday sun. Overlooking the valley, we observed a family of wild buzzards flying high above our heads. The birds were moving on motionless outstretched wings. Circling in broad spirals, without any visible exertion, they were soon only visible as small black specks in the sky until the glare of the sun made it impossible to follow them further with the bare eye.

Alistair—a falconer I knew from my fieldwork in Britain and whom I was visiting in Italy where he was working as falconer and gamekeeper on a hunting estate—explained that the birds were catching a lift on thermal currents to reach cooler spheres in the air higher above. Thermal currents, he pointed out, were particularly strong during the hottest time of the day and when flying a falconry bird one had to watch out for them. To underline his point, he threw a handful of dry leaves from the ground that immediately spiraled upwards, fol-

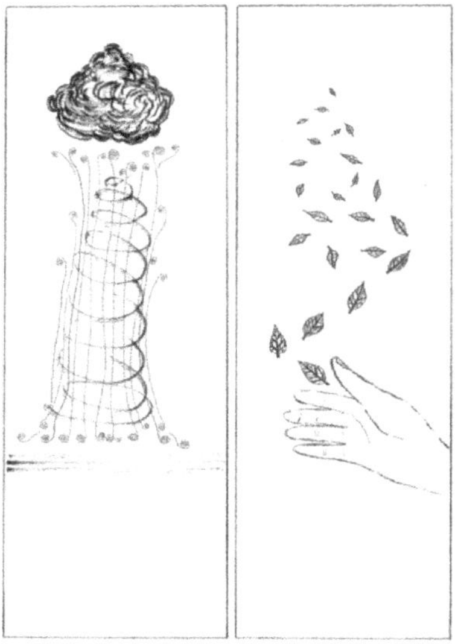

Figure 4.1. The texture of air © Aina Azevedo.

Figure 4.2. Soaring on thermal currents © Aina Azevedo.

lowing a trail of warm rising air that had escaped my awareness until then. For a few seconds, the leaves, just as much as the lines of flight of the soaring birds, made visible the texture of the moving air in which we were immersed.

The air currents could be a supportive force for flying creatures in some situations as much as dangerous and difficult to maneuver in others. "Birds need to progressively learn to use the wind when flying," Alistair explained, "and as a falconer you need to give them the opportunity to gain as much experience as possible in varying wind and weather conditions." His gaze still on the birds above us, Alistair pointed out when a buzzard would fail to soar within the rising air and would "drop out," by being slightly thrown out of balance when exiting the air column and flying into the area of cold descending air that flows down the sides of the thermal. "When you fly your own falconry birds," Alistair warned, "you need to keep an eye out for thermals as birds love to go on a soar to cool off." Indeed falconers often described the temptation of thermal currents for birds in the summer who when catching one would be in a state of "trance" in which they forget about the pathetically waving and despairing falconer on the ground and go up to join other birds in their spiraling ascent. The only thing left to do in such a situation is to wait until the later and cooler hours of the day when thermals fade and the birds return closer to the ground.

Thermal currents are of course not the only movements of air that become relevant when flying birds. Especially in hilly or mountainous country the air becomes what a falconer referred to as "the white water" of the falconer. Compared to lowland country, hilly areas have a much more turbulent and irregular flow of air currents and therefore pose a greater challenge to the falconer who has to be able to anticipate how these flows influence the flights of both their own birds as well as the animals they hunt on the ground and up in the air. In fact, when talking about the air people often drew comparisons to the element of water, or rather rivers and the ocean, possibly to give a more tactile impression of the air and its currents. Another falconer, for example, compared flying falcons to surfing waves:

> I would imagine that being a falconer looking at the air is quite similar to how the surfer looks at the ocean and its waves, not just because he enjoys their beauty but also because he can see the potentials they offer. Also, just like a surfer you have to understand how the shape of the land and most importantly the prevailing weather conditions create the waves or—in my case as a falconer—air currents you are looking for.

Indeed, in many ways, the air and its movements, as they were progressively revealed to me throughout my fieldwork, do share certain characteristics with the fluid medium of the river or ocean. Their movements are created by the landforms through which they are channeled and dispersed, while the form of the land, on the other hand, is also created through the fluid movements of wind and water. It therefore does not seem to be adequate to speak of "landscapes," "seascapes," or "airscapes" in this context as these terms seem to conjure up separate domains rather than the co-constitutive character of a world in constant formation or a "weather-world" (Ingold 2010).

The atmospheric phenomenon of the weather plays a crucial role in all of this. These varying atmospheric intensities and forces have a constitutive influence on the way falconers and birds interact and experience their environments and other beings. I do not understand weather here in its scientific or meteorological sense, where it becomes an object of scientific inquiry. With regard to falconry practice, weather is better understood in a phenomenological perspective as directly experienced by humans and nonhuman sentient creatures. It is such a central aspect of their immersion into the environment, it is usually not talked about divorced from context but always as embedded in the actual executions of particular tasks. Rather than understanding the weather of something that has an effect on the world (following the logic of cause and effect), it seems to be more apt to regard it as an activity of weathering in which the weather is its on-

Figure 4.3. Surfing waves
© Aina Azevedo.

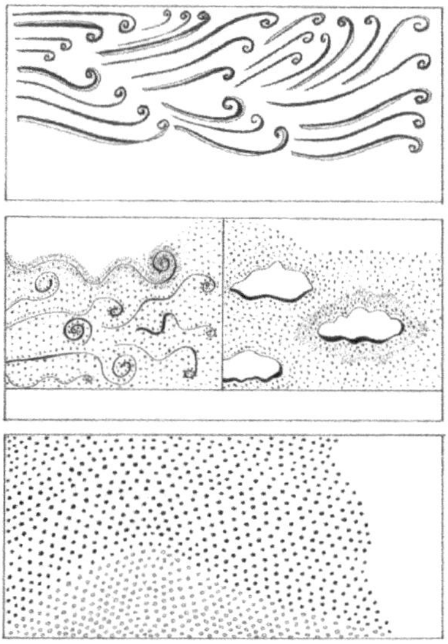

Figure 4.4. Weathering
© Aina Azevedo.

going effect. Even the airborne bodies of the birds are seen as being interwoven with the ebbs and flows of weathering, which influences their metabolism, strength, and moods.

Weathering

The ways falconers come to perceive this weathering environment is not only about observing birds in flight but also includes direct, bodily contact during training and handling practices. Particularly when carrying birds on the fist, falconers need to develop sensitivity toward the forces and intensities of the wind and position themselves accordingly in order to make a comfortable perch for the birds. I learned this when I was taken, together with a few other novice falconers, out into the hills by a falconer to gain experience of carrying falcons being trained for the upcoming hunting season.

After we embarked from the vehicle and got the birds on our fists—protected by strong leather gloves—I started to feel the wind blowing into the hills, and it dawned on me that this was not going to be a relaxing stroll. The strong wind seemed to blow from many directions; at times I needed to lean into it, other times it pushed us forcefully from the sides. The grass on the hillsides was bending and twisting in many directions, and there did not seem to be a single spot within reach that offered cover from the wind.

Having a lightweight and winged creature on my fist, I felt how much an adequate positioning of my arm and fist was necessary in order to keep the bird in a steady and calm position despite the tearing winds. The others who were walking ahead of me seemed to walk through a completely different place. While their hair and clothes were blown about by the wind just as mine were, their hawks did not move a single feather and perched on the fist easy and relaxed.

My bird, on the other hand, did not have a great time. When the wind was blowing from the front, she sometimes spread her wings and was shakily lifted up; other times, the wind was blowing up her back, pushing up against her tail feathers, which threw her out of balance and made her flap her wings sharply to regain control, painfully hitting me in the face. At still other times, the falcon got so frustrated that she started beating her wings in an attempt to get away; once she realized that this did not work she let herself fall, now dangling from my fist with her head towards the ground, flapping about with her wings. After a while—probably out of concern for the well-being of the falcon—one of the others returned to help me get the bird back on my fist. Clearly amused by my clumsy inability to carry the falcon, I was shown how to adjust my arm, and it was recommended that I try to keep her close to my body, always setting her face into the wind so that the air would flow over her wings rather than get under her tail feathers. I tried it again and in the course of our walk through the hills I managed, progressively at least, to improve the bird's position through trying always to place myself into the wind with the falcon held close to my chest.

Carrying a falcon turned out to be a task that required skill and experience as well as the ability to be responsive to the bird whose signs of discomfort needed to be answered immediately. This negotiation between human and bird, however, is not only dependent on both of them but is crucially shaped by the air currents that flowed around us (and through us), forcefully influencing our movements.

Fieldwork Aloft

Through their observations of and engagement with birds of prey, falconers learn to respond to the weather in relation to their movements and to understand the connection between landforms, air, and weather. The way falconers talk about the weather and especially the wind as well as the techniques birds and humans apply to use the wind when hunting suggest that in falconry the wind and weather take on material qualities. Air is rarely experienced as completely still, but rather in continuous movement of more or less turbulent wind currents. Amplified through the movements of the birds, air is revealed as possessing a perceptible texture, consisting of currents that at times can be supportive or dangerous and unpredictable at others. Here earth and air are experienced as co-constituting each other, rather than as belonging to separate spheres divided by the surface of the ground.

During fieldwork, I progressively learned that to work together with an airborne creature means not to superimpose an earthbound perspective, but to become sensitive to the aerial experience of the birds. The activity of the weather and its transformational forces on the movements and ways of experiencing the environment can perhaps be best described as weathering. Putting an emphasis on a weathering-world in movement, in which the weather is its ongoing effects, helps to broaden anthropological approaches to human-environment relationships, by drawing our attention to the role of atmospheric phenomena in the formation of human and nonhuman lifeworlds.

Acknowledgments

I would like to thank Aina Azevedo for allowing me to reproduce some of her drawings that resulted from our previous collaboration. I also would like to thank Tim Ingold for inspiring conversations and the contributors to our jointly organized panel "Life in Atmospheric Worlds: Everyday Knowledge and Perception of Weather" convened at a meeting held in May 2016, London. I also would like to acknowledge the International Rotary Foundation and the Falconry Heritage Trust for funding during my doctoral research as well as the ERC (grant number 295458).

Dr. Sara Asu Schroer, University of Aberdeen, is a social anthropologist with a longstanding interest in environmental perception and enskilment. Having considered questions of more-than-human perspectives on learning, knowledge formation, sociality, and intimacy, her current research is concerned with the broader ecological relationships that intertwine human and avian lifeworlds in a time of rapid environmental change and extinction. She is the author of several peer-reviewed articles and is a co-editor of *Exploring Atmospheres Ethnographically* published with Routledge in 2018.

Notes

1. This essay is based upon in-depth ethnographic fieldwork conducted with falconers and falconry birds mainly in the UK but also including shorter fieldtrips to Italy and Germany (Schroer 2015).
2. The drawings, inspired by the author's writing, are by anthropologist Aina Azevedo. They derive from a previous a collaboration exploring the possibility of using drawing and text as interconnected media in anthropological research, analysis and writing, resulting in the publication of a graphic essay, also exploring the weathering environment as perceived by falconers and their birds (Azevedo and Schroer 2016).

References

Azevedo, Aina, and Sara Asu Schroer. 2016. "Weathering: A Graphic Essay." *Vibrant: Virtual Brazilian Anthropology* 13(2): 177–94.

Jefferies, Ricard 1843. "The Breeze on Beachy Head." In *Nature Abounding*, ed. E. L. Grant Watson, 139–141. London: The Scientific Book Club.

Ingold, Tim 2010. "Footprints through the Weather-World: Walking, Breathing, Knowing." In *Making Knowledge: Explorations of the Indissoluble Relation Between Mind, Body and Environment*, ed. Trevor H. J. Marchand, 115–32. Special issue of the Journal of the Royal Anthropological Institute. Oxford: Wiley-Blackwell.

Schroer, Sara Asu. 2015. "'On the Wing': Exploring Human-Bird Relationships in Falconry Practice." Ph.D. dissertation. Aberdeen: University of Aberdeen.

Schroer, Sara Asu. 2018. "'A Feeling for Birds': Tuning into More-Than-Human Atmospheres." In *Exploring Atmospheres Ethnographically*, ed. Sara Asu Schroer and Susanne Schmitt, 76–88. London: Routledge.

PART II

Moving

Chapter 5

TRAVELING THROUGH LAYERS

INUITNESS *IN FLIGHT*

Willow Scobie

> Intergenerational trauma is real. We have people who work up here but don't stay. It goes back generations. Learn inuktitut [*sic*] + make friends with elders. Your Anthropology work is bs and your work experience is wasting our time. Move over and make room for us. Be our ally #Inuit
>
> —@Allakariallak, 26 November 2019

> Research in itself is a powerful intervention, even if carried out at a distance, which has traditionally benefited the researcher, and the knowledge base of the dominant group in society. When undertaking research, either across cultures or within a minority culture, it is critical that researchers recognize the power dynamic which is embedded in the relationship with their subjects. Researchers are in receipt of privileged information.
>
> —Linda Tuhiwai Smith, *Decolonizing Methodologies*

The dynamics described in @Allakariallak's tweet reach beyond the work of anthropologists, connecting a number of contemporary frustrations with historical injustices, and apply broadly to itinerate southerners[1] and the (painful) residue they leave in their wake. In 284 characters, she moves succinctly, connecting the trauma that previous generations of Inuit experienced—including but not limited to forced settlement, residential schooling, nutritional experiments on children, forced removal for tuberculosis treatment, forced resettlement in the high arctic, the dog slaughter, educational experiments, Eskimo [*sic*] number identification tags, etc.—with the more contemporary experience of colonialism at the hands of anthropologists and other researchers. Her directives include learning the language; connecting meaningfully with Inuit elders; and respecting the time, energy, and interests of Inuit when it comes to research. When she types, "Your Anthropology work is bs," she simultaneously invokes and revokes: she revokes the privilege of anthropological pursuits that seem unencumbered by a growing insistence that research with Indigenous communities follow their protocols; it also invokes the work of Indigenous scholars like Linda Tuhiwai Smith. Smith's text, *Decolonizing Methodologies: Research and Indigenous Peoples* remains a key manuscript in a growing body of literature that challenges the power dynamics and underlying ideological frameworks (1999). Challenging anthropologists who presume that it is their privilege to "accumulate knowledge without impediment" (Menzies 2001: 26), Smith lays out in detail how anthropologists and others are to engage Indigenous communities in all aspects of the research, including its central purpose.

In this chapter I pose two questions: how can we enter the field to work with Indigenous communities, and how do I negotiate these challenges in my own research. I work through these questions by drawing on a literature that identifies practices for decolonizing anthropology and consider my fieldwork experiences through that lens. I then analyze these reflections using the concepts of nomadism, fluid subjectivity, and lines of flight. Within this chapter are two vignettes that advance my methodological tactic to engage with content on the Internet (Stalcup) and that delve more deeply into the meaning of reconciliation when working with Indigenous communities (Dokis).

Reconciling Anthropological Fieldwork

Marie Battiste (2002) critiques the assumption that Eurocentric research can reveal an understanding of Indigenous knowledge and Eurocentric ways of knowing. "A literature review," she writes, "is an oxymoron" because Indigenous knowledge is typically embedded in the cumulative experiences and teachings of Indigenous peoples rather than in a library (Battiste 2002: 2). This, at the very least, takes us out to the field. From this point, there are a number of ways anthropologists have engaged with "radical critiques" from Indigenous communities, broadly summarized by Charles Menzies in terms of complete withdrawal, proceeding without acknowledging these critiques, or engaging in "self-consciously committed, cooperative, and/or community-based research" (2001: 26). Honoring relationships involves awareness of Indigenous histories, place-based existences, and engagement with struggles against "shape-shifting colonial powers" (Corntassel 2013: 48)—powers that permeate knowledge systems (Todd 2016) and practices (Connell 2014). Building on these reflections, I add that it runs deeper than questions of postcolonial ethics and politics, but that there are also ontological and epistemological challenges. As Vanessa Watt points out, Indigenous peoples are finding ways to affirm the connection between places, nonhumans, and humans, and this requires and enables accessing the "precolonial mind" (2013: 21). Watt's argument about decolonization is a challenge to the Euro-Western epistemological-ontological divide between the human world and the nonhuman world and the inclusion of land and nonhuman beings in an understanding of agency (2013: 28). Zoe Todd (2016) elaborates on what she describes as the "Ontological Turn," referring to embodied expressions of stories, laws, and songs from the perspective of Indigenous Place-Thought or self-determination.

For Julie Cruikshank,[2] the relationship between traditional storytelling practices and the demands of academic research require some thought. The significance of oral traditions and storytelling, Cruikshank argues, is that they "confront hierarchies of power in very precise ways" (2005: 61) and that they are best understood by listening to/absorbing the personal messages conveyed in repeated tellings (2005: 60; Donald 2013). Inasmuch as they can be processes in Indigenous knowledge recovery, research partnerships are deeply local, center relationships to land, and are both formal and informal (Corntassel 2013).

Fieldwork Negotiations

It was with this in mind that I reached out to make connections that would lead to other connections in different communities across Nunavut. Stacy Rasmus and Olga Ulturgasheva point out that contemporary social science researchers challenge the "trope of the polar explorer/hero or 'lone wolf' that has characterized many contributions to circumpolar ethnology" (2017: 224). They describe two approaches: the first is a multifaceted and multivoiced methodological process that captures the "multi-layered and rapidly changing complexity of contemporary Indigenous lives and knowledge" (2017: 226); the second involves turning the anthropological gaze back on ourselves in order to produce "points of orientation and disorientation in the ethnographic encounter" (2017: 227).

I thought I was prepared to be that kind of researcher. Ready to identify and follow "points of orientation and disorientation," I listened to myself and others. I followed where they led me, shushed feelings of shyness and discomfort—I was elated, for example, when I received a warm invitation to join a sealskin textile workshop in Iqaluit. I was in Iqaluit, Nunavut, for several weeks on that trip trying to learn about the everyday lives of Inuit youth in that community. Traveling across the northern territory, I was loosely following up on Richard Condon's 1987 study of Inuit youth in Holman Island, NWT. Conducting fieldwork in 1982, Condon described the following:

> As would be expected in a community where adolescents have a great deal of sexual autonomy, premarital pregnancies are fairly common. While parents of young unwed mothers may mildly disapprove of early pregnancies, they tend to be extremely tolerant and accepting. Part of this tolerance is due to the adults' great pleasure in having infants around the house. The infants resulting from premarital pregnancies are managed in a number of ways. The first is that the young mother may decide to take on the primary responsibility for child care, while obtaining occasional assistance from parents and siblings. Generally, only the more socially mature young mothers opt for this arrangement since having and caring for an infant places significant constraints upon the mother's social life. If, however, the young mother is unable or unwilling to take on the burden of child care, she may offer the child for adoption to her parents or another household. (1988: 150–51)

There is an unmistakable paternalism in this description of young women's sexuality, their relationships, and how they are situated in complex arrangements of adoption. They also remind the reader of the long shadow of Christian missionaries and their influence on the lives of generations of Inuit. Based on conversations and casual observations, it was not my impression that women understood becoming a mother to necessitate becoming a wife, but perhaps in the thirty-five intervening years some people had disentangled themselves from Judeo-Christian prescriptions.

Thus, although initially I was interested in asking women about becoming mothers, I was quickly dissuaded by the people I met early in my visit: "That isn't interesting," many told me. Folks who grew up in the south—teachers, government workers, nurses, doctors—encouraged me to push on. They could see it as a "problem" (particularly in terms of high school completion rates), and I needed to study it. I began from a place of curiosity and had no specific agenda. "This is exploratory," I told the Nunavummiut. "I'm not committed to this plan." That seemed a little reassuring, and they agreed to keep talking to me if I kept my mind open, if I agreed to listen to their stories about their own lives and be attentive to how they described them, what they experienced, and how they saw the world.

"How do I get rid of the smell of fish? I can't get this smell out of my hands." This was the question I put to one of the men who facilitates a training program for youth in Iqaluit. He is Inuk and spends all of his spare time training kids and youth in traditional Inuit games. We were about to talk about his program when I interrupted myself to both apologize and ask for help. As a long-time hunter, he had some advice: wash your hands with Vaseline. "Thanks," I said before we got back to our conversation about his program.

I am embarrassed to admit that one of the things that preoccupied me most while participating in the sealskin textile workshop was what was happening to me. The fishy smell on my hands was the result of my attempt to help a group of women scrape the fat from some of the skins. An elder was showing a room of young, adult Inuit women how to work with seal skins in preparation for some sewing projects. These women would go on to make kamiks (outdoor boots), mittens, head bands, jewelry, and more. With permission from the elder in charge I dropped into the program to meet some of the women and chat informally afterward. There was an awkward silence when I entered the room (late! more embarrassment) and sat on the floor between two women who were scraping their own seal skins. I felt overcome with my own shyness and was grateful when someone brought me a skin and an ulu (women's knife). I watched the two women on either side of me and tried to copy them. It turns out that it is incredibly difficult! The room erupted in laughter and everyone generously turned my fumbling attempt into a moment of shared fun. I laughed too, relieved that the focus was shifting from how terrible I was with the knife to how (unintentionally) hilarious I was. The conversation from there was about their sewing projects, about the things they wanted to make for their kids and other family members, about the upcoming bingo game, and generally catching up with each other on their personal news. Most of the women spoke English, but many also spoke to each other in Inuktitut. It was a fluid and seamless flow between languages and topics. I had spoken to the elder on the phone beforehand, and she was the one to invite me to the class, but once I was there she did not engage with me directly. It was up to me to make my way through the room and follow the conversations already occurring around me.

I considered my own role in that moment and thought about how I could move forward with these feelings of disorientation. Later, in response to the way in which an Inuk man framed the research question that informs his own artistic work, I began to orient my fieldwork focus toward the ways youth across the Inuit Nunangat (Inuit homeland) were searching for Inuitness. Reflecting now on my fieldwork experiences in communities in the eastern and western parts of Nunavut, in online fora, and at Ottawa events, I worked hard to become epistemologically attuned to the contemporary methods and content of the stories that Inuit youth were telling. What interested me most were the layers that emerged, which were evident in their search for Inuitness. I thus came to think of this epistemologically as a form of nomadism, such that the methods and content move through all of these spaces and take many forms.

Stories, in 280 Characters or Less

Nomadism can be, as Claudio Aporta describes, a process of interweaving life histories with the land, where well-known trails are like the "roots of a rhizome" forming a "mesh of interlaced itineraries" (2016: 260). The itineraries that I followed/conversations that I had were in coffee shops, in living rooms, and at kitchen tables, at youth center drop-ins, at craft markets, while walking around a department store. The itineraries that I pursued took me through dozens and dozens of YouTube videos, postings on Bebo (a social media site that was popular in the North before Facebook dominated the market), messages on Facebook and Twitter. These sites I visited/stopped/stumbled upon were not simply where the stories were told but are interwoven into contemporary experiences of landscape.

It seems provocative to include the Internet in a discussion about landscapes. *Ikiaqqivik*, the Inuktitut word for the Internet, means "traveling through layers" (Soukup 2006). This idea interweaves what elders describe as a shaman's capacity to travel across time and place to find answers; it also describes a present-day process of bringing together contemporary realities and technologies (2006: 239). Following the lead of a group of social media savvy Inuit artists, I moved across tweets and videos associated with the hashtag #sealfie. The catalyst for this campaign was Inuk teen Killaq Enuaraq-Strauss who used the YouTube platform to digitally link Nunavut to Hollywood: she called attention to the work of US-based non-governmental organizations who, with financial and campaign support from Hollywood celebrities, were having a devastating effect on Inuit economies by calling for a ban on commercial seal hunting. Her video garnered a significant amount of online attention (at one point it was up to 58,000 views and almost 780 comments) when she attempted to digitally draw in celebrity Ellen DeGeneres as an intimate audience of one with her vlog, "Dear Ellen," uploaded to YouTube on 23 March 2014. At the core of Enuaraq-Strauss' video there is a line between culture, practices, becoming, and being alive. The #sealfies leaves markers in the digital landscape that connect food, clothing, tradition, geography, language, history, and culture.

Particularly in the early 2010s, Inuit youth were uploading videos to YouTube on a number of subjects that featured a variety of scenes and scenarios. Nancy Wachowich and I argue in a piece entitled "Uploading Selves: Inuit Digital Storytelling on YouTube" that Inuit youth were tactically using this platform to explore their Inuitness in ways that were serious, but also playful: "I'm going to talk about throat singing and why everybody likes it. I mean, come on! . . . Just think, you're listening to some rap music or some rock 'n' roll and all of a sudden there's a disturbance of throat singers. Yeah, it does sound like a car wreck" (2010: 93).

On the more serious side, thematically, they covered such topics as historical and contemporary depictions of Inuit culture (videos of two women throat singing, training for an Inuit games competition to the soundtrack of "Eye of the Tiger"), political advocacy (challenging other Inuit youth to create spaces where their voices can be heard in contemporary territorial politics, expressing frustration at the Food Mail Program, raising awareness of lobbying efforts in the EU in response to seal product bans), and videos designed to forge links between Inuit youth to create a "digital community" based on "pride" and "positivity." Inasmuch as the filmmakers and vloggers were actively engaged in the process of bringing into being their Inuitness, some of the conversations I had in the course of my fieldwork brought to bear their perception of the instabilities inherent in this process (feeling vulnerable, dealing with trolls, ultimately wanting to be out on the land). The epistemological puzzle of both bringing Inuitness into being and studying this process, therefore, is how one conveys that which is in the making.

That Which Is in the Making

Claire Colebrook (2002: 21) describes: "A problem is a way of creating a future. When plants grow and evolve they do so by way of problems, developing features to avoid predators, to maximize light or to retain moisture." Many of the Inuit that I met and worked with conceptualized Inuit identity as a "problem"—they were creating a future that involved the active constitution of Inuit identity. This included divergent ends and thus lines of flight: intentional disruptions, breaks, and new beginnings. They open up to new futures and multiple identities through various actions and interventions (Braidotti 2006). The active creation of hybrid spaces in which these creations took place incorporated technologies such as filmmaking and social media.

Part of this landscape can be found on social media sites, but also within a space that is Inuit-controlled. Isuma Productions is a collective of professionally produced Inuit film art. They are involved in creating and maintaining a video portal of Indigenous films, film-based Inuit storytellers, and documenting Inuit testimonies before, during, and after resource extraction project community consultations. Isuma's work connects the politics of Indigenous advocacy, resistance, and activism through media (Huhdorf 2003) and is part of a multivocal node in the links between contemporary Inuit art and politics (Evans 2008). Many of their own film projects tell stories with painstaking attention to details such as historically accurate clothing, shelter, travel methods, and language. Beyond the aesthetic value of retrieving and showing historical events and conditions of everyday life, Isuma's films connect contemporary audiences to a historical period before colonialism transformed everyday lives in the Arctic (Santo 2004). These films in effect make real again the experience of the freedom of the Inuit (Santo 2004) and use web space and storytelling in interesting ways.

Movement between these spaces—Nunavut communities/landscapes, Canadian urban settings, and online environments—raises crucial methodological questions. In the following vignette, Meg Stalcup describes the study of the Internet as a field site. Working with a group of students, the research techniques demonstrate that contemporary methods blend the online and the offline, noting that Internet activities are part of our everyday lives; part of the human experience; integral to our relationship to the present. Stalcup's students thus direct their questions and observations to the content and algorithms they find on the web.

Vignette 4
Internet Techniques for an Untimely Anthropology
Meg Stalcup

GM: But what again is untimeliness? How do we teach students to produce that?

> PR: Well, I think that's a big question. The term is taken from Nietzsche's *Untimely Meditations* and used to mark a critical distance from the present that seeks to establish a relationship to the present different from reigning opinion.
>
> —George Marcus and Paul Rabinow, *Designs for an Anthropology of the Contemporary*

Picture a classroom: the students are seated with their phones in front of them or an open laptop. A piece of paper and a pen are at hand. Voices merge into a low hum as they point at the screens, explaining to one another an experience so familiar that they have never before put it into words.

The task is to go to a website and use it. They take notes on what draws the eye, where they want to click, and such thoughts as occur to them, by habit or summoned through the curious externalizing nature of the exercise. We come back together as a group, and one student walks us through his navigation of the foreign-language version of a popular video repository. "Even though I don't know what is written, the site makes it easy. I kind of automatically knew what they wanted when the box popped up––I had to allow cookies." The other students chime in, discussing the colors and layout. He continues,

> I like to look at videos when I get home at the end of the day. I just click around. So here I did what I usually do, which is scroll down to see the number of views and comments. I watch something and let the next video come up, because it knows the kind of thing I like. I don't have an account here though and so the video that came up was random.

The goal of the exercise is to practice participant observation where many people now spend a significant portion of their time: online. Individuals access the Internet throughout the day, from work, school, a public street, or home. It can be a required component of those parts of life, or a break from them. As Annette Markham writes, "We carry the internet with us in our pockets"; for her research subjects, it is "so ubiquitous we don't think much *about* it at all, we just think *through* it" (2016: 1, emphasis in original). In the context of the exercise, the students pay attention to this infrastructure. They begin to see things, such as the algorithmic experience of having videos chosen for them. They agree that this kind of scrolling is physically relaxing. It is a pastime they note they have in common, even though they do it largely alone.

Another student poked around a site where people post medical questions and doctors respond. She went on to do a semester-long project examining how young women get information on reproductive health and found that they do not "just Google it" (Richards 2018). Their approaches included Internet searches and pornography. Rather than an endpoint, however, online information was fodder for debate and conversations with friends, family, clergy, and clinicians. Her research, too, tacked back and forth between the Internet and other sites. She met with members of a university-based sexual health promotion team; did interviews with them, a women's health blogger, and a nurse practitioner; and talked to peers about their personal histories and experiences learning about their bodies, birth control, and sex.

The students were employing Internet techniques, which are practices in the fieldwork repertoire adapted to blend online and offline, much as they are blended in people's lives. A list, which can only ever be partial, includes:

- maintaining and making relationships through social networking services and mobile instant messengers;
- observing the ways that people interact in and with online spaces;
- participating in wholly or partially online groups;
- learning skills for and in these milieus;
- asking digitally mediated questions (whether formally in arranged interviews or not);
- and exploring the many ways that all of this can be recorded and archived.

Casual conversation in a messaging app will produce an exportable file, but to remember the experience of that chat, the researcher might still take notes and incorporate them later. Understanding the other person's experience could require meeting face-to-face. Technology can be the focus of the research but not necessarily. As in the study of women's health information, Internet techniques come into play because digital technologies are part of people's lives. Their addition to anthropology's toolbox has come about as computer-mediating assemblages have become ordinary for many research subjects. Algorithms, big data and machine learning producing artificial intelligence (AI), access and lack of access to the Internet, and other aspects of the digital are significant shapers of existence (human and nonhuman) today. To the extent that lives involve these technologies, anthropological inquiry will too.

Just such making "the familiar strange and the strange familiar" is what anthropology has long claimed as its expertise (see Myers 2011). The Internet and its broader technological problem space pose methodological challenges, however, for a discipline that has traditionally drawn on the authority of "being there" to ground its claims to knowledge. What do we do when a phenomenon has global ramifications, but we still need to choose specific places to go? As we analyze what is available to us through social media, how can we get a sense of what remains unsaid? How do we identify anthropological objects when technological ones are always changing? More broadly, what kind of anthropology might be able to address the movement that materializes in, but is not unique to, technological innovations?

Internet techniques are not answers, but ways of taking these questions to the field. They are tools to be employed in response to specific situations and goals. Developing anthropological practice for an ever-moving world is, withal, more than just a matter of techniques. Critically, it is about a mode of inquiry that can be called the "untimely" in which such techniques are used. The untimely is, as Gilles Deleuze put it, a state of becoming that is inopportune (*intempestif*), and, in Paul Rabinow's conceptualization, ill-timed, inconvenient—and thus appropriate for thinking (2011: 60–62). The digital connotes speed and the ongoing emergence of novelty, inviting similarly timed and urgent responses. This makes it both harder and more requisite for the anthropologist to seek, per our epigraph, "a relationship to the present different from reigning opinion" (Rabinow et al. 2008: 59). Although discussed in breathless terms of futurism or, alternatively, as sensationalistic doomsaying, the issues that concern people about the Internet or algorithmic governance—trust, truth, privacy, security, freedom, individuality, intimacy—are better thought of as "perennial" (Langlitz 2013: 251). Such terms reference enduring ethical and political problems, now showing up in contemporary circumstances and configurations deeply entwined with digital media and related technologies.

If anthropology is to have anything of importance to say, it will not move strictly in time with the world it studies and problems as they are presented, by the news media, tacit disciplinary norms, or academic fads. It will seek instead an untimeliness that comes, at least partly, George Marcus suggests, from being in time with, and holding oneself accountable to, the substance and relations of one's fieldwork (in Rabinow et al. 2008: 60). The recompense is the possibility of producing something inopportune in that it "disrupts those existing things and relations and changes their tone, register, and directionality," yet appropriate, "at least retrospectively in that it reconfigures existing things and relations" (in Rabinow 2011: 60).

In an untimely mode, one might design a project that, as Christine Hine proposes (2015), takes as preliminary problem-spaces the "embedded, embodied, and everyday." Digital phenomena are thoroughly embedded in people's lives. It is untimely to argue that what the Internet is for different people is surely multiple and not yet settled, when most have already leapfrogged to trying solve the problems "it" presents. Observation and asking questions are therefore necessary to grasp meaning and significance they are ascribed in those contexts. One would also look at how being online or the subject of algorithms is an embodied extension of the ways we are gendered, racialized, and classed in the world more generally. Underlying inequalities still structure access to the Internet, while facial recognition and search engines have racial biases (Hine 2015: 6; Noble 2018). Research therefore needs to attend to the discursive erasures yet continued reality of embodiment (Amrute 2016). Finally, the Internet, algorithms, and artificial intelligence are in many ways the infrastructure of the everyday. The dual task this presents is studying when and why this infrastructure takes center stage, as it has with fears about online radicalization to violence or electoral manipulation, and calling it back to attention when naturalized and overlooked.

Turning the Gaze

At my own screen, from my office, side by side and face-to-face, I have posed (naïve) questions and have in turn been redirected toward people, projects, and perspectives that were more in tune with the folks with whom I was working and who were integral to my research. What I came to understand is that as members of an intensely researched population, Inuit in communities across Canada's North strategically negotiate the terms under which they will participate: the research must foreground their interests and priorities. The phrase "not about me without me" refers to a sovereignty of subjectivity both within our interactions and across academic work. And so, my journey as a researcher meant that my own curiosities were set aside and I learned to begin projects by first asking people about their own interests and concerns. It became a multiview, multitextual, multidimensional journey with the intention of understanding and conveying multiple perspectives and variant stories.

Cruikshank argues that storytelling is a practice that is part of everyday life; it is a "framework for understanding historical and contemporary issues" (2005: 60). Part of my story in this telling is a mix of hubris, education, and coming to understand some things. In a chat about dogs with a young man, for example, I assumed that I was adding something thoughtful to a conversation about the traditional importance of dogs to the Inuit: "Some people think of them like their children," I said. "Except that you can eat them," my lunch companion replied. I could not tell if he was pulling my leg, but I was pretty sure that I saw a flash of irritation on his face. I had a pit in my stomach and worried that I had betrayed my lack of experience, my naïveté, my southerness. My impression of the guy on the other side of the table was that he could move easily between being on the land and being in town; vividly describe the lives of his grandparents; talk about his advocacy work on language issues and traditional learning in Nunavut schools. I am reminded of the "two worlds" thesis—a thread that runs through some of the literature about Indigenous youth (Henze and Vanett 1993; Kral et al. 2011). Michael Kral et al., for example, write that younger Inuit feel as though they are part of a globalized economy and at the same time drawn to the traditional values and practices of their elders (2011: 435). In their work, the "two worlds" thesis is shorthand for a sense of self that is incoherent, bifurcated, and contradictory. Perhaps, however, rather than interpret this as a failure to achieve ontological certainty, we acknowledge that the contemporary experience of being Inuit is about traveling through layers. They contend with a colonial logic by making all things possible in every moment. Indigenous epistemologies are flexible and adaptive (Pierotti 2011), and rather than assuming a Eurocentric, Cartesian understanding of the self, these lines of flight reflect a plurality of possibilities and cosmologies.

In another community in the western part of Nunavut, I thought that I was off to a great start when the airport employees discovered that I did not have a way to get myself and my bags to the house where I was staying. Through contacts and conversations and one particularly helpful filmmaker originally from this community and temporarily based in Iqaluit, I found a host with a room in their house to share. When I heard that the local hotel was almost full and that there was a chance that I would have to share my room with a mine worker if a plane landed and men needed somewhere to sleep for the night, I opted to look for a different arrangement. "We'll give you a ride," an airport employee said as he and his colleagues proceeded to shut down the airport and load me and my stuff into their work truck. "Working here is going to be great," I thought to myself. However, although the initial reception was warm, I had a hard time connecting with anyone else for a few days until a man crossed the road in order to speak to me directly. "Who are you?" he asked. I told him my name, but he pushed on, "No, what are you doing here?" When I explained that I was a researcher and here to learn more about youth he looked at my Gore-Tex coat and hiking boots (the uniform of a southerner in Nunavut) and said, "Yeah, I figured you were either a scientist or a drug dealer." His smile widened at his own joke (was he joking?), and he suggested that I check out the craft market at the community arena. While running my hands through furs and picking up earrings and small carvings, I tried to make eye contact with other people at the market. Each time I arrived in a new place I struggled to find a way in. I finally caught a break when I was able to chat with someone who ran the community youth sports programs. That meant that I could start subsequent conversations about the sports program, which turned out to be a popular topic.

Feeling attuned to their importance and being ready to engage deeply with stories is part of the dynamic, but we also often struggle to find ways to connect with storytellers. Anthropological fieldwork on the Internet produces its own methodological challenges, but when we work to connect with someone in a community shortly after stepping off a plane, how do we start that conversation? In the vignette below, Carly Dokis finds her own way into a community by becoming useful. Traveling across layers of colonialism, distrust, histories of exploitative research, and contemporary conditions that are complex and deeply political, Dokis moves with people in the community collecting and hauling water.

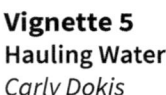

Vignette 5
Hauling Water
Carly Dokis

When I arrived in Behdzi Ahda First Nation in 2004, there was no water treatment infrastructure in the community. Nestled along the shores of Colville Lake, people living in the small Dene community in the Sahtu Region of the Northwest Territories continued to draw the cold, clean water from the lake to drink and for all of their water needs. I was staying with elders Marie and Hyacinth Kochon, and I would watch from their kitchen table every morning as people went out to the lake to get water. Later in the day, Marie and Hyacinth's grandchildren would come and bring them water, and they would visit and laugh and speak to each other in Slavey. Collecting water shaped the daily rhythm of life in the community. Every morning people would go to the water; in summer they would collect water near the shoreline, in winter they would cut holes in the ice with an augur or an axe, marking the hole with a cut tree branch so that later they would only have to break through a day or so of ice, and let the water bubble to the surface.

While living in the community, I also went out to the lake every morning to collect water, and I came to appreciate our daily engagement. I grew to know the water in different ways; the sound she made as her waves lapped gently on the shore or as she came rushing up through the hole in the ice, the way she smelled as she mixed with land, crisp and inviting on a cold fall day, and the sweet, cold taste of unchlorinated water. Over time, I grew to be attuned to small alterations in her with the changing of the seasons or the weather, and became mindful of how much I took and how little I needed, things I never thought about at home when water was available simply by turning on the tap. My engagement with water also deepened my relationships with people. When I look back at my fieldnotes now, I am surprised to find how much I wrote about water, not only about how water felt and tasted and about the physicality of hauling water, but about how many conversations I had while collecting water, about how the water drew us to her and to one another. For me, hauling my own water was not a community problem to be solved or managed, or even so much an activity of inquiry, but because I too had to participate in the gathering of water, I was able to see the connections between that which is done in the everyday and larger webs of social practice.

When I arrived, my initial thoughts were that the absence of water treatment infrastructure was a result of poverty, a lack of resources, or inadequate government funding. I later learned that for many years the government of the Northwest Territories had pressed Behdzi Ahda First Nation to implement water delivery service in their community. Like most communities located in areas of continuous permafrost, the government proposal was to deliver treated water to community households a few times per week. But the community has vehemently opposed government efforts to implement water delivery programs. Residents of Behdzi Ahda First Nation prefer, in fact insist, that they continue to haul and drink water from the lake on an as-needed basis, rather than to have treated water delivered to their homes. When I asked Chief Richard Kochon about this he told me that people did not want to have their water delivered in truck. "Getting water out of the lake keeps us Dene," he said, "people feel better when they can live on their own and when they can be on the land. If we depend on the government to provide things, then they can take them away." Chief Kochon identified two important changes for his community that would result from depending on water from a water treatment plant: there would be a reorientation in peoples' relationships with water, and by extension with each other, when mediated through technology, and the sustainability of their water supply would become unpredictable when brought under the purview and control of the state.

The magnitude of Chief Kochon's words did not strike me until years later when I was working with another Indigenous community on concerns around access to clean drinking water. Their water treatment facility was built in the 1950s and was now ranked, as are a disproportionately high number of drinking water systems in First Nation communities in Canada, as high risk. Community members there remember that prior to the water treatment system, they too would go down to the river to collect and drink the water. They recalled the same sweet taste of unchlorinated water, and how when they went out on the land they would carry a cup with them so that they could dip it in the water for a drink. They talked about a time when they lived without fear of contaminated drinking water.

Living in the Anthropocene, an era defined by increasing disruption of earth systems that has escalated since the industrial revolution, it is not surprising that many of the changes in water quality are human induced: increased agricultural runoff, the discharge of sewage and other industrial material into the lakes and waterways, increases in boat traffic and associated oil skims on the water, the release of toxic chemicals into the water from tailing ponds, pulp mills, hydrological fracking, and other industrial processes. It is also not surprising, given the underlying presumption of human triumph over nature that characterizes the Anthropocene, that many of the solutions proposed or imagined by the state or through normal science are technological in nature; that if we only design or implement the right kinds of technology, we can engineer our way to clean water, to clean air, to a livable earth. This focus on technological remediation of water contamination eclipses the wider political ecologies that contribute to environmental injustice both within Canada and globally.

Anishinaabe scholar Deborah McGregor (2015) has suggested that water has experienced alienation through the same processes that characterize colonization and that addressing the traumas inflicted on water by legal and technical means are not likely to achieve water justice. Rather, she calls on us to restore loving relationships with water as a form of reconciliation and healing. Her words, and her call to know water through intimacy and care, always remind me of Richard Kochon and the lessons offered up to me, and to all of us, by hauling water.

Similarly reflecting on forms of reconciliation, I tried to move to and through the spaces and communities to which I was directed, working to understand the relationships between the past, present, and future; to the Internet spaces and the places where Inuit meet and pass on their teachings to each other. Inspired by Henri Bergson's (1991) philosophy of movement—the affirmation of life, time, the future, and the new—and thinking about Rosi Braidotti's (2006) zones of indetermination (that produce a kind of sieve that enables objects to enter unexpected connections in order to make something new), I consider what nomadism creates. Based on my encounters it produces experiences of becoming subject: either by design as a communication tactic or in response to actions and decisions taken outside of their communities. I met, talked with, and followed Inuit youth who experiment with lines of flight as they simultaneously deepen and weaken ideas they have about themselves and others have about them. They move through time and place (historical context, community-specific dynamics); through media (Facebook, Isuma.tv, YouTube); they position themselves as authors and broadcasters, and story my research. These processes perforate and penetrate the boundaries of subject matter. Braidotti's (2006) nomadic subjects move between being dispersed and fragmented and being at other times coherent and accountable. In her work, she wonders about the subject that is in transit, fluid, and in process, sometimes a hybrid. While we sat in a coffee shop in Iqaluit a young, Inuk filmmaker described his own fluidity in terms of the spaces he occupied. He moved seamlessly between the timescapes and the landscapes of seal and caribou hunting and uploading videos to the Internet. He described specific events and projects, and a continuity, a *durée,* interwoven through grandmothers and grandfathers and his son. "Sometimes I fear we may be witnessing the last generation of Inuit," he told me. And so I shifted the focus of my research from inquiry, from study, to witness, to co-author, to co-archivist; from becoming mother to becoming Inuit.

A Problem Is a Way of Creating a Future

What interests me deeply is how people understand and explain changes: changes in their lives, within their inner circles, or the social context. How do scholars account for changes and how do people with whom they are in conversation describe them? Researchers drawn to the North may be curious about ruptures in linguistic, spiritual, and various quotidian practices. However, contemplating the multiplicities within the *durée* is more pertinent, described by Elizabeth Grosz as:

> Singular, unified, and whole, as well as in specific fragments and multiplicitous proliferation. There is one and only one time, but there are also numerous times; a duration for each thing or movement which melds with a global or collective time. As a whole, time is braided, intertwined, a unity of strands layered over each other; unique, singular, and in-

> dividual, it nevertheless partakes of a more generic and overarching time, which makes possible relations of earlier and later. (1999: 17)

Interested in stories that revealed durations, I was drawn to the cord around the waist of a woman I met in a northern Baffin Island community. The strands of wool intertwined and cinched her *amauti*, her son in the back chewing on her jaw and kissing her cheek to get her attention. We began our conversation, but within a short period of time she wanted some air. She put her sealskin kamiks back on and went outside for a cigarette.

When she came back in, I followed her lead in the discussion of a series of events from years previous. The initial focus of that research project was to learn more about the potential impact of a mine that would begin operating nearby. The stories that I followed brought me to this community in this moment to ask about conversations among youth in response to the proposed iron ore mine. This young woman was interested and her story was about being out on the land, taking one of the mining company consultants to areas where people in her community pick berries and where they camp.

She also talked about some things that had just happened in the community, at public meetings about the proposed mine. She talked about translating—for the consultant, for her colleague, for others in the community. She sounded tired. She seemed to be tired of negotiating between the priorities of elders, feeling competent and useful in one moment and tossed aside and invisible in another. Later, back in Ottawa, poring over my fieldnotes I think of lines of flight—speaking English for work and for fun; speaking Inuktitut for work and to stay alive, continuously becoming Inuk. She signed up for that job for a reason: to protect her community, to protect all of the ways of being Inuit, for her great-grandmother, for her son. She is simultaneously oriented toward and away from the mining company and its consultants. It means a paycheck (which she needs), but she worried that her neighbors were upset with her, that she had let them down. I was not sure if that was specifically related to that project, or if it is a longer running theme, in her, in that community.

All of that work—all of those hours on the land with the consultant; the hours of translating conversations with elders, the data, the points on a map—have been beautifully assembled in a printed document that we found in a box in the archives in a room in the community center. "I think they're there," she said. But she was not sure. She had not seen the results herself. She was pretty sure no one had—with the possible exception of whoever received the package once it arrived from southern Canada.

My colleague and I found the box and pulled out the booklets. There were pages and pages of maps with legends that identified all of the things that she mentioned: picnic areas and camping areas and berry picking areas, all significant in a long, continuous set of practices that connected her to her parents and grandparents and great-grandparents. And now there was a map. That was new. She was anticipating a rupture, however, and the rupture would come when the mining company put a road through that area to haul out their rocks. The mountain—referred to by locals as "Buttocks" ("because it looks like buttocks!")—would be dug up, moved onto ships and sent down the east coast and then on to Europe and Asia. In this scenario, the rocks would move and transform, the mountain would be gone, and the people would stay—habits and comings and goings transformed by a new landscape. The elders were sure that the people and the land animals and the sea animals would adapt. The elders told her and told the mining company and told the representatives from the government that animals move away when it is dangerous (blasting, digging, hauling, shipping), but return when it is safe again. The woman across from me seemed uncertain about this future.

Protocols

That particular period of fieldwork emerged after observing fragments of worry about the mine in online discussions. A partnership was struck via Facebook before flying north. As more and more anthropologists undertake collaborative research (see Gordon 2017; Rasmus and Ulturgasheva 2017), community-based projects such as Ikaarvik (2018) have emerged to assert and coordinate an active role for Inuit and Inuit Qaujimajatuqangit (IQ, Inuit Principles) in the design, implementation, and impact of field research. As I learned from attending one of their workshops, the Inuit youth involved in Ikaarvik have outlined a number of specific criteria for working with Inuit communities, such as "allow your Inuit guide to be in charge and trust them; when on the land, they call the shots," and "become a teacher and a student—pass on your knowledge and learn from the community at the same time" (Ikaarvik workshop, 13 December 2018). Projects like Ikaarvik move beyond regional and community-based research permit granting offices that facilitate consultation and oversight (see Menzies 2001; Nunavut Research Licensing Institute 2015). They formalize their role as a bridge between researchers from the south and communities in the north, and in the process create an experienced network of Indigenous research facilitators. Incorporating IQ into research includes asking local Inuit about the land, weather, and wildlife; it does not mean "simply 'mining' Inuit for knowledge" (Ikaarvik 2018: 4). Their role in research is also informative on a basic level, including the practical suggestion: "If you are planning a field camp, please consider bringing your own food. Buying your groceries in town may appear to benefit the community, but groceries are limited in town and you could leave the community without foods they need" (Ikaarvik 2018: 8).

As the national Inuit organization, Inuit Tapiriit Kanatami (ITK), outlines in its own report, *National Inuit Strategy on Research*, the "number of peer-reviewed publications and dissertations that focus on Inuit and Inuit Nunangat has increased at a rate higher than the increasing population of Inuit. Between 1996 and 2011, the population of Inuit in Canada increased 48 percent from 41,080 to 59,440. For the same period, the number of Inuit Nunangat-related publications increased by approximately 200 percent" (ITK 2018: 17). ITK asks, as do an increasing number of anthropologists: in whose interest?

A foundation of respectful relationships (Cruikshank 2005) is thus "we" work. We together, in conversation and showing and being shown; we together scraping fat and laughing joyfully about an Inuit name that translates to English as "big thumb"; we together explaining and understanding becoming a YouTube phenomenon, turning thousands onto the importance of seal hunting; we together remembering all of the times she traveled by boat to an inlet up the coast on Baffin Island, me thinking of these words:

> The past would never be constituted if it did not coexist with the present whose past it is. The past and the present do not denote two successive moments, but two elements which coexist: one is the present, which does not cease to pass, and the other is the past, which does not cease to be but through which all presents pass. (Deleuze 1991: 59)

Thus the virtual form of the past is accessible through varied forms and practices of remembering (Hodge 2007: 38). For the Inuit that I have met, I see the significance of forming those lines intentionally, thoughtfully, rigorously, politically, digitally, and autonomously.

When I assemble the pieces from my fieldnotes and interviews and the observations that I have made along the way—scheduled meetups, invitations, ad hoc conversations on the road and at community craft markets; my handwritten notes in Moleskine notebooks, reminders to myself on an app on my phone, screenshots from exchanges on social media—I think about the tangible elements that I experienced:

sewing projects using sealskin, teaching kids traditional games, explaining the significance of naming of children (*my son is my little grandmother*), and presentations about different ulus. But there are also the significant intangibles: the silences, the absences, the deletes, the suspicion, the assumptions, the refusals to participate, and more. An important aspect of my itinerary involves learning the meaning of "move over and make room for us." Reflecting on the relationship between anthropology and (de-)colonizing practices includes responding to community interests, building connections, listening to stories, confronting hierarchies, as well as unpacking what @Allakariallak means when she tweets "Be our ally #Inuit."

Willow Scobie is an Assistant Professor in the School of Sociological and Anthropological Studies at the University of Ottawa. She began working with Inuit youth in 2007 on projects related to YouTube, Twitter, Facebook, and Isuma.tv. She is currently working with youth and young adults in Inuit communities documenting their responses to mining projects operating in the Inuit Nunangat. Her most recent publication, "Diversions, Distraction, and Privileges: Consultation and the Governance of Mining in Nunavut" with Kathleen Rodgers, was published in *Studies in Political Economy* 100(3): 232–51.

Meg Stalcup is Assistant Professor of Anthropology at the University of Ottawa. Her research examines intersections of technology and data with science, security, politics, and ethics. Currently, her main project is in Brazil; she has also worked in the United States, France, and Canada. She is the director of the Collaboratoire d'Anthropologie Multimédia/Multimedia Anthropology Collaboratory (CAM/MAC), a forum for explorations of research methods and pedagogy.

Carly Dokis is Associate Professor in the Department of Sociology and Anthropology at Nipissing University. Carly has worked with Anishinabeg communities in northern Ontario and Dene communities in the Northwest Territories with a broad focus on the political ecology of environmental governance, particularly in the areas of extractive industries, land rights, water, and contamination. Carly is the author of *Where the Rivers Meet: Development and Participatory Management in the Sahtu Region, Northwest Territories*, and co-editor of the book *Subsistence under Capitalism: Historical and Contemporary Perspectives*. Her current work, funded by the Social Sciences and Humanities Research Council of Canada, explores land-based storytelling and stories of the land in Dokis First Nation.

Notes

Epigraph: Smith 1999: 176. Epigraph in Vignette 4: Rabinow et al. 2008: 59.

1. From the perspective of Inuit, Canadians who live outside of Inuit Nunangat are in the "south." This chapter reflects that viewpoint.
2. Dr. Julie Cruikshank is the recipient the of 2019 Northern Science Award for her research with Athapaskan and Tlingit elders exploring and recording their knowledge systems and for building "a foundation of respectful relationships" that have helped "Yukon First Nations recognize and honour the strengths of their cultural traditions" (Polar Knowledge Canada, 2019).

References

Amrute, Sareeta. 2016. Encoding Race, *Encoding Class: Indian IT Workers in Berlin*. Durham, NC: Duke University Press.

Aporta, Claudio. 2016. "From Inuit Wayfinding to the Google World: Living within an Ecology of Technologies." In *Nomadic and Indigenous Spaces: Productions and Cognitions*, ed. Judith Miggelbrink, Joachim Otto Habeck, Nuccio Mazzullo, and Peter Koch, 247–58. London: Routledge.

Battiste, Marie. 2002. *Indigenous Knowledge and Pedagogy in First Nations Education: A Literature Review with Recommendations*. Ottawa: National Working Group on Education and the Minister of Indian Affairs, Indian and Northern Affairs Canada.

Bergson, Henri. 1991. *Matter and Memory*, trans. N. M. Paul and W. S. Palmer. New York: Zone Books.

Braidotti, Rosi. 2006. *Transpositions*. Cambridge: Polity Press.

Colebrook, Claire. 2002. *Gilles Deleuze*. New York: Routledge.

Condon, Richard G. 1987. *Inuit Youth: Growth and Change in the Canadian Arctic*. New Brunswick: Rutgers University Press.

Connell, Raewyn. 2014. "Using Southern Theory: Decolonizing Social Thought in Theory, Research and Application." *Planning Theory* 13(2): 210–23.

Corntassel, Jeff. 2013. "Insurgent Education and the Roles of Indigenous Intellectuals." In *Transforming the Academy: Essays on Indigenous Education, Knowledges and Relations*, ed. Malinda S Smith, 47–51. Retrieved 18 October 2019 from https://www.ualberta.ca/-/media/D2916F31E07E43B5BFF8AF3FE2923920.

Cruikshank, Julie. 2005. *Do Glaciers Listen? Local Knowledge, Colonial Encounters, & Social Imagination*. Vancouver: UBC Press.

Deleuze, Gilles. 1991. *Bergsonism*. New York: Zone.

Donald, Dwayne. 2013. "On Making Love to Death: Plains Cree and Blackfoot Wisdom." In *Transforming the Academy: Essays on Indigenous Education, Knowledges and Relations*. ed. Malinda S Smith, 14–18. Retrieved 18 October 2019 from https://www.ualberta.ca/-/media/D29 16F31E07E43B5BFF8AF3FE2923920.

Evans, Michael Robert. 2008. *Isuma: Inuit Video Art*. Montreal-Kingston: McGill-Queen's.

Gordon, Healther Sauyaq Jean. 2017. "Building Relationships in the Arctic: Indigenous Communities and Scientists." In *Northern Sustainabilities: Understanding and Addressing Change in the Circumpolar World*, ed. Gail Fondahl and Gary Wilson, 237–52. Cham: Springer.

Grosz, Elizabeth. 1999. *Becomings: Explorations in Time, Memory, and Futures*. Ithaca, NY: Cornell University Press.

Henze, R. C. and L. Vanett. 1993. "To Walk in Two Worlds—or More? Challenging a Common Metaphor of Native Education." *Anthropology and Education Quarterly* 24: 116–34.

Hine, Christine. 2015. *Ethnography for the Internet: Embedded, Embodied and Everyday*. London: Bloomsbury.

Hodge, Matt. 2007. *The Ethnography of Time: Living with History in Modern Rural France*. Lewiston, NY: Edwin Mellen Press.

Huhdorf, Shari. 2003. "Atanarjuat, The Fast Runner: Culture, History, and Politics and Inuit Media." *American Anthropologist* 105(4): 822–26.

Ikaarvik. 2018. *ScIQ: Science and Inuit Qaujimajatuqangit: Research and Meaningful Engagement of Northern Indigenous Communities*. Retrieved 15 November 2019 from https://ocean.org/our-work/arctic-connections/ikaarvik-barriers-to-bridges.

Inuit Tapiriit Kanatami (ITK). 2018. *National Inuit Strategy on Research*. Retrieved 15 November 2019 from https://www.itk.ca/wp-content/uploads/2018/03/National-Inuit-Strategy-on-Research.pdf.

Kral, Michael J., Lori Idlout, J. Bruce Minore, Ronald J. Dyck, and Laurence Kirmayer. 2011. "Unikkaartiuit: Meanings of Well-Being, Unhappiness, Health, and Community Change Among Inuit in Nunavut, Canada." *American Journal of Community Psychology* 48: 426–38.

Langlitz, Nicolas. 2013. *Neuropsychedelia: The Revival of Hallucinogen Research since the Decade of the Brain*. Berkeley: University of California Press.

Markham, Annette N. 2016. "Ethnography in the Digital Internet Era: From Fields to Flows, Descriptions to Interventions." In *Sage Handbook of Qualitative Research*, ed. Norm Denzin and Yvonne Lincoln, 650–68. Los Angeles: Sage Publications.

McGregor, Deborah. 2015. "Indigenous Women, Water Justice and Zaagidowin (Love)." *Canadian Woman Studies/Les Cahiers de la Femme* 30(2–3): 71–78.

Menzies, Charles. 2001. "Reflections on Research with, for, and among Indigenous Peoples." *Canadian Journal of Native Education* 25(1): 19–36.

Myers, Robert. 2011. "The Familiar Strange and the Strange Familiar in Anthropology and Beyond." *General Anthropology* 18(2): 1–9.

Noble, Safiya Umoja. 2018. *Algorithms of Oppression: How Search Engines Reinforce Racism*. New York: New York University Press.

Nunavut Research Licensing Institute. 2015. "Nunavut Research Institute (NRI)." Retrieved 18 October 2019 from www.nri.nu.ca/nunavut-research-institute-nri.

Pierotti, Raymond John. 2011. *Indigenous Knowledge, Ecology, and Evolutionary Biology*. New York: Routledge.

Polar Knowledge Canada. 2019. "Dr. Julie Cruikshank awarded Polar Knowledge Canada's 2019 Northern Science Award." 6 December. http://nationtalk.ca/story/dr-julie-cruikshank-awarded-polar-knowledge-canadas-2019-northern-science-award.

Rabinow, Paul. 2011. *The Accompaniment: Assembling the Contemporary*. Chicago: University of Chicago Press.

Rabinow, Paul, George E. Marcus, James D. Faubion, and Tobias Rees. 2008. *Designs for an Anthropology of the Contemporary*. Durham, NC: Duke University Press.

Rasmus, Stacy, and Olga Ulturgasheva. 2017. "From Lone Wolves to Relational Reindeer: Revealing Anthropological Myths and Methods in the Arctic." In *Northern Sustainabilities: Understanding and Addressing Change in the Circumpolar World*, ed. Gail Fondahl and Gary Wilson, 223–36. Cham: Springer.

Richards, Gabrielle. 2018. "Women's Health Seeking: Understanding Different Authorities." Ethnography of New Media. Retrieved 18 April 2018 from http://www.cammac.space/womens-health.

Santo, Avi. 2004. "Nunavut: Inuit Television and Cultural Citizenship." *International Journal of Cultural Studies* 7(4): 379–97.

Smith, Linda Tuhiwai. 1999. *Decolonizing Methodologies: Research and Indigenous Peoples*. New York: Zed Books.

Soukup, K. 2006. "Report: Travelling through Layers: Inuit Artists Appropriate New Technologies." *Canadian Journal of Communication* 31: 239–46.

Todd, Zoe. 2016. "An Indigenous Feminist's Take on the Ontological Turn: 'Ontology' is Just Another Word for Colonialism." *Journal of Historical Sociology* 29(1): 4–21.

Wachowich, Nancy, and Willow Scobie. 2010. "Uploading Selves: Inuit Digital Storytelling on YouTube." *Études Inuit Studies* 3(2): 81–105.

Watt, Vanessa. 2013. "Indigenous Place-Thought & Agency amongst Humans and Non-humans (First Woman and Sky Woman Go on a European World Tour!)." *Decolonization: Indigeneity, Education & Society* 2(3): 20–34.

Chapter 6

ALEX LA GUMA AND THE SMELL OF FREEDOM

Giovanni Spissu

In his novel *A Walk in the Night* (1962), South African writer Alex La Guma describes the world of District Six during apartheid through a particular narrative style in which the urban spaces of the working-class district are brought to life through the movement of the novel's protagonists. La Guma never uses the third person narrative voice to comment on apartheid's political and social conditions. Instead, he lets it emerge through finely detailed descriptions of the streets, private homes, and public places as he follows its inhabitants wandering in the district's streets like "ghosts in the night." Its narrative style can be understood as a form of re-signifying or reterritorializing the city's urban spaces, in contrast to the process of deterritorialization put in effect by urban planning enacted during apartheid. "The city is not represented as a knowable totality by La Guma, on the level of, for example, the plan or map; instead, he allows its physical and symbolic structure to unfold contingently, phenomenologically" (Jackson 2003: 76). La Guma's novel denounces the politics of apartheid by minutely describing the state of degradation in which it forces its people to live. His characters' urban movements can be understood as a tactic for transforming and recreating its territory. Taking inspiration from this approach, I allowed the post-apartheid city of Cape Town to unfold through my own anthropological work.

In addition to my reading of *A Walk in the Night*, my project was inspired by the map of District Six located inside the District Six Museum in Cape Town. The map was created almost entirely by former residents of the district and is one of post-apartheid's most important art pieces. Annie Coombes noted how the act of writing on the map and the other museum installations served to establish a direct dialogue "without mediation between the ex-residents and its visitors. By inscribing the district map with their thoughts, hopes, memories, and dreams, District Six's ex-residents sought to give voice to the district's 'dehumanized' places" (2003: 143). The District Six map covers almost the entire area of the museum's first floor and is used by the guides and museum attendants to describe the district's history and transformations. Although it appears to be a regular representation of the district, not unlike the anonymous topographic representations made by apartheid's planners that were "manipulated in the interests of those in authority" (Coombes 2003: 143), it does so much more.

On the floor of the museum, the map began as an "empty" representation, however the District Sixers' "articulation of memory and walking provide for it a totally different meaning, one which resists the apartheid regime's judgment, while at the same time criticizing its acts of destruction" (McEachern 1998: 506). It thus takes on a special meaning when we walk on its surface and can explore the different meanings that its residents attribute to the surrounding urban places. On the surface of the installation and around it, there are sheets, molds, and objects imprinted with the ex-residents' writings. When they explore the map, visitors discover different meanings once attributed to places and spaces within the district. In this sense, the District Six map should be seen not only as a representation of a territory, but a territory itself that can be inhabited. Walking on the map can be understood as "making place," giving meaning and substance to the spaces represented therein. By creating the District Six map the ex-residents projected the stories of their inner lives onto its surface, and by moving ourselves over the map we bring those stories back to life.

Following the dissolution of long-entrenched infrastructures of power, including physical barriers, legal restrictions, and policing that categorized, isolated, and divided Cape Town's citizens during apartheid, new forms of social and urban movement have begun to emerge. These have allowed previously separated populations to engage with the city's territory through new and different forms of becoming and ways of experiencing the urban spaces. People actively make new ways of living in, relating to, and signifying the city through their movements, radically shaping and transforming the social, political, and moral landscape, including how they imagine, understand, relate to, and live within those spaces. Beginning with people who were connected to Long Street, one of Cape Town's oldest, best-known streets,

I delved into the processes of re-signifying post-apartheid Cape Town. Wandering through the city with people affected by forced displacement, passing through the places that evoked memories and imaginations, taking pictures of these places to discuss them afterwards, I started to explore the city alone as well. I started to reflect on how my memories and my personal life experiences were ways to enter into a dialogue with the city, as well as a means to do my research.

The Smell of Freedom

One afternoon in June 2011, I was walking on the waterfront of Sea Point di Cape Town with Marleane, a young woman of Xhosa origins living in Philippi, one of the city's poorest townships. I had met Marleane in her neighborhood while I was having a conversation with one of her neighbors. Later, I asked her to tell me her story and we set up a meeting downtown. We started from the central station and ended at Sea Point. Here we stopped to admire the magnificent view of the Bay of Cape Town. It was a windy day and the waves were coming all the way up to the road. At one point Marleane said, "I smell the smell of freedom." I asked her what she meant, and she explained that in Philippi she was often forced to spend her days confined to the small space of her home. Because there were gangs and drugs in her neighborhood, her aunt (her guardian) decided to restrict her social acquaintances as much as possible. She thus saw the chance to go downtown as an exceptional occasion to move freely and not experience her surroundings as a constant threat. Marleane was both virtually and actually smelling the scent of freedom, breathing in salty air and sensing wind, a feeling connecting her desire to escape (from her room in Philippi) with walking on the waterfront of Sea Point. Later, I thought about the link between my meeting with Marleane and the urban pathways of the District Six residents (particularly as they are described by Alex La Guma), and to my own experiences.

I had been in Cape Town ten years earlier for the tenth anniversary of South Africa's liberation. When I returned for this research, I realized that my arrival had awakened a desire to experience the city once more. I wanted to see specific places I had visited in the past, such as Cape Agulhas where the Indian Ocean meets the Atlantic. I wanted to walk along the promenade at Sea Point on a stormy day. Every place in the city I had been, music I had listened to, and aromas that I had smelled evoked a particular sensation. I walked through the city, letting myself be led by memories and thus returned to the places that had been significant during my previous visit. Just like for the characters in La Guma's novel, I considered the practice of walking as a way to re-inscribe myself in urban spaces. I wanted to experience certain feelings, such as meeting friends I had not seen for years. That is when The Snap came to my mind—a nightclub where I first met Kay one Wednesday evening in 2005.

Kay's Road

Kay, a woman originally from Western Cape who left her birthplace at the age of twenty-three, discovered in Cape Town a place full of work opportunities, and, more importantly, a place where she thought she could live regardless of racial categories and political affiliation. Of significance to Kay was her romantic relationship with Yuri, a young man of Russian origins, who had immigrated to Cape Town. With Yuri, Kay told me, "I had the feeling of being accepted by that social environment (whites) that had rejected me up until then." But after some time together, Kay and Yuri's relationship started to deteriorate and she often felt like an outsider. At one event in particular—a party that she went to on Christmas Day, 2010—she was convinced that she had to break up with Yuri and reflect on her sense of self. She told me that she gave up spending the holiday with her family in order to attend this party with Yuri. The guests were all white, mostly of Afrikaans origin. She was the only person there who was non-white. Despite being greeted politely, Kay felt unwelcome. Her impression was confirmed when a guest alluded to her being with her boyfriend for financial reasons. Kay explained how the "politeness prevented her from knowing how to respond." She decided to leave and return to Sea Point. The trip home gave her a chance to think about her whole experience in Cape Town and consider how she thought of herself and her social group. I asked Kay to take the same route with me to remember the thoughts and feelings of that day.

> At a certain point, I left the house without saying a word to anyone and started walking. There was no one on the streets. I walked past various villas in Camps Bay and headed for the beach. There was no one there and I started walking in the hope that a bus would pass, but it didn't because it was Christmas. I started walking towards Sea Point, even though it was a long way. From time to time I looked at my mobile to see if Yuri had called me because he'd realized I wasn't there, but he didn't call me. I walked for hours and hours and finally arrived in Sea Point, dead tired and soaked in sweat. It was now evening. When I got back, I saw a colored prostitute who was out working the streets every night

> on Main Road in Sea Point. I realized that every time I'd seen her I'd look on her as my inferior, someone who didn't know how to look after herself and who I didn't want anything to do with. That evening I felt I almost wanted to hug her. It was Christmas and she was alone, just like me. Once I'd passed her with Yuri and we'd made fun of her. Look at her, the catwalk model, etc. I felt like a queen with him and she was the lowest of the low; now I felt very close to her as a person. I got home, took off my boots and realized the phone was ringing. After more than three hours Yuri had realized I wasn't there. I switched off the phone and the light and looked at the view over Sea Point. It was beautiful. The moon lit the ocean and there were lots of stars. I put out the light and left the roller blinds up so I could keep watching the moon until I fell asleep.

Kay later explained to me that she had experienced her return to Sea Point as an imaginary return to her home in Worcester. She was leaving behind the world of the whites; the very world she had been pursuing so assiduously since she had arrived in Cape Town. That world now seemed foreign and dangerous to her. In "La Mémoire collective chez les musiciens" (1939), Maurice Halbwachs defines individual memory as the confluence of two collective memories. Taking the example of the audience at a concert, Halbwachs notes that it is possible to experience contemporaneously the state of belonging to a group of music lovers present at an event and other experiences evoked by the music itself. By allowing ourselves to be transported by the musical notes, we can in fact evoke situations such as belonging to a family or a love-affair that has ended or our place of birth, all while

Figure 6.1. Main Road in Sea Point, 2015. Photo by Giovanni Spissu, thoughts by Kay.

still forming part of a group enjoying the concert. In the same way, on her way home Kay had superimposed the images of Worcester, that of the party, and her panoramic view of the road on an imaginary return to her origins.

Ibraim and the Sounds of Security

Another telling encounter during my research was with Ibraim, a twenty-five-year-old man born in a small village in Somalia who had moved to Cape Town. Ibraim dreamt of going to Europe, but it proved too difficult to travel there so he decided to go to Cape Town, "the only place I knew of on this continent where homosexuals could live in freedom." He left Somalia, via makeshift transportation, on a journey that took three years. He told me how when he arrived in Cape Town he slept rough for several weeks and managed to survive by begging. Thanks to a chance encounter he was able to find work as a waiter. Once he received his first wage, he decided to go to Century City to buy a pair of shoes. I asked Ibraim to bring me to the Century City shop where he had made that purchase and tell me about that day. Century City is a megastore in Cape Town's northeast section and is a major destination for shopping and entertainment, drawing thousands of people a day from throughout the city and its surroundings.

Raphael Marks and Marco Bezzoli describe Century City as a post-modern symbol of the changes of Cape Town, "[c]ombining retail, leisure, offices, residential and ecological components under one proverbial roof, Century City represents the ultimate commodification of urban spaces and services" (2001: 27). It is a "cathedral of forgetting" where representations of reality can distract people from memories of the horrors of the past. Marks and Bezzoli point out that here history is erased, that there is "[n]o low-cost housing project here, no public schools or libraries"; there is only merchandise "that can be conveniently repacked, reprocessed and reimaged" (2001: 27).

For Ibraim, however, this place took on a special meaning in his life. It was here for the first time, after a long period of poverty, that he could buy a pair of shoes. When we started to walk around the shopping mall, listening to the sound of cash registers, he started to remember the sense of security he felt, hearing the same noise the day after he got a job. "Hearing this ticking sound made me think that there was something ordered which worked well, and of which even I was a part." Ibraim related his entrance into this society to the "ordered and reassuring" mechanical sound of the cash registers at

Century City. In this case the shopping mall had evoked in him the recollection of a difficult period in his life and how it had been resolved. As La Guma describes of those who conceived of the urban spaces of District Six as the spatial incarnation of apartheid's temporality, I discovered with Ibraim the territory of post-apartheid Cape Town as an urban chronotope in which the time/space configuration of post-apartheid's Cape Town intersected with the intimate time/space configuration of one of its residents.

On "After" Method

In the introduction to *A Thousand Plateaus* (1987), French philosophers Gilles Deleuze and Félix Guattari explored the relationship between literature and the "real world." The authors maintained that a literary work cannot be conceived as a mere representation of the world but as a generative source of it: "the book is not an image of the world. It forms a rhizome with the world, there is an aparallel evolution of the book and the world" (1987: 11). Writing, in this sense, can be compared to mapping, as neither are reproductions of the territory but are acts that generate it. This is similar to how La Guma describes a kind of performance unfolding contingently, phenomenologically.

The current interdisciplinary debate about the relationship between literature and cartographic practices examines the concept of mapping and the proliferation of the mapping metaphor. Scholars of literary criticism argue that this empties of meaning the concept of "mapping." For example, Keith D. Lilley remarks how the term mapping has progressively shifted away from its cartographic roots: "At a time when figurative and metaphorical 'mappings' are becoming particularly prominent . . . it is perhaps worth underlining the benefits of still thinking about maps and 'map-making' in a more conventional and literal sense" (2011: 30–31). According to Lilley, the overwhelming attention to spatiality in literature and the arts in general should lead to greater self-reflection, rather than an uncritical, inexact use of the term "mapping" (2011). Similarly, David Cooper (2012) criticizes the improper use of the term mapping by literature scholars. He remarks that literary critique of cartography should stop at the textual and authorial analysis of maps, rather than improperly borrowing the term "mapping" and thus risk emptying it of its hermeneutic power. For these authors, the relationship between literature and cartography is considered only within the critical and analytical dimension, seeing any kind of conceptual hybridization as a risky crossing of disciplinary borders. Yet, it is this pursuit of conceptual purity and the rejection of cross-pollination of terms among exponents of recartographization that obstructs new methodologies and illuminating concepts.

Sébastien Caquard points out that neither cartography nor literature alone are able to capture the essence of places: "Both are required to get a better sense of it" (2011: 26). He believes that these tensions, torments, and anxieties that define the debate within literary criticism of cartography can be tied to the hidden conviction that there is a presumed objectivity of the territory and a correct methodology to represent it. According to Caquard (2011), literary cartographic criticism is unable to fully grasp the intrinsic potential of the non-representational trend. This becomes possible precisely through the cross-pollination of different approaches.

My own cross-pollination of the District Six Museum's map with La Guma's novel enables me to envision a particular form of urban mapping through movement. I experience Cape Town as a mnemonic and imaginative place filled with the inner worlds of its residents. Urban movement is a prolific, generative act that continuously transforms the territory. The three urban pathways here discussed are a walk along the waterfront of Green Point with Marleane, taking the scenic road at Camps Bay with Kay, and the last one is the visit to the Century City shopping center with Ibraim. I conceive of a sensorial map of post-apartheid Cape Town through La Guma's literary work and through experiencing these places with people. La Guma's ability to observe the urban territory through a dual perspective that simultaneously describes the territory while transcending it inspires my work. I likewise take urban movement as a tactic to transcend the territory and give it new significance and meaning. Urban movement/urban mapping are acts that generate the territory, enabling a performance that conceives of Cape Town through a sensorial ethnographic experience made up of countless voices, smells, tastes, and feelings. In this sense, the process of reterritorialization is both the theory and the method of this project.

Giovanni Spissu was awarded a Ph.D. at the University of Manchester in Social Anthropology with Visual Media in June 2014, with a dissertation on the transformation of the relationship between the city's inhabitants and urban spaces in post-apartheid Cape Town. From 2012 to 2016, he worked as a teaching assistant at the University of Manchester. From 2016 to 2018, he taught anthropology and social research methodology and supervised five Master's in Social Sciences candidates at St. Augustine University in Mwanza (Tanzania). After completing his doctorate, he conducted research on unemployment in Sardinia.

References

Caquard, Sébastien, 2011. "Cartography I: Mapping Narrative Cartography." *Progress in Human Geography* 37(1): 135–44.

Coombes, Annie E. 2003. *History after Apartheid: Visual Culture and Public Memory in a Democratic South Africa*. Durham, NC: Duke University Press.

Cooper, David. 2012. "Critical Literary Cartography: Text, Maps and a Coleridge Notebook." In *Mapping Cultures: Place, Practice, Performance*, ed. Les Roberts, 29–52. Basingstoke: Palgrave Macmillan.

Deleuze, Gilles, and Félix Guattari. 1987. *A Thousand Plateaus*, trans. Brian Massumi. Minneapolis: University of Minnesota Press.

Halbwachs, Maurice. 1939. "La Mémoire collective chez les musiciens." *Revue Philosophique de la France et de l'Étranger* 127(3/4):136–65.

Jackson, Shannon M. 2003. "Being and Belonging: Space and Identity in Cape Town." *Anthropology and Humanism* 28(1): 61–84.

La Guma, Alex. 1962. *A Walk in the Night and Other Stories*. Ibadan, Nigeria: Mbari.

Lilley, Keith D. 2011. "Digital Cartographies and Medieval Geographies." In *Envisioning Landscapes, Making Worlds: Geography and the Humanities*, ed. Stephen Daniels, Dydia DeLyser, J. Nicholas Entrikin, and Douglas Richardson, 25–33. London: Routledge.

Marks, Rafael, and Marco Bezzoli. 2001. "Palaces of Desire: Century City and the Ambiguities of Development." *Urban Forum* 12(1): 27–48.

McEachern, Charmaine Ruth. 1998. "Mapping the Memories: Politics, Place and Identity in the District Six Museum, Cape Town." *Social Identities* 4 (3): 499–521.

Chapter 7

(RE)TURNING MANIFOLD-ISH ALONG WITH MONGOLIAN REINDEER HERD(ER)S

TRIAL(S) BY VAGARY

Nicolas Rasiulis

> . . . in well-being and adversity there is a divine trial.
>
> —Ilyas

Approximately two hundred reindeer pastoralists nomadically inhabit the alpine tundra and boreal forests on the Mongolian side near the border with the Russian Republic of Tuva. In the West and East Taigas of Mongolia, the Dukhas[1] move with their herds across the landscape. Performing fieldwork among Dukhas in 2014 and 2018, I witnessed how the world's inherent unpredictability makes both herding and anthropology fundamentally uncertain vocations. Continually improvising decisions and actions in concert with the vagaries of happenstance, I endeavor(ed) to sympathetically align my improvisation in step with the lessons of my Dukha mentors, as well as of the horses, reindeer, trees, and other living beings with whom they share their homeland.

Nestling, Tripping, (Re)assuring

I first arrived in Tsagaannuur, the northernmost village in Mongolia, in August 2014, eager to begin my MA fieldwork in the nearby taiga (coniferous forest). However, I had not yet established contact with any Dukhas, and, although there was a loose notion and agreement—with the Dukha community-run Tsaatan Community and Visitors Center (TCVC)—that I was to be an "independent volunteer" with the TCVC, I was not part of a project with any established infrastructure for integrating scholars to the community. Rather than try to execute a planned cookie-cutter methodology, I was open to becoming submerged in the unfamiliar: a whirligig of nomadic social constellations and experiences that involved improvising decisions and taking opportunities to doing whatever is going on, much of which is ongoing.

I arrived in the taiga in much the same fashion tourists do. Following fourteen hours of faring off-road-ish roads, a driver left me at a guesthouse. The owner said he would equip me with horses and guides for traveling in the taiga—services and logistics I wanted and that I had planned to coordinate with the TCVC. However, my attempts at phoning and emailing the TCVC were unsuccessful, and I suddenly felt a path opening beneath me. I was compelled and inspired to discard what had been planned and simply let things unfold. We agreed on dates for one venture to both the East and West Taigas, leaving time for two lengthier follow-up trips.

Planning (again) to evenly split my time in each region, my second trip to West Taiga turned out to be lengthier than anticipated. This was partially due to the departure of my translator (who took leave to return to the capital to attend a job interview). This made my party—now of one—take up less space and made me feel like less of an imposition. No longer depending on external wranglers and guides, I began dealing directly with my hosts and their families and friends for transportation. Pre-established travel dates carried less weight in such informal arrangements. Modifications to plans also happened as a result of my commitment to helping a friend build his winter cabin from start-ish to finish-ish. Furthermore, my hosts and I were quickly growing close(r), and did not want to separate for four years.

One night in their winter settlement, I asked two of my West Taiga friends if I was a *zhuulchin* жуулчин (Mngl.: tourist)—a name that is loaded with connotations of lacking integral local aptitudes and relationships (a name that some people in the taiga and many in Tsagaannuur called me). They answered that I had been a tourist, and still was a *gadaad* гадаад (Mngl.: alien), adding that I *manaĭ khün bolson* манай хүн боолсон (Mngl.: became *our* person). Becoming increasingly productive in the life projects of my hosts and mentors, feeling less and less alienated, I was garnering a new belonging. I was becoming their

Figure 7.1. Stockpile of firewood after a productive few hours of chopping. West Taiga, 2018. Photo by Nicolas Rasiulis.

alien. I was turning into *our* alien. I was becoming all this and more. I was and continue to become manifold-*ish*, branching out into new openings.

During my first trip to each taiga region, I reached out to my hosts by asking if I could help in any way. Once some trust was established, I also helped according to my own initiative and sensibilities. Fetching water, as well as harvesting, cutting, and chopping firewood were movements toward mutual acclimatization and trust—not only concerning livelihood practices but also and especially getting to know one another. In West Taiga, I lived in a pay-to-stay guest tipi. I sustained my household and contributed labor to neighboring households. This afforded me with increasing invitations for tea or meals with my neighbors. This way I developed an affinity with my hosts and, incidentally, with their family and friends. I began participating in more technically difficult and broadly demanding livelihood activities.

In East Taiga, I joined a household in which the husband was nursing a leg he had broken driving his motorcycle in the taiga a few months earlier. I tended to the household's water and firewood needs. Once I asked his wife if I could participate in the herding of reindeer through pasture. She had assessed me as capable and so granted me the request. I excelled at this practice and bonded with the people with whom I worked. Eventually I was afforded the responsibility of herding our camp's reindeer through pasture without any supervision, and with only the assistance of three tourists under my own supervision.

Acknowledged for accomplishments that are integral to this landscape and the Dukhas, on subsequent trips to each Taiga I was able to engage in activities requiring and involving increasing expertise and teamwork. Acknowledged also for my failures, I improvised a balancing act, reflecting on my successes and shortcomings. I realized that it was surely my failures that grounded me. My growing affinity with my mentors, and having them recognize me as a locally "response-able" (van Dooren and Rose 2016: 77) person was an ongoing process that afforded me with a continual interplay between ingratiating oneself, striving toward humility, and being humbled. It was an experience that in its entirety felt like an ongoing set of trials and tribulations.

In August 2018, as part of my ongoing PhD fieldwork, I found my way back among friends in West Taiga. When it was time to migrate from one camp to another, I suddenly felt like I had become a heavy burden. I added the weight of my body and baggage that the horses or reindeer would have to bear, while I would contribute just basic help packing and saddling animals, herding livestock along our migratory path, and so on. Even the stirrups on the saddle my hosts provided me with were tied and, yes, even adjusted, by my patient mentors. Ready for departure a friend, one year my junior, held my horse—a horse that one of my hosts told me was *zòrüüd* зөрүүд (Mngl.: stubborn)—by the lead rope and told me to climb on. I frequently mounted horses unassisted throughout my fieldwork in 2014 and 2018 and thought my friend's help unnecessary. I feared that this was an indication that my capabilities—which are always questioned, and rightly so—were being doubted. I said I could do it on my own. My friend simply reiterated that this horse was stubborn. He did not hand me the lead rope until I was sitting on the horse, feet "safely" in the stirrups. One kilometer or so into our migration, our caravan stopped atop a swampy knoll. My friend descended from his horse, and I followed suit. He refastened luggage on some of the reindeer while I stretched and played with a match—"your metaphor, my literality" (Taussig 1997: 4)—while watching, wishing I were more useful.

Once we got going again, I became increasingly aware of my frustration with my steed's reluctance to follow the pace set by my friend's horse, let alone obey my commands. This feeling grew and something along the lines of shame and, in hindsight, sadness, loneliness, as well as, surely the most difficult feeling for me to admit let alone share, fear, and, certainly the tenor that terrifies me the most, doubt, set in. I was scared, but not for my safety. I felt the creepy fingers of doubt merci-

Figure 7.2. Dukhas leading horses and reindeer down from Uvaalagiĭn mountain pass. West Taiga, 2018. Photo by Nicolas Rasiulis.

lessly tickle my spine. I feared letting down my mentors, the Dukha community, my family, friends, and colleagues. Yet I did not doubt my path or azimuth.

After leading our *bêtes de somme* (Fr.: beasts of sum/packsaddle), our beasts of burden, on foot along a sinuous path down a breathtakingly steep mountain pass, we convened in order to refasten the luggage. I held halters and provided a little heavy lifting. My friend, on the other hand, was busying himself with the tasks of redistributing weight and refastening knots, voicing frustration with my luggage. When it was time to leave, he took my steed by the lead rope. When I protested, he let go and resignedly walked away, seemingly incredulous at my stubbornness and indignation. Like steed, like rider? Once he was on his horse, his mother asked me if I was certain I could do the same. Answering "yes," I clasped the rope and reins in my left hand, put my left foot in the stirrup, and lifted up my right leg. Once my body was over the horse and I began searching for the other stirrup with my right foot, the animal's back was no longer beneath me. Instead, what I saw below as I fell toward the ground was the horse's hind legs flailing while it bolted. Rather than suffering the dangerous kick I was expecting, I merely fell (in)to the ground.

Vindicated, my friend left me there, followed by his mother. My amazement at not having hurt myself, and my instinctual avoidance of displaying weakness in moments of shame overshadowed the embarrassment I felt. I quickly stood and looked for the horse, which my friend's older brother had caught. Before giving me the reins, in a rare instance of a Dukha instructing me in the mechanics of a technique, my older friend told me to hold the reins tighter when mounting. He did not, however, give me the lead rope until I was "safely" atop the horse.

Within a matter of minutes, the stubborn horse and my stubborn self were traveling at a snail's pace, far behind (out of sight and out of earshot) of the caravan. Stuck several times on this unmoving horse, I took in the gorgeous cascades darkening in the twilight and thought: "This is a good 'ego check.'" I had to roll with the punches, "tumbling and fumbling" (Jensen 2007: 101), and reconsider a seemingly deep desire to (always) be a hero. Nonetheless, I could not bear falling from grace with my hosts and, by extension, others in their community—a community into which I was weaving myself. These insights about myself made me recognize that I was exceeding/receding/preceding/interceding/trailing a multiplicity of selves, that I am-in-becoming. Although I contributed what labor I could that night, it was not until the following day that I felt as though I was—and, hopefully, am—(re)deeming myself as broadly and locally capable and as integral to the caravan.

Early the second day of our migration, as I brought up the rear, I noticed that three reindeer had separated from the caravan. After grabbing hold of the lead rope that had snapped off from a reindeer being led by my friend's mother, I caught up to her and delivered the strays. A few kilometers later, I was again out of sight and earshot of my companions. Once I caught up to my mentors, they asked me if I had seen any other strays. I said "no," and dismounted my horse after seeing my friend do so. Together we walked into the forest to find the stray reindeer. Rather than following my friend, I went in my own direction, expanding our search area, and affording us the ability to outflank the reindeer.

As if prayers were answered, I spotted the stray. Without startling the yearling, I called to my friend—out of sight—that I had found the reindeer. I heard no answer. Without hesitating or really thinking, I reached into my pocket for an empty candy wrapper. I rubbed it while making a distinct noise with my mouth as I walked toward the stray, emulating sounds reindeer hear when they are seduced with salt, and then reached for its halter just as it was bolting away from my grasp. I returned it to my friend and his mother, both of whom were pleased with the find. My friend took my steed's lead rope to help me mount, paused, then doubled back and tied it to a tree, affording me control over the reins as I climbed up.

Figure 7.3. Photo taken while leading stray reindeer eating mushrooms back to the migratory caravan. West Taiga, 2018. Photo by Nicolas Rasiulis.

I mount(ed) my horse on my own from then on. Nonetheless, my friend's mother kept asking me if I was certain I was able to do this. How could I (re)assure her? As we descended into the valley where we would make an autumn camp, my steed and I once again found ourselves far behind our companions. Noticing my friends' water jug and ladle along the path, I saw another opportunity to (re)assure and, more importantly, contribute to my hosts' travels. I dismounted the horse and recovered the stray items, wondering how I would remount the steed while bearing the ladle and bulky jug. I squeezed them in-between my back and overcoat, then mounted. When I handed my friend's mother her canteen and ladle, she took in what I had done to retrieve it. My ability to mount a horse were not questioned again on that trip, yet might be again and anew someday—surely rightly so. My improvisation and the continual interplay of modifying and being modified, of adjusting, pleading, (re)assuring, striving toward humility, and being humbled are exhibited in a course of a few decisions made and played out during the winter of 2014.

(At)tending to the Home(land)

A few days after helping my friend and his family move into their new winter cabin that I had helped build in West Taiga, I found myself in a shop in Tsagaannuur getting supplies for my upcoming trip to East Taiga. There I would rejoin the household with whom I had cohabited in autumn. Or so I thought. A friend I had made in East Taiga happened to be running errands in the same shop at the same time. When she asked me if I would house- and dog-sit for her and her husband during their upcoming trip to the capital, I made a quick decision, and I accepted her proposition and the opportunities it afforded, even though it meant forsaking plans previously made with former hosts.

The householders expressly requested that, while dwelling in their cabin, I ensure the maintenance and stewardship of the hearth fire. Complying, I tended the spirit of the hearth and the *ongod* онгод (Mngl.: spirit guardian), who each watch over the sanctity of the home and the well-being of the household(ers). By feeding the fire wood, tea, and food, and by cleansing the air in the home and around the guardian's cloth-bound shrine with holy juniper smoke, I maintained the householders' relationship with the spirits. In turn, the spirits' benevolence is not assured but rather voluntarily shared, so long as the householders and their kin reciprocally and appropriately share of their own volition.

Based on Benedikte Kristensen's (2004) description of Dukha shamanic knowledge and perception of the landscape, I grasped that my friends' domestic spirits were enmeshed with(in) the broad(er) spiritual ecology of the taiga. In their place, I sincerely and intuitively worshipped *Oron Khangaĭ* Орон Нангай (i.e., the whole taiga as subjective actor), *Tėngėr* Тенгер (Mngl.: Sky), and Rechindlumbe Mountain *ėzėn* эзэн (Mngl.: master) spirit with prayers, libations, and an earnest effort to steadfastly attend to the spiritual forces in the taiga. I was grateful and, arguably, respectful. I strove to be non-obstructive and symbiotic, nurturing through an adjustment of my lifeline(s) in "sympathetic correspondence" (Ingold 2015) with the local places. I conspired with/in the meshwork in which it/we swim—with varying degrees, intensities, and frequencies of submersion—"as octopuses and anemones" in the sea, "floating in [our] milieu[x] and in [our] sentiments" (Mauss 1923–24: 103, my translation).[2] I wondered if these practices were just symbolic, until I (twice) saw a seemingly yet, in a visceral manner, uncertainly human form, later discerned to be a spirit by three Dukhas to whom I told my tale.

The following day I visited Öwah, an elder. When I described my sightings and encounter, he told me that the spirit was evil. I shuddered—seemingly *par-delà* (Fr.: passing the threshold between somewhere and beyond)—struck by the more-than-visceral realization of the grave, immense reality of it all.[3] Öwah asked me if I had dreamed of the spirit. "No." "Good." I told him what I dreamed during my first night in the cabin. Dreaming, I opened the cabin door and watched three white-headed eagles fly above me, heading north to south. I then found myself on the crest of a snowy mountain peak and saw my sleeping bag lying on the ledge atop a crag in a cliff. I slipped into the bedding and relaxed, rejoicing in the place, before descending into the grassy valley folding and growing in the pits of the geological sinuses beneath the mountain. There I watched a herd of horses, a few of whom were blue or green and surreally luminescent, canter around me.

Öwah was (re)assured and even pleased with my dream, saying that the eagles flying from the north were protecting me, keeping danger away. He added that the shiny horses I encountered were likely of Rechindlumbe Mountain master spirit's herd, and that exposing me to its herd was an act of good grace on the part of the mighty, powerful spirit. Tides were turning, astral bodies twirling, and time crystallizing into a kairos. Issues (e.g., religiosity, spirituality, etc.) that had heretofore been rarely and limitedly addressed with other Dukha mentors were now being explored extensively in dialogue with Öwah.

I asked Öwah whether trees were *sėdėgėltėĭ* сэдэгэлтэй (Mngl.: spirited). He told me that *böö mod* бөө мод (Mngl.: shaman tree[s]) are. He then invited me to visit such a tree at an indeterminate future date with him, adding that he would tell me once it was time. The following day, a Mongolian crew filming a cooking show for television arrived. They invited me to appear on camera the next morning and to prepare a "Canadian" meal on their show. When morning came, Öwah came by and asked if I still intended to visit a tree with him. If so, the time was *now*. In that moment I decided to pass on the chance to be on television—a seemingly glamorous and enticing opportunity—and instead followed the elder along a path, as it turns out, heading toward and *par-delà* my existential stead.

Öwah and I walked northwest for over an hour until we passed into a grove in the northeastern foothills of Rechindlumbe Mountain. Here, hands clasped at our foreheads, we worshipped Rechindlumbe master spirit and two shaman trees, each bearing most of their branches in one gnarly bunch mid-trunk. When I tenderly and intimately touched one in particular with my left hand, warm energy gushed from the tree along my arm into my thorax. I wanted to make an offering for the tree and was prepared with juniper and white cloth. Öwah helped me burn the juniper on a piece of wood balanced on a narrow stump and tie cloth strips to branches of nearby pine saplings. We breathed in and out over the fabric as we knotted them, tying our respective prayers into the land. Afterward, as I followed Öwah home, he turned toward me and asked whether I understood what I had become. I did not, although I suddenly felt that it was something significant. He said *Kanad zaĭran* Канад зайран (Mngl.: Canada male shaman) before turning away and continuing down the path.

Figure 7.4. Self-portrait with shaman tree. East Taiga, 2014. Photo by Nicolas Rasiulis.

A few hundred meters further, we resumed our weird and strangely comfortable discussion. Öwah said that the tree and I were now knotted together. He added that if I am to pursue this path—which in hindsight I now perceive more clearly—earnestly, I must "learn," largely from my "ancestors," how to appropriately, effectively, and (potentially) even "with great might," act as a shaman in my own way(s), manner(s), words, and deeds. He would later add that no one else, shaman or otherwise, could teach me this. Perhaps the strand of wisdom plucked by Öwah's counsel that resounded most with(in) me was to *not boast* about any of this. The chance of these circumstances led me to set out quickly albeit patiently to meet my ancestors, to tend to my ties with a special tree, and to pray through the knotted ties and thus bring it all into being.

(Re)turning, (Re)tying

Years passed—as if both slowly dripping and quickly zooming—in-between my 2014 and 2018 fieldwork trips. In that time, I pursued a shaman-ish practice as a (co)creative, broadly inspired personal application of the techniques, sensibilities, ontological bearings and tenors, and attentiveness(es) to which I had attuned myself through dialogue and shared experiences with Dukha shamans and laypeople. Kristensen's (2004: 2015) work describes seeing and being whelmed by the reality of a particular(ly) grave spirit. In these narrative ethnographies, Kristensen (2004, 2015) conveys how she became identified as a shaman among the Dukhas, and how she somewhat reluctantly accepted the frustrating and puzzling responsibility (Kristensen 2015: 30).

I might be a particularly unsettling/disrupting vessel of shaman-ish-m for Dukhas, especially if they perceive me—as many very well likely do—to be a "like shaman[s]" (*böö shig* бөө шиг) or "half-shaman[s]" (*khagas böö* хагас бөө) (Pedersen 2011: 7), an "indigenous notion" in northernmost Mongolia (Pedersen 2011: 222) that harnesses the modifier *shig* шиг (Mngl.: like, as if, almost tautologically convergent with). In some respects, *shig* approximates the English suffix -ish, hence both my emphasis on this suffix and my invention of the term "shaman-ish-m." Pedersen makes reference to the notion of *böö shig* in English with the translation "not quite shaman[s]" (Pedersen 2011: 222). Characteristic of the post-socialism experienced by the Darhat people in Ulaan Uul during the 1990s–2000s (a time when people said there were no longer any "genuine shamans") not-quite-shamans were—and, one might argue, still are—problematic insofar as they "attracted the restless souls of dead shamans and living animals without being able to control them" (Pedersen 2011: 222). Kristensen demonstrates how Dukhas experience the potential for, and material effects of, grave danger in the lack of spiritual control plaguing people who struggle to (consistently) answer (a) shamanic call(s) (2015: 135–36).

Symptomatic of this lack of (complete) spiritual control, not-quite-shamans may be frequently "subject to *agsan*" (Pedersen 2011: 222), a type of altered state of consciousness, named after "fiery tempered horses . . . particularly difficult to break in," characterized by a loss of self-control typically coupled with a "drunken rage" and "downright 'crazy' (*galzuu*) behavior" (Pedersen 2011: 1, 7). We might say random behavior, intentionally striking the chord of the adjective's etymological rootedness in the Old French word *randir*, meaning to run or gallop.

The situation is nonetheless not as bleak as it might seem. Pedersen's closing statement in *Not Quite Shamans*: "and they alone, are imbued with a hyper-shamanic capacity to mold, extend, and apportion emergent social, political, and economic realities into new impossible forms, making it possible to ride on the edge of change" (Pedersen 2011: 224) links shamanism to the chaos of the transition to post-socialism in Mongolia (Pedersen 2011: 223).

I returned to the taiga in 2018 with growing awareness of my approach to and practice of shaman-ish-m—which I then still referred to as "shamanism," albeit (somewhat) cringing(ly). I had loosely planned dates for a return to East and West Taigas, intending to spend more time in East Taiga in order to make up for my past challenges with time allocation. I also intended to visit the oh-so-very-dear tree, which I knew to be walking distance from an area in which many households camp during autumn. Aside from my devotional practices, shaman-ish-m did not surface much in my daily interactions and activities. I was focused on reaffirming and tending to bonds I had forged with people here in 2014, knotting together new ties, and grasping at how Dukhas were adjusting to the newly instantiated Tengis-Shishged National Park's regulatory framework (the primary focus of my PhD research). It would seem that every day I (re)considered my travel dates. Somehow, the decisions and other adjustments I improvised somehow made me stick to my anticipated dates.

Two days before the first of my two 2018 departures from East Taiga, a neighbor had a serious medical emergency. After several hours of collaborative efforts trying to stabilize the man's cardiac condition (including contact with a doctor on my satellite phone), he died. Not knowing what to do, and profoundly affected by the death, my instinct was to give the grieving family space, room to breathe. I spoke with an Estonian anthropologist who was visiting Dukha friends while on vacation. I told her what had happened and about my reticence. After half an hour or so, with her counsel and with gifts in hand, I visited the family. My time with them in their home over the following forty-odd hours deeply touched my heart. Everyone in the camp joined together and caringly supported the grieving family—with visits, labor, provisions, and more.

The good humor, kindness, emotional resilience, as well as cooperative disposition and work of everyone passing through that home—not the least of which the members of the family themselves—impressed upon me a profound feeling of "*communitas*" (Turner [1969] 1977). It helped with my own trauma from having witnessed his death. Sitting beside the widow in her home and playing cards, finding solace in moments of shared playfulness, joy, and care, with her sister, children, and their friends, I realized how much my relations with Dukhas—and the people of my community of care anywhere and everywhere they happen to be—necessarily precede and take precedence over my research. Yet I also note how my presence and research might affect Dukhas, might affect people and communities. I left here feeling deeply knotted into their fabric.

One month later, I rejoined this community, now inhabiting an autumn camp a few hours ride north of the shaman tree. While traveling to the camp with a friend, Öwah's son-in-law, I spotted the tree along with a nearby young pine to which I had tied white cloths and prayers. I slowed to a stop while my friend continued onward. The atmosphere around the tree was different. The electricity of this place was palpable—we might say holy—and within it my attentiveness amplified, my animic vigor and might invigorated. The day was growing late and so I had to leave the place without properly worshipping. Catching up with my friend, I realized how close the tree is to a highway, so to speak. Having worshipped it during the winter, I initially did not notice this route. However holy the place might be, it no longer felt (as) private. As if it owed me that.

Further along the way, my friend's wife's cousin joined us after preparing hay for the horses for the winter. Riding into camp, I exclaimed at the number of tents, which suggested that there were a lot of tourists present. My companions agreed. The cousin added that I am "not a tourist," marking the second of three times during this trip a Dukha said this to me, unprompted. On two of those occasions, I was instead called a *Tsaatan* Цаатан (Mngl.: reindeer person), and on the last a *taĭgiĭn khün* тайгийн хүн (Mngl.: person of the taiga).

Nonetheless, my hosts and I remain distinctly different. Among the most important differences are our tempos. Whereas Dukha mentors inhabit the taiga in the "*très longue durée*" (Bergson [1907] 2002:

Figure 7.5. Photo taken while leading pack reindeer. East Taiga, 2018. Photo by Nicolas Rasiulis.

212), the "very long duration," my presence in the taiga and in my mentors' lives is ephemeral. I come in and out with a slowness relative to most foreigners, yet with great quickness, almost haste relative to the time signature of movements of the taiga's rich community of life. I come, stay longer, and involve myself more than most visitors, but eventually leave. I return, and will continue returning as long as I can. But I always leave. I am a foreign anthropologis(h)t nestling and (at) tending a unique place as I come and go again.

A few days later, most households migrated from the higher altitude location southward to various smaller autumn camps, if not all the way to Tsagannuur. After helping Öwah's son-in-law fasten his household items onto reindeer, involving myself more than ever before in this task, he, his parents-in-law, and I set off. Bearing more responsibility than ever before during a migration, I rode with a *somme* (Fr.: packsaddle, sum, doze) holding precious, fragile items belonging to—and entrusted to me by—mentors. I also led three pack reindeer and felt that I was providing more than basic labor. As Öwah chose to travel the more direct, less muddy paths we did not pass the shaman tree.

It was not until my last full day in the taiga in 2018 that I visited and properly worshipped the tree. I ventured on foot two kilometers or so through forest and swamp to find it. As I prepared my worship, various friends of mine appeared along the path in three different movements, so to speak. When they asked me what I was doing way out here, I—not untruthfully—brandished my camera. Once "alone," I burned juniper in a sacrificial piece of wood (broken off from a nearby stump much like Öwah had done four years before) and worshipped Oron Khangaĭ, Rechindlumbe Mountain master spirit, this place, and the tree. I then ritually knotted and breathed my prayers into white cloths that I tied around branches of two newly joined pines nearby.

Ultimately, I knotted new white cloths over the ones I had tied in 2014, rejoining and reaffirming my committed devotion to those original prayers for (the) well-being (of a few of my dearly beloved, of the taiga, and of the Dukha community) with not quite the same branches. Tremoring in the breath of Oron Khangaĭ, I conspired with the wind(s) and turbulence(s) of our planet twirling through space, throughout the swirling whorl of the whole, strange(ly familiar) world (re)turning on(ward).

Acknowledgments

This research was supported by the Social Sciences and Humanities Research Council of Canada. I extend my gratitude to the Dukha people, and to all other inhabitants of their homeland.

I extend warm and special thanks to Julie Laplante for her unwavering support, inspiration, and faith ever since that fateful day in 2012 when she first welcomed me into her office and life.

Nicolas Rasiulis is a Canadian-Lithuanian anthropologist. As both an undergraduate at the University of Ottawa and a canoe expedition guide, Nicolas researched transformative effects of open-air nomadism on relations with oneself, others, and nature. During his master's at the University of Ottawa, Nicolas researched ways Mongolian Dukha reindeer pastoralists realize livelihoods through largely collaborative and playful acrobatic improvisation. Currently a PhD candidate in the Department of Anthropology at McGill University, Nicolas's work now attends to Dukha adjustments to nature conservation regulations within the Tengis-Shishged National Park, and vice versa, as well as to avenues toward collaborative conflict resolution.

Notes

Epigraph: Quotation rendered by Stefania Pandolfo, "Dreaming at the Threshold of the Law: An Islamic Liturgy of Healing." Lecture, part of the Islamic Encounters Lecture Series, McGill University, School of Religious Studies/Institute of Islamic Studies/Department of Anthropology, Montréal, 14 March 2019.

1. For more information on Mongolian reindeer pastoralists and their various appellations, see chapter 1 in Rasiulis, Nicolas. 2016. "Freestyle Bearing: Work, Play, and Synergy in the Practice of Everyday Life among Mongolian Reindeer Pastoralists." MA thesis. Ottawa: University of Ottawa.
2. I am grateful to Tim Ingold's *The Life of Lines* (2015) for guiding my attention to this passage from Marcel Mauss's classic essay.
3. A lyric from the song "Demon Host," by Timber Timbre: "I know there's no such thing as ghosts / but I have seen the demon host / Ooh, oooh."

References

Bergson, Henri. [1907] 2002. *L'évolution créatrice*. Digital version, Paquet, Gemma (prod.), part of "Les classiques des sciences sociales" series. Chicoutimi: CEGEP de Chicoutimi in partnership with Université du Québec à Chicoutimi. Originally published in Paris: Les Presses universitaires de France.

Ingold, Tim. 2015. *The Life of Lines*. New York: Routledge.

Jensen, Aage. 2007. "The Value and Necessity of Tumbling and Fumbling." In *Nature First: Outdoor Life the Friluftsliv Way*, ed. Bob Henderson and Nils Vikander, 168–78. Toronto: Natural Heritage Books.

Kristensen, Benedikte. 2004. "The Living Landscape of Knowledge: An Analysis of Shamanism among the Duha Tuvinians of Northern Mongolia." *Specialeafhandling til Kandidateksamen* 317: NP. Institut for Antropologi, Københavns Universitet. Retrieved 10 December 2013 from http://www.anthrobase.com/Txt/K/Kristensen_B_02.htm.

———. 2015. "Returning to the Forest: Shamanism, Landscape and History among the Duha of Northern Mongolia." Ph.D. dissertation. Copenhagen: University of Copenhagen.

Mauss, Marcel. 1923–24. " Essai sur le don: Forme et raison de l'échange dans les sociétés archaïques." *l'Année Sociologique*, second series. Retrieved 6 January 2020 from http://dx.doi.org/doi:10.1522/cla.mam.ess3.

Pederson, Morten Axel. 2011. *Not Quite Shamans: Spirit Worlds and Political Lives in Northern Mongolia*. Ithaca, NY: Cornell University Press.

Taussig, Michael. 1997. *The Magic of the State*. New York: Routledge.

Turner, Victor. [1969] 1977. *The Ritual Process: Structure and Anti-Structure*. Cornell Paperbacks edition. Ithaca, NY: Cornell University Press.

van Dooren, T. and D. B. Rose. 2016. "Lively Ethography: Storying Animist Worlds." *Environmental Humanities* 8(1): 77–94.

Chapter 8

ENSKILMENT INTO THE ENVIRONMENT

THE *YIJIN JING* WORLDS OF *JIN* AND *QI*

Elisabeth Hsu and Chee Han Lim

The *Yijin jing* 易筋經 (the Canon for supple sinews; also known as the Sinews transformation classic)[1] is well-known as a martial training method found in a variety of styles practiced by Chinese communities. This chapter discusses two of them, one learned as *qigong* 氣功 meditation, the other as a basic training method for the martial arts. Elisabeth Hsu learned a version of the postures outlined in the *Yijin jing* from a *qigong* healer in the backstreets of Kunming city, the capital of Yunnan province, in the People's Republic of China (PRC) during her doctoral fieldwork in 1988–89. Chee Han Lim learned another version in Singapore from Lau, an ex-triad member and practitioner of various Eastern martial arts. Both were taught what their teachers called a *gongfa* 功法 (skills-enhancing method). In March 2010, Hsu showed Lim her version and asked to be taught his. This chapter is thus based on auto-ethnographic fieldwork in a college squash hall at Oxford, undertaken by both co-authors daily for one to two hours between 1 and 31 March 2010, after each had received training in this martial method independently. Our comparative lens allows us to reflect both on the embodied routines we learned and on the materiality of the environments into which we as practitioners enskilled ourselves. As we will see, the martial routines we learned strengthened a common bodily disposition, namely that of aiming to expand one's self into the universe. Even though this fieldwork experience was primarily bodily, it predisposed us to recognize in it a salient cultural trope when encountering it elsewhere in our research, for instance, in ancient texts, contemporary medical practice or religious rituals.

We discuss what Bruno Latour (2000) would call the "thing," namely, the techniques that practitioners learn in the course of enacting the *Yijin jing* postures (*shi* 勢). This fieldwork method of "participant experience" combines participant observation with the process of going through a sufficiently thorough learning experience to gain competence in the practice itself (Hsu 1999, 2007). We take a distinctively phenomenological stance (e.g., Csordas 1994; Merleau-Ponty [1945] 1962) and attend to the intentionalities that trigger practice as well as to the sensory dimensions of the self, as experienced in the course of it. Rather than engaging in a de-contextualized comparison of the different forms of *Yijin jing* practice, we aim to discuss the peculiarities of the environments with which we as practitioners became engaged. Tim Ingold (2000) calls this process by which an organism attunes itself to its perceived environment "enskilment." It is a learning process that involves the learners' active engagement with their surroundings and the negotiation of the tangible resistances the environment poses. As Ingold (2000) notes, it is a relational process through which living organisms become involved with their social and material environment in order to "dwell" in it.

The Text of the *Yijin Jing*

The *Yijin jing* of 1624 is an epitome of late Ming syncretism, according to Meir Shahar (2008: 149–65). It is attributed to a certain Zongheng 宗衡 from Mount Tiantai in Zhejiang province, whose sobriquet was Zining Daoren 紫凝道人 (Man of the Way from the Purple Mist) that in the Ming could refer to either a Daoist or Buddhist affiliation. Apart from the opening and closing movements (discussed in Hsu 2018), the movements it presents are generally considered to be derived from Daoist *daoyin* 導引 gymnastics.

The *Yijin jing* became integral to martial arts exercises, and presumably originated from them. As Shahar notes, it was "the first to explicitly associate military, therapeutic, and religious goals in one training routine" (2008: 165). Its two prefaces link it to the martial tradition, namely Damo (Boddhidharma).[2] One is signed by the Tang dynasty general Li Jing 李靖, the other by the Song dynasty general Niu Gao 牛皋. However, scholars of the time already considered both forgeries, based on anachronisms in the text. Zining Daoren clearly did not have their scholarship, rank, and status.

Perhaps *Yijin jing* practices survived mostly in popular contexts, as it is precisely from an adept of a living tradition in a popular neighborhood that Hsu learned it (1999: 21–87). *Qigong* master Qiu (pseudonym) traced this style to Mount Wudang. For him, it combined therapeutic, martial, and religious aspects.[3] The version Lim learned, however, insists on its predominantly martial roots and relevance (in accordance with the Damo legend) that comes with certain health-enhancing effects but acknowledges no religious roots.

The *Yijin jing* that Lim learned in Singapore in the context of martial arts training consisted of eight postures and a closing movement; the version Hsu learned in the context of practicing *qigong* consisted of ten movements.[4] Despite these subtle variations, Qiu's and Lim's forms of the *Yijin jing* have family resemblances with one of the four styles of *jianshen qigong* 健身氣功 (health-building *qigong*)[5] advocated by the PRC's Chinese Health Qigong Association (CHQA)[6] and known to the authors through a video in Mandarin Chinese (CHQA 2003).[7] The video presents a performance of the *Yijin jing* version edited by Wang Zuyuan 王祖源, which was published in the *Neigong tushuo* 內功圖說 (Illustrated exposition of internal techniques) of 1882 and reprinted in 1956.

The *Yijin Jing* and the Notion of Enskilment

Body techniques differ, Marcel Mauss ([1935] 1973) tells us, depending on culture; even if bodily movements like swinging one's hips when walking, may appear to be natural, they, in fact, involve cultural learning. Treating *qigong* and the martial arts as body techniques allows the researcher to identify symbolic aspects and the socio-political context in which these arts evolved but reveals little about the experiential dimensions of practicing *Yijin jing* movements, and any insights that may ensue from these experiences about the *Yijin jing*'s purpose, structure or history.

We wish to widen our investigation away from a focus on the body enveloped-by-skin, as the study of body techniques tends to do, to the body-in-interaction-with-its-environment in order to identify the experiences and realities that these movements generate. As noted above, Ingold's notion of enskilment proves useful. While Mauss stresses that body techniques are culturally acquired through social transmission, Ingold (2000: 34–39) provides a critique of this notion of "enculturation" by emphasizing the practical involvement of an organism with its environment. He notes that, rather than the acquisition of rules, learning a craft is "inseparable from doing it" (Ingold 2000: 416). This process, which he calls "enskilment," requires an "education of one's attention" (2000: 22; Gibson 1979: 254), which typically happens through negotiating the materiality of the physical environment (Ingold 2000: 356).

Enskilment attends thus in a Latourian sense to the "thing," even if the "thing" may be *qi*, which for a natural scientist is not "thing-y" (in other words, not a "material" entity), but which for *qigong* practitioners is insofar "thing-y" as it is a tangible, resistance-offering, impersonal aspect of the environment that is experienced, at times, even as possessing sentience. While body techniques are often discussed as entities detached from their environment, an enskilled movement is always directed toward it in acts of constituting it. The practitioner interacts creatively with the physicality of the environment in the course of becoming enskilled into it. The process of enskilment involves both the shaping of the body and the transformation of the environment.

Learning the two different *Yijin jing* routines had us experience the emergence of a common substance constitutive of both the body and its environment. Depending on whether the environment was constituted of *qi* 氣, as in the case of the *Yijin jing* being practiced as a form of *qigong*, or a human opponent brimming with *jin4* 勁 as in the martial arts, will have an effect on how the movement is enacted and how the body is felt. Where *qi* has become, with its entry in the Oxford English Dictionary, a vaguely understood English term with a semantic stretch from wind to breath to energy, *jin4* is a sort of power that has so far scarcely been discussed in academic writing. It is a tangible entity central to the practice of the Chinese martial arts (Chen [1943] 2014) that simultaneously exudes qualities of power, strength, balance, and sensitivity.

In the following, we account for variations in the movements and postures of Qiu's and Lim's *Yijin jing* routines with particular attention to their techniques of enskilling themselves into their respective environments. We first discuss the version Lim had learned in Singapore in 1998–99 and taught Hsu in March 2010 at Oxford, and then reflect on the version Qiu taught Hsu in 1988–89 in Kunming, PRC.

The *Jin* of Lim's *Yijin Jing*

Lim learned his version of the *Yijin jing* as part of his training in Hong Fist, a southern form of Chinese martial arts that involves stances with bent legs and powerful hand techniques. In the early days of Singapore's independence,[8] the martial arts were associated with triad activities, as they were during the late eighteenth and nineteenth centuries in China (Henning 1999: 327). It would appear that this is no longer the case in Singapore, where currently particularly the middle classes indulge in them. With Singapore's increasing urbanization, martial arts training moved into residential areas like community badminton courts or training schools located in multistory buildings. When Lim learned his *Yijin jing* postures from June 1998 to December 1999, he did so in Lau's living room, which contained several pieces of training equipment that offered various forms of resistance, such as punching bags and a wooden mannequin.

The versions of the *Yijin jing* practiced by Lim and Qiu both began with an opening gesture that involved placing the palms together. Qiu would then stand still for a moment and silently gather himself in concentration. As the fingers were pointing upwards, this posture looked to Hsu like a gesture of prayer,[9] and her inclination was to hold the palms gently together. However, Lim taught Hsu to press her palms together with all her might, and to then recite the following verse (*koujue* 口訣):

> 下顎回收找喉頭，喉頭找玉枕，玉枕找百會，百會上頂。
> *Xia e hui shou zhao hou tou, hou tou zhao yu zhen, yu zhen zhao bai hui, bai hui shang ding.*
> The chin is retracted and reaches for the larynx, the larynx reaches for the *yuzhen* 玉枕 acupoint [at the back of the head], the *yuzhen* reaches for the *baihui* 百會 acupoint [at the top of the head], and the *baihui* props upwards.
>
> 垂肩落肘，含胸拔背，小腹收起，大腹鼓起，會陰向前，命門向後，尾閭向下。
> *Chui jian luo zhou, han xiong ba bei, xiao fu shou qi, da fu gu qi, hui yin xiang qian, ming men xiang hou, wei lü xiang xia.*
> Drop the shoulders and the elbows, relax the chest and expand the back, contract the lower abdomen, expand the upper abdomen, push the *huiyin* 會陰 acupoint [between the anus and the genitals] forward, push the *mingmen* 命門 acupoint [between the kidneys] backward, and push the coccyx down to the ground.
>
> 膝蓋微曲，脚趾內扣。
> *Xi gai wei qu, jiao zhi nei kou*
> Bend the knees slightly, point the toes inwards, and lock them into position.

This mnemonic described the opening movements of the first posture. Lim explained that this verse revealed that the surroundings were experienced as issuing *jin4* (勁) power-energy, perpetually and indiscriminately. More recently, in the course of co-authoring this piece, Lim specified that this mnemonic expresses a specific enskilment strategy that requires the practitioner "to expand" (*peng* 膨) themselves.

This strategy of *peng* is seen most evidently in the choice of the word *ding* (to prop up) in the phrase *baihui shang ding* 百會上頂, which requires one to use the tip of the head to lift the weight of heaven bearing down as an adversary. By contrast, *ling* 領 (to be lead) in the phrase *baihui shang ling* 百會上領, a term used in several *qigong* styles (but not Qiu's) elicits sensations of dangling on a rope that comes down from heaven. Lim underlined that if one were to merely dangle from heaven, the spine, rather than being taut and upright, would be relaxed as the practitioner would surrender to their weight and dissolve into the environment. The word *ding*, to prop up, made very clear that the opening movement was one of expanding and puffing up one's self in an act of stubborn resistance to an adverse environment.

To learn how not to surrender to an environment of *jin4*, Lim underwent a grueling training regimen under Lau's tutelage. Lau not only required Lim to manifest the mnemonic in his postures, but also to administer movements individually against various adversaries that were cast at him, from having to punch the wall, stamp on the floor, to being struck by Lau's kicks, punches, and even a steel-jacketed wooden pole, while remaining immovable and without temper. This made Lim's body taut and constantly attentive, ever ready to *peng*-expand from a state of tranquility to retaliate the *jin4* issued from the environment with the *jin4* dynamism from within his body.

In a strict but not abusive way, Lim would strike Hsu, without informing her, in parts of her body tasked with *peng*-expansion, and accordingly, Hsu experienced the training environment as one of strikes from different sides. To cultivate her *ding*-propping in the opening posture, Lim slammed his palm vertically onto her shoulders to make sure that a pathway between them to the heels of her feet had been cleared. Hsu should extend her spine, open her hips, and stretch her hamstring. If performed well, Lim would be able to feel the ground's *jin4* being rechanneled, through Hsu's taut structure, back into his palm, and Hsu would be able to feel the *jin4* from Lim's palm administered through her heels into the ground, rather than being hit off balance.

Lim understood the *Yijin jing* to build up one's martial skills by training one's *jin4* and *jin1* 筋 (sinews), where the former is administered by the latter. Where the spine is portrayed as "natural" in Western anatomy books when curved in the S-shape, Lim told Hsu to stand by a vertical wall, stretch her *jin1* to straighten the spine, also in its lower parts, such that she could feel each vertebra one by one pressing against the cold cement wall. Simultaneously, she should contract her lower abdomen, the *dantian*, as prescribed in the mnemonic, point her *huiyin* forward as if it was towed on a hook, let her *mingmen* 命門 expand from within and point backwards, and drive the coccyx vertically down into the ground. The taut *jin1* sinews withstood the *jin4* power of the wall, the ground, Lim's hitting, as they themselves exerted *jin4* power. Control over one's *jin1* are the very "thing" that *peng*-expands in the administration of *jin4*. Without the internal strength to maintain a state of *peng*-expansion, Hsu would sometimes start to bob up and down and even spontaneously shake and tremble in pain, while perspiring profusely. She evidently was struggling to respond with the *jin4* of her *jin1* against the environment's *jin4*.

Jin1-sinews and *jin4*-power have different tones but are homophones that express a martial principle. Lau taught Lim another homophonous martial training principle: enskilment into *jin4* required *fang song* 放鬆. Although *fang song* generally means "to relax," Lau insisted on its literal translation as "to let go and be a pine tree." Although this translation is grammatically incorrect, it plays on a homophony that carries practical implications. To *fang song* while practicing the *Yijin jing* requires one to relax while remaining unmoved. As Lim had learned from his teacher, "a tree stands alone doing nothing and thinking nothing while it is battered by wind and water, but the moment you punch it, your broken bones will teach you that remaining unmoved is the tree's way of striking back." The pine tree thus not only stands for the pinnacle of martial excellence, but also represents how to respond to powerful strikes by assuming a calm and ever-present *jin4* within a state of tranquility.

Enskilling into *Jin* with Lau's *Yijin Jing*

The manipulation of *jin1* characterizes all the postures and movements found in Lau's *Yijin jing*, and Lim jokingly claimed that his version was the more authentic one because it explicitly seeks to transform the sinews. In the movements of the first posture, the *jin1* that are being manipulated are found in the shoulders and shoulder blades. From the "prayer gesture" discussed in the previous section, Lim then rotated his palms so that his fingers pointed forward. He then pushed his palms forward, pressed tightly against each other, straight in front of his chest until his elbows could almost touch each other. He thereupon turned his palms upward, such that they faced the ceiling, stretched out the arms to both sides and lifted them until the hands were high above the head, with palms facing each other. Finally, he pressed the palms against each other, slowly lowering them until he reassumed the initial prayer gesture. All these techniques, as Lim explained, exerted tremendous demands on the *jin1* that connect the shoulders to the upper arms. The posture ended in a movement that consisted of opening and closing the space between the palms three times. This last movement extends and contracts *jin1* between the two shoulder blades, expanding the cavity between them and thus administering *jin4* laterally in two opposite directions.

Lim tried to explain the different ways one can work on the *jin1*-sinews between the shoulder blades. If he did it correctly, the horizontally held forearms would be parallel to the ground and parallel to the surface of the chest during this movement. By contrast, if he used his trapezius and *latissimus dorsi* muscles, the forearm would be raised at the elbows. As a trained practitioner, Lim could perceive the *jin1*-sinews in terms of their tactile quality. If he did this movement correctly, Lim would feel a sustained *jin4*-power emanate from his heels rooted to the ground, expand outward, and offer resistance to any incoming forces that were assaulting the body.

Hsu, who had been totally unaware of the existence of this aspect of her bodily structure, was told to pay attention to the visual cues. Lim also showed how a minor movement, such as a slight inward rotation of the palms that were pressing against each other, effected a sinewy stretch on the outer side of the forearm and simultaneously gave one the feeling that the shoulder blades were opening. However, even though Hsu gained awareness of her *jin1*-sinews between the shoulder blades over the course of the month she trained with Lim, she never acquired the skill to work them. This small episode shows that Hsu was introduced to the plausible existence of a "thing," but it remained an intractable materiality.

The second posture, "to pluck the stars and reverse the dipper" (*zhaixing huan dou* 摘星換斗), was in Lim's version of the *Yijin jing* a strike. It was a side-kick, which involved a diagonal extension of one's spine, shoulder blades, and one straightened leg. Along this diagonal line, the elbow of one arm pointed upwards, with the forearm dangling down in relaxation, while the other arm was stretched out with a taut forearm that rotated the horizontally held palm inward. If one placed the shoulder above the heels precisely in a diagonal straight line, Lim explained, it was possible to issue the kick with ease, simply by contracting the lower abdomen and thereby straightening the spine.

The notion of *jin4* encompasses not merely power and strength, but also sensitivity and a sense of balance. The third posture, called "twisting and pulling the oxen's tail" (*dao zhuai niu wei* 倒拽牛尾), developed these qualities, as did the sixth and seventh. The third posture began in the same position as the first one where the feet were kept parallel to each other, side by side, but then required the practitioner to take a step back. It consisted of a combination of pushing and pulling movements, as the weight of one's body shifted from the front to the back leg, and vice versa. Lim told Hsu to push with one arm forward, as the other arm went backward, palm facing down, and held horizontally parallel to the ground. Once the arm was horizontally stretched out, Hsu was told to concentrate her volition on the palm that was held erect and widely opened, each finger being kept as distant as possible from the other one, *peng*-expanding the *jin1*-sinews within the hand. As this hand was turned around, the fingers were folded into a fist, which was pulled horizontally back to underneath her armpit. Meanwhile the other stretched out arm was retracted and extended to the fore, shoulder locked into position through rotating the opened palm such that the smallest finger was on top and the thumb pointed to the ground. These movements trained the *jin1*-sinews of the hand, the wrist, the shoulder, and the lower spine, without which one could not sense and control the exchange of *jin4*-power between two persons as they resist one another by pushing a push and pulling a pull.

The following postures each had an explicit objective of transforming one's *jin1* and administering *jin4* in different parts of the body. Lim's sequence comprised eight postures, followed by a closing movement:

1. Skanda offers his *vajra* club (*weituo xianchu* 韋馱献杵)
2. Pluck the stars and reverse the dipper (*zhaixing huandou* 摘星換斗)
3. Twist and pull the ox's tail (*daozhuai niuwei* 倒拽牛尾)
4. Draw the horse saber (*bamadao* 拔馬刀)
5. Extend the claws and spread the wings (*chuzhua liangchi* 出爪亮翅)
6. The crouching tiger lunges at its prey (*wohu pushi* 卧虎扑食)
7. Three plates drop to the floor (*sanpan luodi* 三盤落地)
8. Wag the tail (*diaowei* 掉尾)
9. Scoop *qi* and pour it onto your vertex (*pengqi guanding* 捧氣灌頂)

Each posture targeted specific *jin1*-sinews in the body. In posture 1 those in the shoulders and between the shoulder blades; in posture 2 those connecting the shoulders to the lower spine and the heels; in posture 3 those between the fingers, in the wrist, between the ribs, in the lower spine and the abdomen; in posture 4 those between the ribs and in the spine; in posture 5 those between the shoulder blades and between the fingers, and in the shoulders and the wrists; in posture 6 those in the spine and the entire frontal torso from the chest to lower abdomen; in posture 7 those connecting the torso to the hands and feet; and lastly in posture 8 those in the lower spine, the waist, hips, and neck.

The manipulation of *jin1* was so central to Lau's *Yijin jing* that whenever Hsu spoke of muscle ache and muscle power, Lim corrected her, "You must stop thinking about this thing called 'muscle.' The book is called *Yijin jing*, not *Yiji jing* 易肌經 [Canon for supple muscles]; the muscles are external and fragmented, while the sinews are internal and integrated. Muscle power is crude, the *jin4* administered via the *jin1* is subtle."

While sports mechanics and physiology attempt to measure their impact, the *jin4*-power events Lim spoke of are not recognized as such by Western biomedicine. Meanwhile, Hsu's training centered on acquiring sensitivity to this subtle tangibility through repeated imitation of precisely choreographed movements that expanded and contracted parts of her body she never knew existed. The negotiation of this tangibility—*jin4* traveling through *jin1*, indispensable for combat—enskilled her into an environment of very tangible forces, materializing in Lim's punches and strikes, "attacking" her from all directions.

Lim noted that the *Yijin jing* did not provide a complete body-building repertoire. Therefore, he trained daily for ninety minutes another set of exercises that strengthened his *jin1* and developed his *jin4* more comprehensively. For Hsu, however, a month of daily one-hour sessions led to subcutaneous fat loss, the most evident loss resulting in her lower abdomen becoming completely flat. More importantly, the training had a lasting effect on her posture and her awareness of it in general.

Enskilling into *Qi* with Qiu's *Yijin Jing*

Some twenty years earlier, Hsu had learned movements of the *Yijin jing* from a *qigong* master in Kunming. Qiu worked as a *qigong* healer on what was commonly called "the street of the poor" (*pinminjie* 貧民街)

where petty enterprise flourished. Qiu too considered the *Yijin jing* movements discussed here suitable only for beginners. It was insufficient if one wanted to attain a state in which one can "see the light", and feel the glow central to recovering one's own vitality. The latter was particularly important, he said, after a day's work of treating patients by emitting his *qi* onto them for restoring theirs. In autumn 1988, shortly after Hsu became acquainted with him and his family, Qiu agreed to teach her. This happened in daily sessions of about an hour at dusk over two months in a nearby park (Hsu 1999: 21–87).

When asked, in 1988, Qiu did tell Hsu the names of the movements, but because the martial arts were veiled in secrecy, Hsu refrained from asking him to write the names down. Twenty-one years later into the reform era, in the summer of 2009, an acquaintance with a foreigner was no longer as unusual as it had previously been. Qiu now agreed to name the movements, while seated in front of his medical practice, and a "friend" who referred to himself as one of his disciples, wrote them into my notebook:

1. Skanda makes an offering to Buddha (*Weituo xianfo* 韋馱獻佛)
2. Topple the mountains and overturn the seas (*paishan daohai* 排山倒海)
3. Pluck the stars and reverse the dipper (*zhaixing huandou* 摘星換斗)
4. The immortal presses onto the water (*xianren yashui* 仙人壓水)
5. Turn your head backwards and look at the moon (*huitou wangyue* 回頭望月)
6. Nine oxen, pull them by the tail (*jiuniu bawei* 九牛拔尾)
7. The blue-green dragon surveys its claws (*qinglong tanzhua* 青龍探爪)
8. The hungry tiger lunges at its prey (*ehu pushi* 餓虎扑食)
9. Welcome the wind while looking at one's palms (*yingfeng kanzhang* 迎風看掌)
10. Receive *qi* and return it to the primordial origin (*shouqi huanyuan* 收氣還元)

Some names were exactly the same as those in the other three versions,[10] others differed. Their sequencing was evidently not the same, an observation discussed in more detail below. Unlike Lim, Qiu barely gave any explanations when he taught Hsu. The names of Qiu's movements hinted at the body ecologic, a body that is ontologically continuous with its environment and that extends beyond a body-enveloped-by-skin into the surrounding ecologies (Hsu 1999: 78–80,

2007). Qiu's names of the movements referred to the mountains, the sea, the stars, the dipper, water, the moon, wind, and *qi*. Or they referred to animals known for their strength: the nine oxen, the blue-green dragon, and the hungry tiger. They also mentioned body parts, such as the tail, the head, the claws, and the palms. Apart from the Buddhist allusion to Skanda and the Buddha, the names invoked the immortals and the primordial origins, *yuan* 元, which are particularly vivid in the Daoist imagination.

In Qiu's, as in Lim's, version of the *Yijin jing* routine, the word *qi* is mentioned only in the names of the closing movements. However, there are hints that *qi* may have been central to all of Qiu's movements. First, Qiu taught movements rather than postures (in Chinese they both are "*shi* 勢"), He performed each seven times, very slowly, which had the effect that Hsu experienced them as flowing into each other. Meanwhile, he occasionally took pleasure in performing just for her, or some other passersby, similar sequences of martial movements. They consisted of a series of quick strikes ending in discrete postures. Second, he always practiced the *Yijin jing* in parks, among the trees, *en plein air*. Third, although he spoke neither of *jin1* or *jin4*, as did Lim, nor of *qi gan* 氣感 (feelings of *qi*) and *qi* circulation, as many *qigong* practitioners in the commercial sector did, some of the movements clearly indicated an intense engagement with the environment. Once, Qiu even spoke of pushing hard, all the way, to the end of the world. This last point will be discussed in the following section largely from the viewpoint of Hsu's participant experience and the phenomenology of the movements learned (since we are talking about felt experiences, the first-person singular is used in what follows).

> Qiu never provided explanations on how to do the movements and what to pay attention to. He merely demanded that I imitate him and he only occasionally, rather gently, pulled and pushed me into the right position. Today, I still do not dare to claim to have reproduced the movements accurately, although Qiu did review my practice on my post-fieldwork visits after seven, fifteen, and twenty-one years respectively. Nevertheless, it does not feel right to aim to provide a detailed description of the movements Qiu taught me. I can however comment on the effects they had on me. These movements caused distinctive but unusual and sometimes painful sensations of sinewy stretches in my body, some of which I was told to conceptualize as activating the flow of *qi*. Furthermore, the movements affected my breathing, although this was an observation I made but never communicated to Qiu, nor do I remember

him to have spoken about breathing. When practicing for years the entire sequence on my own over the course of approximately thirty or more minutes daily, I noted that my breathing became increasingly deeper; I never managed to practice the seventh movement, "The hungry tiger lunges at its prey," without panting. Details of how my breathing was affected are outlined below.

The second movement "Topple the mountains and overturn the seas," would usually slow down my breathing, as I exhaled while pushing and inhaled while pulling my arms back. The movement involved, with broadly placed feet but bent legs, stretching forward both my arms and pushing very hard. Qiu's hands sometimes trembled from the efforts of pushing when he did this movement. The self was thereby made to expand and reach out to the end of the world. As each of the movements Qiu taught was to be repeated seven times, a recommendation found also in Wang Zuyuan ([1882] 1956: 52), the breathing would become very regular before a new posture was adopted.

The fourth movement, "The immortal presses onto the water," would usually make me breathe more deeply. It was a movement that should be practiced with one's arms only, as the bent legs are rooted to the ground. One exhales while pushing downwards, palms held parallel to the ground, opened face-down, but inwardly inverted so that the fingertips touch each other. One inhales while pulling up one's palms that now are upwardly open, to above the head. This movement had an undeniable effect on deepening my breathing.

The sixth movement, "Nine oxen, pull them by the tail," would deepen the breathing even more. It required me to do a very slow and long drawn out movement of pulling with both arms from the left to the right, or vice versa. This lowered my point of gravity, as the leg on which I rested was now strongly bent. The other stretched out leg was gradually bent as I shifted my body's gravity onto it, while imagining that I was pulling a tail [or nine in a bundle] with the strength of nine oxen. The shifting of my gravity had a perceptible effect on the depth of my breathing.

Finally, the eighth movement, "The hungry tiger lunges at its prey," required me to tilt my body and shift the center of gravity downward toward the five fingers of each hand that I had stuck into the ground in front of myself, on either the left or right side. The face and torso were then slowly pushed forward along the ground, and earthy odors inhaled, as I stretched my chest and lungs, and eventually raised the head and contracted the nape. The tilting of one's gravity, the earthy odors, and the stretching of one's chest all worked toward a drawn out inhalation.

Notably, the above four movements were all performed in a position where the feet were apart, parallel to each other, such that one stood with bent legs and a lowered center of gravity firmly rooted and broadly on the ground while the spine had to be kept straight, and the head was vertically connected to the sky.

While Qiu's movements demonstrated engagement with a resisting environment as the self expanded into it, Hsu's experience of the above four movements was that they filled one with *qi* which, in turn, made one expand. In between them there were three movements, which Qiu practiced with legs crossed over, cross-legged feet parallel and close by each other: "Pluck the stars and reverse the dipper" involved a stretching of the torso, "Turn your head and look at the moon" effected a twisting of the torso, and "The blue-green dragon surveys its claws" resulted in a bending of the torso. These three latter movements likewise stretched the sinews and caused unusual feelings, and, in this sequence, they also deepened one's breathing, and made one feel more compact.

While Qiu never provided a rationale for his movements, over many years of practice, Hsu identified a pattern that gave them a rationale. Accordingly, there would be a pattern of alternation of the broad postures (movements, 2, 4, 6, 8, and 9) and the postures with crossed legs (movements 3, 5, and 7). The former felt like an expansion of one's self, and the latter like a contraction. The rationale for the sequencing of Qiu's movements would be explained through the deepened breathing as the body's center of gravity is increasingly lowered in postures 2, 4, 6, and 8. Although Qiu himself scarcely made any allusion to *qi*, these movements enskilled the practitioner into a universe with which one engaged in an ever more drawn out and deeper on-going exchange of *qi*. This altered breathing would bring with it a sense of tranquility, which resulted in a heightened awareness and increased pleasure of the quiet parks and garden landscapes in which Hsu continued practicing the *Yijin jing*.[11]

Discussion

Lim taught a sequence of postures, rather than a string of movements flowing into each other. Assuming a posture demanded standing rooted to the ground, while accumulating *jin4*-power in one's *jin1*-

sinews. Needless to say, this required enormous imagination-and-concentration (*yinian* 意念) and great endurance of pain. Lim claimed that the version he taught was "minimalist," both in regard of the movements performed and the names those had. For example, the fifth posture, known as "Nine ghosts, draw the horse saber" (*jiu gui ba ma dao* 九鬼拔馬刀) in Wang Zuyuan's text of 1882 and in the CHQA's video, was in Lim's version named matter-of-factly "Draw the horse saber" with no allusion to ghosts. This posture involved a graceful bending of the torso in the CHQA's video, which looked baroque to Lim; such a rounded movement appeared to have no effect on the training of sinews in anticipation of a strike. Rather, the graceful and round movements advocated by the CHQA suggested an enskilment into an environment constituted by *qi*. The environmental modality toward which the two *Yijin jing* styles were oriented we experienced as *qi* and *jin4* respectively.

Since we were dealing with intentionalities, with unusual bodily projections into the world, and with ensuing unusual proprioceptive and tactile perceptions, we took recourse to auto-ethnography, specifically to "participant experience," which requires the ethnographer to learn a technique to a degree of being capable of performing it without depending on external guidance (Hsu 1999: 15, 2006), also called "participant learning" (Wang Yishan, personal communication). As becomes evident from the above, the postures and movements in the different versions of the *Yijin jing* enskilled the practitioners into different "materialities" of their environments. Where *jin4* evoked solid and quick strikes, working with *qi* resulted in more flowing movements. Lim's forward gaze and linear alignment of movements were directed toward retaliating with the *jin4* of the *jin1* against *jin4* while Qiu's multidirectional, diagonal, and rounder movements were comprehended as negotiating a multidimensional "materiality" of an environment constituted of *qi*, which one eventually would become one with.

Regardless of the tangible qualities that the environment posed, the practitioner learning either of the two *Yijin jing* styles was asked to master its "materiality" by generating a feeling of expanding and extending beyond the self's immediate surroundings into the universe at large. Our analytic focus on the "enskilment into the environment," rather than on the cultural transmission of "body techniques" highlighted that bodily routines can affect and transform not merely the body-enveloped-by-skin but also the environment and its "materiality."

Actively negotiating and reconstituting the environment's materialities, certainly effected what Ingold (2000) has called "an education of the senses". Furthermore, our method of acquiring bodily knowledge and auto-ethnographically report on it, also had us develop a sensitivity to cultural tropes in other modalities than the sensory bodily routines of the martial arts. Even though we had not further reflected upon, let alone verbalized and discussed, the bodily sense of expanding and extending into the universe, it illuminated our reading of ancient Chinese texts.

In an earlier study (Hsu 2000), it was interesting to find that the term *shen*, meaning "spirit, divine, superhuman" (Karlgren 1957: 109–110), was listed among the words that since ancient and archaic times had as a phonological marker the homophone *shen* 申. Furthermore, in lexicography the homophone *shen* 伸, meaning "to extend", "to stretch out", was used to explain why the living body *shen* 身 was pronounced as *shen* Although, while practicing the *Yijin jing*, Hsu had not been taught a specific term like *peng* that meant "to expand," the bodily experience of extending into the universe gave her the certainty that the lexicographic observation was not irrelevant and encouraged her to search for further textual evidence, . . . and she found it in Roger Ames's comment: "This is suggestive that the person was seen as 'extending' or 'presencing,' having correlative physical and spiritual (or psychical) aspects denoted by *shen* (lived body) and *shen* (spirit) respectively" (1993: 165). Although a statement of this kind might have appeared unfounded and speculative, the text gained contour and weight by treating the above bodily practices and their auto-ethnographic analysis as a heuristic device.

More recently, when analyzing the different shades of the meaning of the word *bing* 病 in an early Chinese text, namely in the *Zuozhuan* of circa the third to first century BCE, this word, which today means "to be ill," was shown to describe the inner state of persons of rank who felt they had been wronged, *bing zhi* 病之. This was a serious condition that could result in death (Hsu 2015). It would arise after non-observance of rituals, or the gossip over it, and after other dishonorable insinuations, as well as disputes over land. To make sense of their hurt and/or indignation, it was necessary to assume that their social self expanded into the lands surrounding them. Accordingly, an honored and honorable person of rank had a large influence sphere, and *bing zhi* referred to a sort of distress that diminished its radius and radiance. Here, the auto-ethnographic, bodily experience that had the practitioner imagine the self as expanding into the universe, provided the basis for interpreting notions of the self as found in ancient texts.

Rigorous training and bodily routines that taught us how to expand into environments opened up new ways of comprehending ancient texts, medical practices, or religious rituals. We experienced that realities are constructed through intentionalities inherent to daily bodily routines, and the above examples highlight that awareness of those can fruitfully enhance textual scholarship. All this happens in ways that are Beyond Method.

Acknowledgments

This research was made possible through the postdoctoral visiting fellowship in medical anthropology at Green Templeton College, University of Oxford, which Lim was awarded from January to March 2010.

Elisabeth Hsu is Professor of Anthropology and co-founder of the two master's courses in medical anthropology, and of the postdoctoral anthropology research group on Eastern medicines and religions (ArgO-EMR) at the School of Anthropology and Museum Ethnography, University of Oxford. She has published widely on the anthropology and history of Chinese medicine.

Chee Han Lim is Senior Lecturer and head of programme for Overseas Experiential Learning, Centre for Experiential Learning, at the Singapore University of Social Sciences. His research interests include the martial arts, meditation, medicine, and religion. He has received over thirty years of training in various martial and meditational styles, and has been teaching them for more than ten years.

Notes

1. *Yi jin* is a verb-noun phrase which means "to transform one's sinews."
2. Damo purportedly invented the Shaolin martial arts and by extension, all styles of martial arts. Legend states that on his visit to the Shaolin monastery, he encountered monks frail and sickly from long periods of meditation; hence he designed a series of exercises that formed the foundation of Shaolin martial arts. Yet scholarly research shows that none of the above is likely (Henning 1999; Shahar 2008).
3. His meditation room on the top floor of his house had Daoist and Buddhist iconography pasted onto the walls.
4. Wang Zuyuan's ([1882] 1956) edition contains twelve depictions of postures (*shi* 勢), as does the version advocated by the CHQA. The latter additionally contains a closing movement (*shoushi* 收勢). For evidence that the twelve images in fact depict nine postures, see Hsu (2018).

5. The other three are called *Wuqin xi* 五禽戲 (Five Animals Frolic), *Baduan jin* 八段錦 (Eight Sections Brocade), and *Liuzi jue* 六字訣 (Six-Worded Mnemonic).
6. This association, which is supervised by the State Sport General Administration, was founded after the Falun Gong incident of 1999 to regulate *qigong* practices in China. It organizes forums and seminars and publishes books and videos (in Mandarin and English) that show the correct movements for all four styles of *qigong*.
7. The differences between the text in the video and in the 1956 facsimile edition are minimal. There are other versions of the *Yijin jing*, among them the *Shaolin Yijin jing* 少林易筋經, the *Damo Yijin jing* 達摩易筋經 and the *Weisheng Yijin jing* 衛生易筋經.
8. The Martial Arts Instructions Act, drawn up in 1974, was designed to prevent "secret society members and criminal elements from using martial arts training to further their own illegal purposes" (MHA 2003). Under the act, all martial arts instructors and trainees had to register with the authorities (Lim received a certificate for doing so in the early 1990s). The act was repealed in 2003 as the authorities felt that triad activities had been brought under control. Lau was indeed involved in gang activities at some stage of his life, as Lim found out much later.
9. Qiu and his family would adopt this gesture as one of prayer in temples while kneeling on a round cushion in front of deities of the Daoist and Buddhist pantheon.
10. Qiu's movement 1 is comparable to Lim's movement 1, 2 to 5, 4 to 7, 3 to 2, 5 to 4, 6 to 3, 8 to 6, and 10 to 8.
11. As Judith Farquhar and Qicheng Zhang (2005) observed in their fieldwork in Beijing, "pleasure" was reported as one of the primary experiences from and reasons for practicing life-nurturing (*yangsheng* 養生) practices. See also Farquhar and Zhang (2012).

References

Ames, Roger. 1993. "The Meaning of Body in Classical Chinese Philosophy." In *Self as Body in Asian Theory and Practice*, eds. T. P. Kasulis, R.T. Ames, and W. Dissanayke. Albany: State of University of New York Press, 157–77.

Chen, Yanlin. [1943] 2014. *Taiji Compiled: The Boxing, Saber, Sword, Pole and Sparring*, trans. Paul Brennan. Retrieved 2 November 2016 from https://brennantranslation.wordpress.com/2014/03/18/taiji-boxing-according-to-chen-yanlin/.

CHQA, Chinese Health Qigong Association. 2003. *Health-building Qigong: Yijinjing*. Chinese Health Qigong Association.

Csordas, Thomas, ed. 1994. *Embodiment and Experience: The Existential Ground of Culture and Self*. Cambridge: Cambridge University Press.

Farquhar, Judith, and Qicheng Zhang. 2005. "Biopolitical Beijing: Pleasure, Sovereignty, and Self-Cultivation in China's Capital." *Cultural Anthropology* 20(3): 303–27.

———. 2012. *Ten Thousand Things: Nurturing Life in Contemporary Beijing*. New York: Zone Books.

Gibson, James. 1979. *The Ecological Approach to Visual Perception*. Boston: Houghton Mifflin Company.

Henning, Stanley. 1999. "Academia Encounters the Chinese Martial Arts." *China Review International* 6(2): 319–32.

Hsu, Elisabeth. 1999. *The Transmission of Chinese Medicine*. Cambridge: Cambridge University Press.

———. 2000. "The Spiritual (*shen*), Styles of Knowing, and Authority in Chinese Medicine." *Culture, Medicine, and Psychiatry* 24: 197–229.

———. 2006. "Participant Experience: Learning to Be an Acupuncturist, and Not Becoming One." In *Critical Journeys: The Making of Anthropologists*, eds. G. de Neeve and M. Unnithan, 149–163. Farnham: Ashgate.

———. 2007. "The Biological in the Cultural: The Five Agents and the Body Ecologic in Chinese Medicine." In *Holistic Anthropology: Emergence and Convergence*, eds. David Parkin and Stanley J. Ulijaszek, 91–126. New York: Berghahn.

———. 2015. "*Bing*-distress in the *Zuo zhuan*: The Not-so-good-life, the Social Self and Moral Sentiment among Persons of Rank in Warring States China." In *The Good Life and Conceptions of Life in Early China and Graeco-Roman Antiquity*, ed. R. A. H. King, 157–80. Berlin: de Gruyter.

———. 2018. "The Iconography of Time: What the Visualization of Efficacious Movement (*shi* 勢) Tells Us About the Composition of the *Yi jin jing* (Canon for Supple Sinews)." In *Imagining Chinese Medicine*, eds. V. Lo and P. Barrett, 89–99. Leiden: Brill.

Ingold, Tim. 2000. *The Perception of the Environment: Essays on Livelihood, Dwelling and Skill*. London: Routledge.

Karlgren, Bernhard. 1957. *Grammata Serica Recensa*. The Museum of Far Eastern Antiquities Bulletin 29.

Latour, Bruno. 2000. "When Things Strike Back: A Possible Contribution of 'Science Studies' to the Social Sciences." *The British Journal of Sociology* 51(1): 107–23.

Mauss, Marcel. [1935]. 1973. "Techniques of the Body," transl. Ben Brewster. *Economy and Society* 2(1): 70–88.

Merleau-Ponty, Maurice. [1945] 1962. *The Phenomenology of Perception*, transl. Colin Smith. New York: Humanities Press.

MHA, Ministry of Home Affairs Singapore. 2003. *Repeal of the Martial Arts Instruction Act*. Retrieved 4 July 2016 from http://www.parliament.gov.sg/sites/default/files/030018.pdf.

Shahar, Meir. 2008. *The Shaolin Monastery: History, Religion, and the Chinese Martial Arts*. Honolulu: University of Hawaii Press.

Wang, Zuyuan, ed. [1882] 1956. *Neigong tushuo (Illustrated Exposition of Internal Techniques)*. Beijing: Renmin weisheng chubanshe.

PART III

Imagining

Chapter 9

LIVE TO TELL

IN AND OUT OF VIEW IN THE INTERVIEW

Ari Gandsman

This chapter is comprised of three texts that take traditional elements of research, the interview and the archive, and view them not as static and closed artifacts circumscribed by preexisting questions or material documents but as living and breathing processes that embrace openings and posit imaginative and creative encounters that examine what is not said or written as much as what is. They highlight the gaps between what anthropologists want to find out, where their interest lies, and those of our interlocutors. They show how predesigned research agendas or interests often preclude us from paying closer attention to what is important to our informants, which they often convey in ways opposed to our own mode of inquiry. Similar to a consideration of the interview as an unbounded space of interaction that can speak in a myriad of different and unconventional ways, the archive, rather than as a bounded form of already existing "accumulation of work," as a living, breathing space that constitutes, in the words of Thushara Hewage, an "immanent system of relations, organizing the production of fields of distinct yet implicitly related statements."

Interviews imply formalized procedure and systematic technique with a standardized approach in a highly ritualized and contrived encounter. Somebody knows something that we want to know; that is, the research question. Ply them with questions in order to extract information that meets the preordained needs of the inquiry. After the prescribed yet arbitrary number (the "target," a term that lends an unfortunate militaristic aura to the process) is reached, research ends, and "data analysis" begins. When to end is often preordained by this target. In applications I review for my university's research ethics board, researchers are told by the ethics officers to adopt a baffling "first come, first served" approach with the implied understanding that once the number specified in their research proposal is reached, they reject any more willing participants, thus lending an even more consumerist and commodified logic to the practice. Once collected, interviews are painstakingly transcribed. To conform to ethical standards of confidentiality, any features allowing for any potential identification are removed or modified as the individual is transformed into pseudonym, guaranteeing to transform interlocutors into generic types (thus vampirically purging them of their individual humanity as they become prototypes or representative vehicles of larger arguments). The same process also often eliminates the interviewer's pesky presence as questions that elicited the responses are conspicuously absent. Language is cleansed, reordered, and reworded, thoroughly polished and scrubbed of all verbal quirks, ticks, and idiosyncrasies, punctuated, truncated, and made grammatically correct so that our speakers no longer resemble speakers (what is called "denaturalized"). Once thus transcribed in a meticulously time-consuming process, results are then filtered and processed through a methodological software that identifies, parses, and sorts common discursive threads and themes. If we are good ethical subjects (among whom I do not count myself since I do not do this) or if we work with Indigenous communities, which justifiably may make this a prerequisite of research, we provide transcripts of our interviews back to our interviewees in order for them to be vetted, corrected, and authorized. In either case, the "raw material" of the interview has now been processed into ready-made quotes to form the building blocks of what gets lumped together as qualitative academic inquiry. The spoken word is now quotation mark text (or in block for bulk) ready for citation. Academic conventions may require a brief identification of speaker like an age and pseudonym and some might even ask for a date of interview. Others may be rendered into more abstract figures like discourses circulating in the ether.

While this may appear as caricature, I have tried to encapsulate the ways the interview appears at loggerheads with anthropological ways of knowing, antithetical to our discipline, which promises the more tacit, sensorial, and intimate. The interview and, correspondingly, the interviewee, are held suspect and considered at odds with participant observation research. Most contemporary work on ethnographic methods decenter the interview to the periphery or margins of anthropological practice, one to be looked at with scorn or distrust. Perusing such works as Harry F. Wolcott's *Ethnography Lessons: A Primer* (2010), one could surmise that anthropologists do not even conduct interviews, which appear contrived and thus a "non-naturalistic" (whatever that means) encounter that does not allow for intimacy, length of time, or in his own description the "authentic" and "real" or even "firsthand." Within a naïve positivist epistemology, anthropological observations have oft been assumed to have occurred as if the anthropologist were not present, something which could never be assumed from an interview. For example, Bruce Jackson's *Fieldwork* (1987), a work that differentiates the interview from "ordinary talk," objects to how "interviewing changes what is going on" rather than naturalistic observation and considered the interview an "intrusion" that "influences the information provided to them" (1987: 66).

Yet most anthropologists regularly conduct interviews as part of their research repertoire, ever despite our intentions or inclinations, even if the interview is often hidden like a shameful secret within the more general confines of what we label participant observation fieldwork. Yet for many projects, in which there may not be formal opportunities for classic participant observation research, the interview becomes base currency that lends research a magic of presence, a form of quantification other than temporal (where a formulae like fieldwork for *x* amount of time in the field ceases to make sense with a destabilized and largely deterritorialized and unbounded field sites, interviews with *x* number of people provide epistemic heft), a metric that provides both legitimacy and authority but also accountability for our research.

With my most recent project on right to die activism, I have struggled over how "anthropological" my research is; research that I hereby embarrassingly declare is largely derived from interviews. Granted, I have, when such opportunities have availed themselves, attended events, workshops, meetings, other organizational and institutional activities, legal hearings, informal gatherings, and so on; however, the interview remains the main currency of my research, the main source from which I have drawn upon when writing about the topic. And I wager that I am not alone. As a basic perusal of many anthropological texts attest, especially within my own subfield of medical anthropology but also works on the past and oral histories or anthropological texts on political violence or memory or futures or any subject where the anthropologist is not a direct witness to events but a chronicler and cataloger of other peoples' narratives, many anthropological projects are similarly interview based.

This may be an unavoidable product of research context and topics, especially since so many contemporary studies endeavor to "study up" and examine institutional or bureaucratic corridors of power or expert practitioners. In doing so, we often run into highly commodified time and scheduling constraints that resistant the kind of "deep hanging out" that we seek and cherish. Rebuffed and scorned, we settle for the interview that exists within a limited and temporally circumscribed moment that makes us feel less friend than stranger. Rather than study specific populations or specific geographic locales (i.e., villages) that allow for a much more immersive experience, we have "topics," the more topical, contemporary, and plucked from the headlines, the seemingly better to brand ourselves. Our aim is to explore the "topic" by engaging with those involved in it one way or another but often as part of their work or professional expertise.

As Jennifer Hamilton writes in a similar research context that highlights some of the problems with this kind of methodological approach in which interviews often conform to an institutional narrative that is already accessible to researchers:

> My own experience reflects a growing problem with the "interview" in certain contexts; I could predict with great accuracy what people were (or were not) going to tell me before I ever went in. At one point, in a scenario that became all-too-familiar during the course of fieldwork, I found myself sitting in an interview with a low-level bureaucrat, my informant nervously and repeatedly checking my tape recorder as though keeping an eye on it would prevent any unintended and hazardous revelations. As he answered my pre-scripted questions in a prescripted way, it became clear to me that I could have crafted his answers myself, begging the question as to why I had made numerous phone calls, left multiple messages on voicemail, and traveled downtown on yet another dismal Vancouver day to do an interview with someone whose demeanor toward me ranged from apathy to discomfort to barely disguised irritation. Why, indeed—other than to say that I had done an interview, done something. (2009: 76–77)

Vignette 6

Against Ethnographic Disappointment, or on the Importance of Listening

Larisa Kurtović

Much of my doctoral fieldwork in postwar Bosnia-Herzegovina focused on a grassroots activist initiative that formed in the aftermath of a series of mass protests inspired by a murder of a sixteen-year-old boy, Denis

Mrnjavac. Mrnjavac was killed in early February 2008, by three other boys riding a tram passing through downtown Sarajevo, but his death became perceived by the public as a symptom as well as a symbol of the collapse of governmental power and biopolitical care in the fragmented postwar state. When I arrived in the field in June 2008, shortly after the street protests had ended, I tracked down one group of activists who had participated in the demonstrations and were now looking to continue their organizing in a different form. They would eventually form a non-governmental organization focused on issues of governmental accountability, and specifically, on responding to the perceived rise of youth crime. As my theoretical interests pivoted around emerging conceptualizations of postwar and postsocialist futurity, their efforts proved to be a fruitful site for my research project.

But my ability to see their activism as a part of a larger story about postwar futures at times also precluded me from grasping the more nuanced and less transparent aspects of their political practice. One evening, very early in my fieldwork, I made my way to the neighborhood of Dobrinja at the outskirts of the city where I was to meet two middle-aged women, "Iris" and "Jasmina," who both participated in the protests and were now working to establish a formally registered activist organization. Iris and Jasmina would both become very important to me as long-term ethnographic interlocutors and good friends, but that summer evening, as I attempted to interview them in an outdoor patio of a neighborhood café, we had not yet gotten to know each other very well. Green and eager to learn more about the protests, I began my informal inquiry by asking: "Why did you come out to the protest?" It was, so I thought, an uncomplicated question, the kind that opened doors for further elaboration on the part of its addressee.

Iris sat in the chair with her legs crossed, looking a bit tired from working all day, smoking a cigarette and gazing at me intently. Then she began to speak. But instead of offering me a systematic breakdown of her political motivations, a critique of the postwar Bosnian state, or the lack of accountability of governmental officials, she responded by recounting her own visceral response the night the public learned about Mrnjavac's murder. Holding her hand to her chest, she recounted, "I felt like something was sitting right here (*sve mi se ovdje nešto skupilo*) . . . crushing me. So, the next day, I went out into the streets." As she exhaled, her eyes welled up with tears and her gaze grew even more piercing. She looked as if she had just told me everything that I needed to know.

But on my end, despite the profound emotional charge of the moment, I could not help but feel a deep sense of disappointment. I could certainly sense the touching intensity of her response, and recognize that it was somehow significant. But I had been hoping for an articulation, for a discursive elaboration of her motivations, a clever quote, an account of my interlocutor's inner world. I wanted to be in the presence of an ethnographic subject who could explain to me, preferably in an expansive way, how and why citizens came into the streets, and why a murder of an underaged boy had managed to do what years of dissatisfaction and millions of dollars of foreign money could not, that is, politically mobilize groups of people that seemed both politically disengaged and preoccupied by their own precarious postwar lives. I wanted something that I myself could recognize as ethnographically significant and valuable, capable of becoming a building block of an argument. What Iris seemed to offer me was a vernacular trope I did not quite know how to handle. Taken aback by my perceived failure to generate the right kind of reflection and articulation, I abandoned my plan to conduct a full interview, and decided to give it some time before I posed the question again.

It was only much later, after my fieldwork had already been completed, that I began to realize the significance of what Iris had said to me that evening. In locating the source of her motivation to come out into the street in her body, specifically the chest cavity, which holds both her heart and muscles besieged by tension from all the stress she endures as a single mother of two sons in postwar Sarajevo, she was indeed offering me a different way of thinking about the political as inextricably linked with the embodied and the affective. What is more, as it would turn out, Iris was not the only one among my interlocutors that used bodily metaphors to capture the feeling of living amid what I would later begin to understand as the "postwar impasse"—an enduring, pervasive sense of political paralysis that trickled down to everyday lives and tissues that were now holding the sedimented traces of trauma, loss, and insecurity. People would speak of not being able to "fit it all under their skin anymore" (*ne može više pod kožu stati*); of bursting into thousands of little pieces (*puk'o sam*), and of not being able to breathe. The postwar period also gave rise to new kinds of body-centered but politically charged practices; some of the other activists I worked among would take valium before sitting down to watch the news, in order to mitigate the corporeal effects of anger, rage, and upset that the newest corruption story stirred. What ultimately most impressed me about these practices is the fact people still chose to stay informed, even though this information was sometimes unbearable. Ultimately, in the case of my activist interlocutors, the body's vulnerability to this kind of stimuli paradoxically created political resolve, not just to seek information, but to protest, to organize street actions, and fight in any other way possible. The corporeal aspects of political life also anchored enormous affective charge that would later fuel subsequent, much larger waves of protest in 2013 and 2014.

That evening in the outdoor café, Iris had, in fact, told me something that I urgently needed to know, but that I, back then, did not quite know how to recognize as wisdom and insight. She had, actually, given me the best, the most useful kind of response, by locating her "why" in the realm of the corporeal and affective. The lesson here is that ethnographers have to learn to really listen and to be open to a wide range of ways people encode significance. It is not simply a matter of, as Charles Briggs (1986) once put it, "learning how to ask," since the interview itself is an uncustomary mode of speech that uproots everyday communicative conventions. It is also that we, the anthropologists, bring to the table a range of sometimes misguided expectations about valid responses to our questions. Becoming more aware of our own desires for particular kinds of ethnographic subjects and answers—and their limitations—will make us better ethnographers.

Scouring the internet for names or institutions, we contact them, often via email but sometimes via social media and ask for interviews (we have not yet reached the point where we can ask if they want to hang out). Hopefully, we may have met our prospective targets in advance, perhaps at meetings or in offices, so they can place a smiling face to our unfamiliar name, but more often than not it is the blind cold call (or, rather, email, since who uses the phone nowadays?) that may or may not be responded to. Perhaps we received their names from one of our other interviewees who, deeply immersed in the milieu, has a vast network that they may share with us. Someone who knows something also knows someone who knows something. We have the temerity to attempt to give this a scientific aura and call it a "technique" known, in the unfortunate metaphor, as "snowball sampling," even if "word-of-mouth" should not qualify as any real form of "sampling," except in a generic "non-probable" sense while "snowball" in its non-precipitation meaning refers to a rapid rate of accumulation that does not even describe the application of this practice.

In sum, this often makes for research that has trouble being recognized as fieldwork both from within and without. A hostile Vice Dean of Research at my university (an economist, as it happens) disputed my use of a federal research grant for this project on right to die activism by arguing that because I was working with professionals in a major city and not, in her words, "living in a tent with the Bedouin or with a tribe in Africa," my trip was not reimbursable because it did not count as "real" fieldwork and count as a legitimate research expense even if the grant was awarded precisely to conduct such research. Even after attempting to denounce me to the Social Science and Humanities Research Council and receiving a response that in fact my research was fieldwork, she still maintained that such a research trip could only be conducted for more than two weeks maximum in order to qualify as research. While this may be extreme, the reality on the ground is that we have to justify our existences through a university accounting system that forces us to quantify our experience in order to conform to bureaucratic norms where our disciplinary research norm practices are frequently illegible.

Even as our research may become, by default or necessity, shackled to the interview, as either a central or non-central component of our research, anthropologists still reject the vision of the "qualitative interview" that I described at the start. We have long striven to differentiate our interview—or what we call the "ethnographic interview"—from those of other disciplines. However, what makes our interviews different from all the rest? As documented in James Spradley's classic text, *The Ethnographic Interview* (1979), we emphasize the spontaneous, contextual, and creative aspects of our encounters. We emphasize a more dialogic encounter that takes connotations of a police interrogation or job interview. Our open-endedness follows the lines drawn by respondents rather than our own boilerplate texts (even if they may include such jaw-dropping open-ended banalities, which I have ashamedly used in the past, as "Is there anything I haven't asked you about that comes to mind?"). In the end, like the shaggy dog discipline that we are, our interviews should look less like interviews and resemble something like conversations. Our interviews should look less decontextualized as we attempt to situate them within the messiness of everyday life. It is in this sense that Martyn Hammersley and Paul Atkinson (1983) question the artificial dichotomy between interviews and participant observation research in which the former can also provide a context for the kind of approach that goes into the latter.

On the other hand, conversations imply a spoken role for ourselves that we might want to move away from. After all, in an interview, it is better to listen than to speak. And I often consult my graduate students, nervous as I have also been, in order to establish our legitimacy and credibility by showing what we know on the topic, to try to talk less. In that sense, our interviews should look less like the disembodied sound bites and talking heads of news programs, documentary films, and, yes, sociological texts. In the end, the challenge of the interview is how not to reduce it to datum gathered and accumulated, disembodied and anonymous, in which the word is privileged above all else.

An additional challenge exists for the anthropological interview. We need to situate the interview within its larger context: we largely live in what David Silverman termed an "interview society" (2017). The interview is already a commonly understood framework for self-understanding, exploring our past, and becomes a key cultural site for what Michel Foucault famously identified in *The History of Sexuality* as our confessing society, an "incitement to discourse and truth" (1978). We need to be careful in our role of perpetuating such incitements. As critical as anthropologists often are, the taken-for-granted role of the interview in our research often goes unquestioned in our methods. In fact, when compelled to justify ourselves in research ethics applications in terms of potential benefits our research offers, we will usually refer to our role as sympathetic listeners who offer people the space and forum to voice their thoughts and feelings, putting ourselves directly in the role of confessors even if we can offer no penance. On the other hand, our theoretical dispositions should dissuade us from making such claims, even as we do. I once tried to fill in the question of benefit on the research ethics application by saying "unknown and uncertain," only to have it sent back to me for clarification. As Foucault famously wrote:

> the confession became one of the West's most highly valued techniques for producing truth. We have singularly become a confessing society. The confession has spread its effects far and wide. It plays a part in justice, medicine, education, family relationships, and love relationships, in the most ordinary affairs of everyday life, and in the most solemn rites; one confesses one's crimes, one's sins, one's thoughts and desires, one's illnesses and troubles; one goes about telling, with the greatest precision, whatever is most difficult to tell. One confesses in public and in private, to one's parents, one's educators, one's doctor, to those one loves; one admits to oneself in pleasure and in pain, things it would be impossible to tell to anyone else, the things people write books about. When it is not spontaneous or dictated by some internal imperative, the confession is wrung from a person by violence or threat . . . Western man has become a confessing animal. (Foucault 1978: 59)

We should be suspicious of being instruments of the same confessional technologies that circulate as modes of truth or, worse, being the vehicles of those "wringing" confessions from others through our interviews. When we see our function as confessional, it is hard not to see the interview in line with a police interrogation in which the goal is to extract a confession from the suspect. For many of us, our experience being on the other side of the interview comes from our own experience on the academic job market as the necessary passage into employment. What we value about the interview in our fieldwork practice is often what we disdain in everyday practice. Job interview questions are remarkably standardized and uncreative, usually coming with a standardized list repeated from institution to institution (a customized gem from my own institution: "Why do you want to live in Ottawa?" a question that I am sure is not asked in Toronto or London). In the world of academic job interviews, it is the "asshole" who asks the left-field question, the one that attempts to destabilize and disorient the candidate. In fact, an entire discussion in workplace interviewing revolves around trying to "really" get to know the person beyond the standardized interview, from undercover interview or direct spying. In a similar way, textbooks on anthropology and introductory methods texts often present participant observation research as a means of exposing "hypocrisy" or at least a gap between theory (how we see our lives) and practice (how we live them). This unfortunate dichotomy misses something: how we talk about our lives is also inextricably how we live them.

In any event, anthropologists taking part in this research program unknowing play into the same dominant strands of power that they ostensibly resist. At the same time, so many ethnographic interviews fill what Joel Robbins (2013) calls the "suffering slot" in which eliciting and diffusing confessional narratives of suffering, injustice, and victimhood become the reason for our existence and what ostensibly lends an activist or political dimension to our work. My own interviews with right to die activists would seem to perform this role. Many of these people were themselves individuals who used their personal narratives of suffering as part of their activism. They would talk about witnessing the prolonged deaths of their loved ones that involved great suffering. They would talk about their own degenerative or terminal conditions that led them to make a demand for the recognition of their own right to die. Conversations with them would invariably involve retelling of stories, intimate confessions that drove their activism, and a strategic deployment of suffering in order to make their appeals, one of the long-recognized prerequisites of human rights demands.

In what follows, I would like to use an example of how we can think of the interview in our research against the interview. As Tim Ingold observes, many, if not most, practices and ways of knowing are inaccessible and resistant to the verbal. He argues that "knowledge of the sort that can be rendered formally and self-consciously explicit is but the tip of an iceberg compared with the immense reservoir of know-how that lies beneath the surface and without which nothing could be practicably accomplished"(2013: 112). In doing so, Ingold breaks down what it means to "tell," which can be differentiated into what can be told in narrative form and what one can see and sense, a more subtle and tacit form of knowing that is often difficult to fully articulate and links back to the use of the term "tell" in poker. As Ingold points out, we can often learn more from the unsaid tells than the said. The following example will show how I came to appreciate what lies outside the interview in the sense of recapturing the etymological origins of the word of how to perceive others (interview from the French *s'entrevoir*, to see each other). One can look to the interview as a culturally recognizable and accessible form to access what lies beyond words and what we see through other means. My example requires a self-critical evaluation of failure and a confrontation with my own blind spots, but many of us will admit that our failures in the field teach us far more than our successes. These are key moments that invite ethical self-reflection, make us question what we are doing, how we are doing it, and, more fundamentally, why we do it.

Brian is a seventy-five-year-old man I met while on a four-month fieldwork trip to study right to die activism in Melbourne. We had already spoken informally at various events and gatherings of Exit, the radical right to die organization he has been an active member of for years. I was given his email address by the national coordinator of Exit, and he agreed to be interviewed. I had already heard about Brian from numerous informants, who had recommended that I speak to him for the wealth of stories and experiences that has accumulated over the years; in particular having actively helped several people to die and thus risk criminal charges. This was a crucial interview I had eagerly anticipated, and, if I am honest with myself, I went in with the explicit aim of extracting those stories.

We sit and exchange pre-interview pleasantries in Brian's parlor in a Victorian bungalow in Melbourne in what was once a lower middle-class inner suburb that in recent decades had gentrified into real estate auction speculation and Scandinavian modern third wave coffee houses. I see the evident pride and care that he takes in home and heritage. He shows me pictures on the wall of his family members, some photos going back to the nineteenth century that mark his ancestor's arrival from England in Australia. Everything seems, to my mind, very British. He tells me that after the interview that he wants to introduce me to his partner, Mick, who, at ninety years old, is convalescing from a second stroke in the other room. Having exchanged all the regular pleasantries of pre-interview banter, I enter the formal spiel of the consent, what my university requires as part of its interpretation of Canadian Tri-Council ethics policy, which in the oral presentation that I give it, I have tried to make appear less legalistic and rigidly formal. This includes asking Brian if I can record the interview, a consent I have already presumed by preemptively placing my phone between us already open to the ALON Dictaphone app I use and just waiting for my finger to hit record. If I had been more perceptive at this moment and not attuned to my own nervous energy—a regularity of pre-interview jitters that I have never overcome—I would have noticed his own nervousness and perhaps his assent being more grudging than not. I hit record on the iPhone that lies on the coffee table separating our velvet armchairs. We both glance at it in acknowledgement of its presence, a third-party chaperone to our date.

Several hours later, I will write in my field journal: "What a disaster. The difference between our pre-interview informal chat and the 'formal' interview [i.e., once the recording gets going] was remarkable. From friendly and garrulous, he became nervous and removed. I think it must be using recording devices. Despite my reassurance, he seemed to have become more embarrassed and annoyed with himself as we went along and the whole thing fell apart." My initial conclusion was that the interview's failure was a product of the formal interview. Going through the official ethics spiel and conspicuously placing my recording device between us made Brian nervous and it spiraled from there. At the same time, only when I later listened to the whole interview, I realize that this was not the entire story, since when the interview finally ends when Brian abruptly asks me to stop recording, we have already been speaking for almost an hour. It is only when we begin talking about what I wanted to find out at the start—his involvement in helping other members of the organization die—that the interview goes completely off track. I try to delicately turn to the question, not asking him directly, but evoking it through a series of questions about his activities in Exit. He wants to tell me, but in trying to answer, he stumbles continually and finally, exasperated, brings the recorded part of our interview to an end:

> B: One [Exit] member—actually my memory of events is not good. Yes, I can't. A year or two ago, I could have told you exactly what I wanted to tell you. Therefore, I really do worry. Are we nearly finished? I'm sorry if you haven't finished. My hearing isn't very good either. And perhaps I didn't completely hear everything you were saying. But I do . . . I should have . . . There was this case in the country, but I just don't remember the details.
>
> AG: I'll turn off the tape. [*recording ends*]

In support of my idea that the problem was the recording device, once I hit stop and the "interview" is over, Brian is visibly relieved, and we continue chatting. Relaxed, more comfortable and his nerves calmed, he starts telling me those stories I wanted as I furiously scribble in my note pad. He helped someone die by sneaking into a nursing home with a nitrogen tank and helped them to set it up. The death is discovered, and he is summoned for a police interrogation. I scribble as fast as I can, getting a general sketch of the action. I lose details, but I suppose I get what I was after, his exploits in what is known as the "euthanasia underground," what he himself refers to as "one of the most interesting parts of my life."

Yet at what cost? From an ethical point of view, the interview is a disaster. In terms of provoking distress, my interview could not have been worse. If in ending the interview, Brian states, "Therefore, I really do worry," what he is worrying about is obvious. In the first part of the interview, he talks at length about his mother's death from Alzheimer's, but also how it runs in both branches of his family. He even mentions a few family cases from a hundred years ago. "It's worrying," he says earlier as he talks about genetic risks of Alzheimer's. I do not ask if he has done his own genetic study, but he talks about his own concerns with his current state "of having to reread things and a lack of concentration." I try to reassure him by joking about my own similar problems as a recent parent, but it does not appear to reassure him and probably comes off as condescending.

Alzheimer's is one of the thorniest problems for right to die activists, but also the one that I found most concerned right to die activists, who largely told me it was their predominant concern. Brian's experience with his mother's Alzheimer's is what initially motivated him to become a right to die activist and get involved in the organization. Even if and when legal reform is achieved, it is often excluded because it involves doctor administration in the context of recognizing an advanced directive (Mentzel and Steinbock 2013). Netherlands is one of the few places that allows it, but even there many doctors are uncomfortable with the idea that they will be administering death to a person who, in that moment, does not have any awareness of what is about to happen, even if their prior wishes were documented. Many controversies have ensued (de Boer et al. 2010). As a member of an underground organization that procures life-ending "medication" and thus exists outside of legal regimes, Brian has already secured the means to end his life that he has hidden away ("not in the house," he tells me). But the foremost problem with Alzheimer's is still a question of timing. Since it requires self-administration, he knows he would need to end his life earlier rather than later when he would still have the capacity to do so. Earlier in our interview, when we discuss this conundrum based on his experience with his mother and other family members, he talks about how "sometimes you are lucid and sometimes you aren't for a while, it seems that the brain is clever enough to elude you. You think you are okay." In his mother's case, he recalls how her friends were the ones who first warned him about his mother's increasingly erratic behavior, so he is now following suit.

> I've asked a few friends if I start not just being slightly forgetful but doing strange things. I think that is the problem. You need to most of all act early. It's sad to need to that. And then that also brings up many people who have prepared for their end of life but in the end, they don't have the guts to do it. I suppose putting it off is not having the guts too.

Brian, worried about being in the early stages of Alzheimer's, is, at the time we are speaking, thinking about the possibility of having to end his life and wondering if he has the "guts" to do it. The interview is shaped by this concern, and his consequent nerves about getting the story right provokes him, although he does not make this explicit during the interview itself, to face this concern more directly. His distress voiced at the end of the taped interview is a clear manifestation of that. After the interview, I send a well-meaning email to thank him for meeting me, and Brian writes,

> I'm sure I demonstrated clearly why I am concerned mentally . . . So many of those happenings, I tried so hard to recall names, and a couple of times the details, even though I had been very familiar with [them]. They say people who criticize others do so because the problem is also theirs. Today, I said some just do not have the guts . . . hope it's not a problem of mine.

I try to offer further reassurance, but Brian uneasily responds, "Appreciate your comments but feel it was more the point I reached with many hints of Exit happenings (from you) that I personally was involved with or knew of and could not recall the names or actual details . . . It was sort of sheer disappointment if not a mild panic."

Much later, when I transcribe the interview, I began to realize the fault lies in how I mechanistically approached the interview, and this also becomes a moment of insight. While asking questions about his right to die activism, he speaks instead about another experience, and when he did, it was a perfectly expressed narrative. He spoke for twenty minutes about how he cared for his mother for over ten years while she suffered from Alzheimer's, launching into the story without much prompting on my part. Rather than recount narratives of helping people end their lives—what I thought I would get—I get a narrative of caregiving for an ailing and aging parent. When he begins recounting this story, I thought he would tell me about how she wanted to die and that he could not help her. This would be a logical entry point into right to die activism that I saw in many other narratives, but his story was far more nuanced than that. In fact, he readily admitted that his mother was not the kind of person who would have availed herself of the option of a medically assisted death even if it were available. Yet as his story goes, when his mother needed care at the age of eighty-four, he stopped working, and moved to where she was living in order to take care of her, a model of filial self-sacrifice and responsibility. Although he initially thought she would die relatively quickly, she ended up living a decade longer and he took care of her the entire time. Caregiving became his fulltime responsibility. He talks about her long decline, problems with incontinence, feeding tubes, but also how he kept her at home, living with her, and refusing to put her in a nursing home. He uses the term "disappointed" to describe her death several times, but it hides a more glaring wound. He speaks of her long, drawn-out death in which the doctor refused to give her adequate pain care. He recognizes his own caregiving to be anomalous and understands that people are "too busy" now but bemoans how readily people abandon their family members to nursing homes, unwilling or unable to take care of them. He speaks of how many people would prefer to stay in their homes if that were an option, but it simply is not because they have no one to take care of them.

Although he could have taken his mother's death as a way of addressing the need for better hospice or palliative care among medical practitioners, he instead became involved in the most radical fringes of DIY (Do-It-Yourself) right to die activism, an organization that believes that any "rational" adult should be able to end their life at the time of their choice, no matter what the cause. This leap would only make sense in the context of his own worry and concern of having the same death as his mother and not wanting it. Though unsaid, this clearly motivates and frames his right to die activism, even if he found himself unable to speak about his activism on the subject. Moreover, at the same time we are speaking, he finds himself again in the role of caregiver to his partner, Mick, who at ninety, is semi-paralyzed and wheelchair-bound after having had several strokes and several mini strokes. Clearly, Brian is acutely concerned by Mick's medical situation and the prospect of his death. He tells me that he needs to be close to him at all times in case he needs help. He speaks of how his friends suggest that Mick's expectations may be selfish, but Brian responds, "I don't know. I think after forty-three years most of us should be hopefully prepared to give some time to your partner." In fact, he sees this in line with his tradition of caretaking. In fact, he says, "I've become so involved in this that I mean . . . that was ten or twelve years out of my life with my mother, and it's happening again with Mick."

If I had followed the lines of Brian's words and became more attuned to what he was conveying through other nonverbal signs and the direction that he set off on rather than pursuing my own preordained interests, I could have learned more about intimate practices of care. In fact, reflecting upon this afterward, this eventually became an important research insight. Although caregiving and palliative care are often dichotomized in the issue of an assisted death as if they are mutually exclusive, in reality, they exist on a continuity of care. An assisted death can constitute an act of love, in particular ways in which people do not want to abandon others to an impersonal medical system but in also not wanting loved ones to witness the suffering of a long, drawn-out death. Brian's caretaking of his mother through her long, drawn-out death is part of this continuity of care that involved later helping members of Exit die at great personal risk and potential criminal charges (the stories that I was originally hunting for). Brian even speaks about how intimate and close one must get with another person in order to ask for their help to die. At this point the interview is unraveling but Brian says, "But of course, to offer or to ask someone [for help to die] is a very big ask. Very big." While I want to hear what this means, this is also the point of the interview where I can no longer go further in eliciting those narratives.

But more than the words, other dimensions outside of the confines of the interview itself become more revealing. After our discussion finally ends, Brian brings me to meet Mick who is waiting in their living room area. I am moved by the love, pride, and tenderness visible when he brings me to meet Mick who is seated in a wheelchair in the backroom. He is impeccably groomed and dressed in English tweed, which goes to show the depths of Brian's devotion, given that these tasks must fall to him. It turns out one of his worries about having Alzheimer's and being forced to confront the prospect of having to preemptively end his life is that he understands nobody would be able to take care of Mick and he would be forced to a nursing home. As he wheels Mick out into the parlor room, and talks about how knowledgeable and intelligent he is, he also provides us with post-interview tea. He brings out an elaborate prepared display of pastries and hot tea, a very British tea-time. Not accustomed to such post-interview rituals, I feel ashamed of myself for having brought nothing, an impolite intruder who has already caused enough harm for the day. Being on a health-mandated sugar-free diet at the time, I break dietary protocol to appreciate the hospitality and eat a pastry. Brian seems disappointed when I hedge on a second, so I take the offer as well. As we eat, watching Brian help Mick and seeing the love between them teaches me as much or more than the interview itself, obsessed as I was with gathering these stories, but missing the bigger picture.

Vignette 7
The Discursive Archive

Thushara Hewage

In this vignette, I want to consider this volume's productive suggestion that we reconsider the conventional, privative, distinction between ethnography as method and anthropology as theory. Specifically, I want to think this provocation through a limited, methodological engagement with my own "field" of the Sri Lankan political, in the theoretical aftermath of anthropology's postcolonial moment. That turn provincialized anthropological objects and arguments, illuminating their colonial patrimony and how this disciplinarity mediates the ethnographic visibility of objects in the field. This revealed the inadequacy of reconceiving an anthropology purely through the resources of the discipline's own compromised archive. After post-coloniality, we are also unable to view postcolonial locations as mere empirical sites for answers to theoretical questions arising elsewhere. All these developments demand a reflexive awareness of how any specific disciplinary contribution is also intelligible as a critical intervention in a more broadly conceived field.

Here I want to gesture to how we might theorize the temporal depth of objects, problematics and arguments, which delimit conceptual spaces of ethnographic investigation in the post-colony and elsewhere. I find Foucault's well-known conceptualization of the "archive" (1972: 126–31) useful for thinking about the abiding presence of this context of inquiry. That is an archive, less in the sense of an accumulation of work, but rather as an immanent system of relations, organizing the production of fields of distinct yet implicitly related statements. Locating archives and their effects is therefore itself an interpretive activity more akin to engaged intervention than abstract mapping.

David Scott's concept of the "problem space" (1999: 3–10) helps us gain uptake on this archive's movement. A problem space describes the present state of play in a discursive tradition. It is a context of argument and therefore intervention, comprising objects and problematics animated by implicit questions, which index its participants' common political stakes. The critical value of any investigation inheres in how it calibrates its questions to the conjunctural demands of this space. If we conceive a discursive archive as a density of such problem spaces, we might then ask how objects normalized within disciplinary paradigms embed political horizons and forms of problematization specific to the contexts of their initial emergence.

I will briefly illustrate what I outline above by describing the "archival" context for my own work on Sri Lanka. This is a discursive archive of Sri Lankan political modernity, which embeds a narrative of the island's development as a once model colony and exemplary new nation-state interrupted by the problem of ethnic violence (Jeganathan 1998).[1] My interest here is the work a normalized concept of ethnicity performs within this archive, the diagnoses it enables, and the forms of thinking it forecloses.

We can isolate three key moments in the constitution of this archive. The first centers on the work of US political scientists, for whom Ceylon's recent status as a model British colony made it a promising case for the development of modern democratic institutions in the independent Third World. On their account, Ceylon's favorable social indicators, and its seemingly stable democratic and governmental infrastructure, promised a steady evolution from the measured constitutional concessions of the colonial period (Wriggins 1960). By the late 1960s and early 1970s however, Sinhala Buddhist nationalism's established political presence, and questions about the character of national integration, prompted explorations of the nature and history of Sinhala and Tamil identitarian movements. In this work, ethnicity describes pre-modern, primordial elements of identity, which distinguish Sri Lankan nationalism from secular-liberal, Western European models (Roberts 1979).

A second moment is defined by the need to understand the political mobilization of Sinhala chauvinism, contingent on the state's conflict with Tamil militancy and especially visible in the anti-Tamil pogrom of July 1983. Here, a body of left-secular scholarship anatomized ethnicity's ideological production, critiquing its overdetermining effect on class consciousness within the Sinhalese social formation (Abeysekara and Gunasinghe 1987). This social constructionist analytic of ethnicity also informs anthropological work of the period that diagnosed a village-level Sinhalese cultural receptivity to ethnic nationalism. In one such scheme, villagers' culturally generated need for politics as a sphere of plain speaking produces a need for nationalism as a remedial idiom of unity (Spencer 2000). The problem is that villagers, in cultural thrall to their own construction of politics and to nationalism, cannot discern the fact that nationalism is itself a form of politics (Spencer 2000). Within such work, it is at times difficult to distinguish culture from the effects of nationalism, ethnic identity from ethnic ideological projects of identity making.

Part of this problem arises from the inherent doubleness of ethnicity's conceptual usage. Ethnicity commonly names the neutral fact of group identity but was leveraged to explain ethnicization, which names an excess and primordialization of identity. The concept retains both referents. A third, contemporary, moment consists in reading the country's manifold recent crises—from authoritarianism to failures of reparative and retributive justice—through this normalized concept of ethnicity (as identity-ideology). All attest to the pathologically "ethnicized" and "ethnocratic" character of the Sinhala polity and the Sri Lankan state.

Notwithstanding their popular purchase, it is doubtful whether the problematics of how a model colony became a dysfunctional nation-state, or why peaceable, smiling people commit murder now frame much serious academic inquiry. I do suggest though that we think more carefully about how the concepts we use embed such considerations. Ethnicity is one such concept. Thinking through how conceptual schemes are context- and tradition-bound, theorizing their mediating effects in our ethnography, understanding ethnography as a kind of theoretical work, threatens area studies' authority and its colonial structure of knowledge production. Sri Lankan area studies is increasingly premised on the salability of field objects, held to be empirically transparent and accessible to the ethnographic labor of "teams" of native collaborators and informants, dependent on project funding from the metropole. I see no reason why the poverty of its empiricism should define the limits of conceptual thinking about Sri Lanka.

Ari Gandsman is a cultural and medical anthropologist and Associate Professor at the University of Ottawa in the School of Anthropological and Sociological Studies. His research examines the intersection of new technologies and rights-based claims. He has conducted fieldwork in Argentina, Australia, and Canada, working on long-term research projects on medical-aid-in-dying and post-dictatorship human rights movements. His work has been published in a wide range of anthropological and interdisciplinary journals including *Death Studies, Anthropologie et Sociétés, The International Journal of Transitional Justice, Anthropologica, The Journal of Latin American and Caribbean Anthropology,* and *Ethos.*

Larisa Kurtović is Assistant Professor of Anthropology at the University of Ottawa. She is a political anthropologist who conducts research on activist politics, postsocialist transformation, and the aftermath of international intervention in postwar Bosnia. Her broader interests include postsocialist studies, political aesthetics, humor, performativity, historical anthropology and ethnology, visual anthropology, infrastructure, and political economy. She is currently writing a book entitled *Future as Predicament: Political Life after Catastrophe* based on her long-term research in postwar Bosnia, as well as working on a future graphic ethnography about syndical struggle and political possibilities with anthropologist Andrew Gilbert and graphic artist Boris Stapić.

Thushara Hewage is Assistant Professor of Anthropology at the University of Ottawa. He is a historical anthropologist of South Asia with an interest in questions of democracy, nationalism, and postcolonial political theory. His work focuses the manifold crises of the Sri Lankan postcolonial state, primarily the unresolved "national question" of the political rights of minorities, and attempts to reconceive how this problem is conventionally framed and its solutions tendered.

Note

1. I thank Pradeep Jeganathan for sharing his work on this narrative with me some time ago.

References

Abeysekera, Charles, and Newton Gunasinghe, eds. 1987. *Facets of Ethnicity*. Colombo: Social Scientists Association.

Briggs, Charles. 1986. *Learning How to Ask a Sociolinguistic Appraisal of the Role of the Interview in Social Science Research*. Cambridge: Cambridge University Press.

de Boer, Marike et al. 2010. "Advance Directives for Euthanasia in Dementia: Do Law-Based Opportunities Lead to More Euthanasia?" *Health Policy* 98(2–3): 256–62.

Foucault, Michel. 1972. *The Archaeology of Knowledge*, trans. A. M. Sheridan Smith. New York: Pantheon.

———. 1978. *The History of Sexuality, Volume 1: An Introduction*. New York: Vintage Books.

Hamilton, Jennifer A. 2009. "On the Ethics of Unusable Data." In *Fieldwork is Not What It Used To Be: Learning Anthropology's Method in a Time of Transition*, ed. James D. Faubion and George E. Marcus, 73–88. Ithaca, NY: Cornell University Press.

Hammersley, Martyn, and Paul Atkinson. 1983. *Ethnography Principles in Practice*. New York: Tavistock Publications.

Ingold, Tim. 2013. *Making: Anthropology, Archaeology, Art and Architecture*. New York: Routledge.

Jackson, Bruce. *Fieldwork*. 1987. Chicago: University of Illinois Press.

Jeganathan, Pradeep. 1998. "'Violence' as an Analytical Problem: Sri Lankanist Anthropology after July '83." *Nethra* 2(4): 7–47.

Mentzel, Paul T., and Bonnie Steinbock. 2013. "Advance Directives, Dementia, and Physician-Assisted Death." *The Journal of Law, Medicine & Ethics* 41(2):484–500.

Roberts, Michael. 1979. "Problems of Collective Identity in a Multiethnic Society." In *Collective Identities, Nationalisms, and Protest in Modern Sri Lanka*, ed. Michael Roberts, 337–60. Colombo: Marga Institute.

Robbins, Joel. 2013. "Beyond the Suffering Subject: Toward an Anthropology of the Good." *Journal of the Royal Anthropological Institute* 19(3): 447–72.

Scott, David. 1999. *Refashioning Futures: Criticism after Postcoloniality*. Princeton, NJ: Princeton University Press.

Silverman, David. 2017. "How Was It for You? The Interview Society and the Irresistible Rise of the (Poorly Analyzed) Interview." *Qualitative Research* 17 (2): 144–158.

Spencer, Jonathan. 2000. *A Sinhala Village in a Time of Trouble: Politics and Change in Rural Sri Lanka*. Delhi: Oxford University Press.

Spradley, James. 1979. *The Ethnographic Interview*. Long Grove, IL: Waveland Press.

Wolcott, Harry F. 2010. *Ethnography Lessons: A Primer*. Walnut Creek, CA: Left Coast Press.

Wriggins, Howard. 1960. *Ceylon: Dilemmas of a New Nation*. Princeton, NJ: Princeton University Press.

Chapter 10

ON FAILING TO LEARN TO SHOOT A GUN

Bradley Dunseith

> Learning does not mean to act on a script received from predecessors but literally to negotiate a path through the world.
>
> —Tim Ingold, speech, 27 April 2010

Upon moving to the state of Georgia, the first thing I want to do is learn how to shoot a gun. It is the summer of 2015. In two days, Donald Trump will announce his intention to run for president. I have two months to complete my fieldwork with gun owners before going back to Canada and think learning how to shoot guns will help me understand what it means to be a gun owner. My assumption is that learning to use firearms and spending long hours in a shooting range with gun owners will constitute the gold standard of anthropological research methods: participant observation. Participant observation, I have been hearing and reading since my first year of university, is what differentiates anthropology from other social sciences, forming the bedrock of any ethnographic research. While other researchers conduct interviews, focus groups, or surveys, anthropologists go further, participating in the everyday lives of the people they study and come out with deeper insights because of it. As far as I am concerned, this somewhat vague research method is what gives anthropology its edge.

Unfortunately, my first attempt at participant observation is a total flop. Too worried imagining how gun owners are perceiving me at the shooting range, I fail to properly learn how to shoot a gun (despite significant amounts of time and money). In my experience at a shooting range, participant observation proves inadequate to prepare me to do research amid so many armed men. What failing to learn to shoot a gun does do is to force me to reimagine what kind of fieldwork I am doing. Failure allows for a new kind of ethical self-reflection, inviting me to question my relationship to my research and how my own views about gun ownership affect this relationship.

In this chapter, I use my own failure to learn the skill of shooting a gun to reflect on the skill of anthropology and what it means to learn in the field. To shoot a gun well requires practice, proper technique, concentration, physical alignment, and (among other things) a general comfort with the power of a firearm. Tim Ingold argues that human beings learn, not by simply picking up ideas and models that represent the world around us, but by exploring the world and "acquiring the skills for direct perceptual *engagement* with its constituents" (2000: 55, italics original). When describing the journey of learning and engaging in the world, Ingold uses the imagery of travelers and wayfarers exploring a physically and socially meaningful landscape, their understanding of which grows in relation to the specific skills (hunting, weaving) they craft within this environment (Ingold 2011: 12). This understanding of skill allows us to think of learning, perception, and being as creative acts that situate individuals in an unfolding, dynamic relation to the world they live in. However, coming to anthropology myself as an awkward and anxious youth, I always found the descriptions of how these individuals learned new skills seemingly too organic, too seamless, and too easy.

To consciously negotiate a path through the world is transformative, but it is simultaneously deeply frustrating and unsettling—especially when that world is rigged against you. Writing about a hotel employee he knew in Barsa, Iraq, who suddenly vanished in 2009, Hayder Al-Mohammad argues that "If, as Ingold maintains, lives are lines entangled and enmeshed in a meshwork of other lines, then we need to introduce a greater sense of instability within the meshwork" (2013: 212). This sense of instability is an important anthropological consideration because, simply put, our lives are marked by both connections and dislocations. As Al-Mohammad elaborates: "Our continuity and embeddedness in the world never comes with guarantees" (2013: 227). My failing to learn how to shoot a gun is a blow to the perceived and hoped for linear progress of doing fieldwork. With only two months at my disposal, I feel as if every day has to be used in some meaningful engagement with gun owners and so am not prepared for the dead ends and missed connections that result from this failure. Traditional research methods did not prepare me for the awkwardness and social disconnect that come from failing to learn to shoot a gun, forcing me to rely on improvisation and imagination in order to get to a more meaningful understanding of my fieldwork. As I explore my own experiences of failure during fieldwork, I argue that failure is an inevitable and important part of research that invites us to reflect upon our relationship with our research and reimagine our engagement with the people we research.

Arriving in the Field

As soon as I find an apartment to stay in, I sign up for a shooting class at the nearest range. The class is at ten o'clock in the morning, and, according to Google Maps, it will take me fifty-five minutes on foot. With a half-liter of water and a few bananas in my shoulder bag, I set out in an unfamiliar city for what feels like the official beginning of my fieldwork. Halfway to the shooting range, the clear blue sky abruptly changes into pouring rain. I take shelter first under a tree, then in an administrative building but cannot avoid getting wet. By the time I locate the shooting range in an out-of-the-way industrial parking lot, I am drenched from both rain and sweat. I have rationed my water poorly; I open the door exhausted and thirsty. The air conditioning fogs up my glasses, and the first thing I do upon entering is sit down and catch my breath.

The interior of the shooting range defies my expectations. There are two sealed shooting galleries, each with six individual lanes and a double soundproofed door. The open-concept reception resembles the lobby of a gentrified condominium, except that original gun-themed art hangs from the exposed-brick walls and a set of matching leather couches are arranged around a magazine rack where publications like *Guns and Ammunition* sit alongside the likes of *Vogue* and *GQ*. I had imagined employees working at a shooting range in the United States would be old, grumpy white men. Almost half of the diverse employees at this range are women and no one working looks over forty years old. All the employees keep a handgun holstered to their side while nearly all of the customers (except for me) bring their personal firearms to the range. A piece of paper taped to the glass counter where the rental guns are kept reads, "PLEASE DON'T FIDDLE WITH YOUR FIREARMS IN THE WAITING AREA; IT MAKES PEOPLE NERVOUS. Thank you!" I did not expect to see a semicolon in a shooting range.

The class is facilitated by a man named Grant who wears jeans and a black T-shirt. Grant guides us through basic safety rules ("Never point your gun at anyone, whether it's loaded or not"; "Only put your finger on the trigger if you're about to shoot") and gives us anatomy lessons on several disassembled firearms. Grant moves on to proper shooting postures and hand positions.

After a coffee break, we are each given a pair of large noise cancelling headphones and safety glasses then led into the shooting gallery. Every lane has a target already pinned to the wire with a participant's name written in the corner. The targets are large sheets of thick paper with the vague outline of a faceless human body. I watch as the first two participants load their 9mm rental Glocks under Grant's supervision. Even with the headphones on, their first shots startle me; my shoulders rise and tense up.

I go last and by the time it is my turn, Grant and I are the only two left in the shooting gallery. I am given a 9mm Glock, a semi-automatic rifle, and a double action revolver. A rush of nervous energy travels from my chest to my hands as soon as I pick up the Glock: it is so much heavier than it looks. I feel as if I am holding a small dumbbell out in front of me and suddenly, I can no longer recall any of the advice from the past few hours. Grant patiently walks me through each step after I overload the clip with too many bullets.

I slowly pull down the trigger of the gun with my index finger, surprised at how long it takes for the trigger to travel to its end point. I hear the small explosive discharge of gun powder first in my right ear. The moment before the bullet torpedoes out of the chamber of the gun, my hands jerk up and to the right. My shot barely brushes the outer white corner of the target.

As I place the butt of the semi-automatic rifle against my shoulder, Grant tells me to aim for the target's head. I pull down on the trigger and the smell of gun powder shoots up my nose: I smother a cough. "Now aim for the chest," Grant instructs. The rifle's butt knocks my shoulder like a light punch, and I feel as if I am standing in a room full of smoke as the strong aroma of gun powder continues up my nose. The bullet casings fly out of the rifle, sometimes they bounce against my forearm or neck. The casings are hot, and I feel the place where they touched my body for half a minute after they have hit the ground. I anticipate the recoil and clench the stock of the rifle too tightly right before firing, throwing off my studied aim at the last second. My wrist is not strong enough to steady the rifle and so it keeps jamming. My arms are exhausted from the weight of the guns and the kickback after every shot. By the time I load the revolver my hands are shaking. For my last shots, Grant moves the target just two feet away from me, instructing me to hit the figure's head, which I managed to do each time. I leave the shooting range feeling physically tired and uncomfortable. Still, I feel like I have done a decent job.

A week later, Grant agrees to meet me for dinner. Before our planned meeting, I visit the shooting range where he works twice. Each time there are new employees working the counter and supervising the shooters. Each visit follows a similar trajectory. I arrive at the shooting range dehydrated and tired from the walk, rent a new firearm for the day, and spend an hour or two by myself shooting at the target. Worn out from the new experience, I take a lot of bathroom breaks.

My dinner with Grant is my first one-on-one meeting with a gun owner. Seeing as I invited him to dinner, I decide against recording the conversation. When I described my research to Grant, he was more comfortable with the prospect of an informal conversation than with a recorded interview. Still, I memorize my interview questions hoping I can naturally weave them into the flow of our conversation.

We sit at a long wooden table at a downtown Mexican restaurant and talk about Grant's side job as a physical trainer, the difficulty of getting a job out of college, and a gun show I recently attended. "Did you see a lot of Nazi stuff?" Grant asks dismissively. ("A few booths.") Grant opines that gun shows attract neo-Nazis and people looking to buy guns with cash. As we grow comfortable in each other's presence, Grant grows critical of the average gun owner. He makes a distinction between the regulars of the shooting range who own multiple firearms and possess a deep knowledge of how guns works and the infrequent visitors who purchased a handgun because they thought it would be good to have but are largely inept when it comes to shooting. According to Grant, the vast majority of gun owners fall into the latter category—people who bought a gun on a whim but would not know what to do with it in a moment of potential danger. Grant goes on to criticize the shooting range he works at for providing insufficient defensive training to its employees. I ask Grant if anything had ever gone wrong at the shooting range. He sighs.

Just a few months earlier, a man had shot himself in the heart with one of the rented guns. Grant was working when it happened: the bullet narrowly missed Grant's head. Employees at shooting ranges are taught to identify potentially dangerous behavior in clients, the man exhibited many of the warning signs; Grant and his colleague had been debating whether to ask him to leave when he shot himself.

I ask Grant what kind of warning signs employees look for. "He showed up alone and on foot," Grant explains. "Most of our members will either drive in on their way from work or come with a friend." Grant elaborates further: the man had no existing knowledge of guns and seemed to randomly chose which handgun to rent; when he arrived, the man was sweating profusely and looked nervous; he had a foreign identification card the employees could not immediately verify; he took a lot of breaks too and would even go to the bathroom in between firing—"probably to splash water on his face and work himself up to do it," Grant ventures. The man's behavior sounds a lot like how I have been acting at the shooting range. Until I met Grant, I thought I was doing a pretty good job; now I worry that Grant's co-workers think I am a threat.

Returning to the shooting range the following week, I feel apprehensive about how Grant's coworkers may perceive me. As soon as I enter, the man at the counter says "Hello, how can I help you?" in a loud, assertive voice I imagine bank tellers use to discombobulate suspected robbers. I feel like he is sizing me up and panic. I unnecessarily begin reciting my standard spiel about being a graduate student from Canada interested in learning about gun ownership. The introductory speech is poorly delivered and received with suspicion, which further fuels my panic.

"What would you like to shoot today?" he asks.

"Nothing too intense," I say. *Why did I say that?* I think.

I worry I am fidgeting too much and, in a final attempt to win the man's confidence, ask if I can pay for the thirty-minute lesson advertised at the counter.

The man at the counter says he will teach me and introduces himself as Craig. Craig hands me the safety glasses and headphones while he carries my rental Glock and ammunition into the shooting range himself. It is the first time I have seen an employee do that. As I load the handgun, my paranoia spirals out of control. Each time I looked at Craig I smile, thinking a quick and friendly smile may help convey my harmlessness. I immediately regret every smile in fear they make me look creepy; yet I cannot stop giving Craig these weird half-smiles every time our eyes meet. I worry Craig has pinned me as dangerous. He whispers something into the slick headsets all employees wear. I am afraid that if my hand jerks the wrong way, Craig will misread my body language and shoot me in self-defense.

After my thirty-minute lesson, I buy another hundred rounds of ammunition, determined to shake the feeling of paranoia. But every round I fire seems pointless, and I feel like a dejected teenager spending all his time and money on a misguided venture to make friends that is destined to make me even more of a laughingstock.

I begin visiting the shooting range with a decreasing regularity. While my ability to handle and shoot firearms continues to improve incrementally, I feel painfully out of place. Firing guns remains physically discomforting, anxiety inducing, and generally a frustrating experience. With the exception of Grant (who finds work as a personal trainer and significantly cuts back his hours at the range), the employees I had hoped to make my interlocutors remain skeptical of me. When I ask whether they would be interested in doing an interview or speaking about gun ownership more casually over a coffee, several employees politely ask me to follow up with them over email. At a time when cell phones are ubiquitous, I think it is safe to say that giving someone an email address in response to a proposed coffee date is a fairly clear "no." Needless to say, my emails do not receive replies.

Awkwardness and Self-Reflection

My experiences at the shooting range make me feel radically out of place in the exact space I had hoped would become my principal field site. This feeling of social vertigo is emotionally exhausting, however, it also forces me to ask certain questions about myself as a researcher. What am I hoping to achieve in a room full of men wearing noise-cancelling headphones and concentratedly shooting various firearms? Strike up a chat? And why have I, a Canadian citizen with no former experience around firearms, decided to pursue fieldwork among gun owners in the American South in the first place? What am I hoping to learn and contribute through this research? These are seemingly simple questions and from the comfort of my university I had ready answers for them. I wanted to study gun ownership in the United States because gun-related violence remains so staggeringly high and because owning and carrying a gun around seemed so antithetical to my own sense of safety and well-being that I wanted to understand why it was so important for other people. Walking out of the shooting range after another unsuccessful attempt at making connections and with my own discomfort around firearms increasing, these questions no longer feel simple and the reasons for doing fieldwork among gun owners seems naïve and insincere.

When I began, I was enthusiastic about doing real fieldwork for the first time. Concerned about making a good impression, I actively present myself as agreeable and empathetic about the need to defend oneself, while internally feeling anxious about shooting and bewildered about much of what I hear. I do not take gun owners' concerns about self-defense seriously, nor am I expressing my skepticism out loud. I am falling into an age-old anthropological trap by approaching gun ownership like something exotic, practiced by a strange and distant people. It is only after my feeling of failure really sink in that I am able to interrogate this discrepancy between how I present my research and how I think about it. Once it is clear that the shooting range is not a viable field site, I meet a group of grassroots gun rights activists in Georgia and begin attending their meetings, workshops, and social gatherings. Conscious of how I failed to create connections at the shooting range, I try to cultivate a more sincere engagement with these activists by not hiding my critical questions as I take their concerns seriously.

My experience with failing to learn how to properly shoot a gun also prompts me to think about failure conceptually within the context of my research. In failing to shoot a gun competently, I feel vulnerable. My concern that more experienced shooters at the range may read my poor skill as being either intentionally or accidentally dangerous makes me fear that a false move on my part can provoke a disproportionate, and potentially lethal, response. I begin to think about being a "good" gun owner (or more readily evoked in US popular culture as "a good guy with a gun") as part tactical skill and part moral goodness brought together by a broader understanding of responsibility. This "responsibility with guns" implies both skill and intent and is used by the gun rights activists I later meet to control the political narrative of firearms in the United States.

The disproportionate attention toward individual skill obscures the inherent danger of firearms, especially those guns that can fire a series of bullets very quickly. Gun advocates argue that the vast majority of people who take the trouble to legally purchase a firearm also learn how to use them competently and responsibly. On the other hand, people they already consider to be responsible individuals are also assumed to be able to become skilled gun owners. This is not an opinion shared by Grant, who oversees countless gun owners' practice as a shooting range supervisor. Nor is it backed up by public health research that estimates only 61 percent of US gun owners have received formal training (Rowhani-Rahbar et al. 2018).

By projecting the image of a competent, safe gun operator onto the category of legal gun owners, gun rights activists turn the skill of shooting a gun into a virtue of instinctively knowing how and when a gun should be used. This circular reasoning absolves firearms themselves from any responsibility for the violence caused in shootings—blaming gun violence instead exclusively on the shooter—while propping up a dangerous dichotomy between "good" and "bad" people. In these imaginings, the individuals who use guns to cause violence are not themselves "real" gun owners but "evil" individuals who would just as likely use their bare hands to wreak havoc. This dichotomy between good and bad people becomes possible when the gun as an object is denied any agency for the violence it is designed to facilitate, and it makes it much easier for gun owners (whether citizens or police) to misread another person as a threat and act with lethal force.

In much of the anthropological writing and thinking about skill, the skilled are idealized practitioners who have perfected their craft. While there is nothing inherently wrong in thinking about skills as they should be performed, it may not accurately convey how skills are actually practiced. By projecting the image of an idealized practitioner onto a category of people who practice that skill, anthropologists risk naturalizing the implicit power relations and hierarchies that define the success of that skill. This risks presenting a narrow picture of a group of people; reverting to an older conception of culture as the culmination of the "best" of what has been thought and done by a particular people.[1] To understand the specific ways and implications of how people learn, we also have to think about how they fail.

Failure as a Safeguard against Certainty

My inability to successfully learn how to shoot a gun is a minor act of failure in terms of the great losses and losers out there. Likely, with an extra year of committed practice and with the help of effective mentors, my awkwardness with guns would gradually diminish. Importantly, too, my failure to shoot a gun is not expedited by systematic roadblocks or societal obstacles. The experience does, however, invite me to ask new questions of my fieldwork, which later formed the bedrock of my research with gun rights activists in Georgia. Failing to learn the skill of shooting a gun also reminds me that the process of learning a skill is often an uphill journey beset with false starts and dead ends. Failing puts me out of synch with the environment around me, and in this unaligned, wobbly space I see my research differently.

Failure is nothing new for anthropologists. Quite often an anthropological insight into the lives of a group of people originates from anthropologists stumbling and messing up. This failure is typically represented in ethnographic texts through the trope of a well-meaning anthropologist accidentally botching a ritual or social interaction, interpreted by their informants as a deeper transgression (Stafford 2010).[2] It is by their very failure and transgressions that researchers are often made aware of underlying moral codes, norms, beliefs, and values that may have been otherwise implicitly understated. While failing in general can act as a lighthouse in revealing how a peoples' ways of life are structured, understanding failure conceptually helps illuminate the (often shaky) ground in which social orders rest—what Judith Halberstam, in *The Queer Art of Failure*, calls the "precarious models of success" (2011: 5). Sometimes you have to un-tune yourself to the environment around you to see what is wrong with it.

To take failure seriously (that is, empathetically) in our research both as a practice and as an idea can offer new, counterintuitive ways of looking at our environments. "Under certain circumstances," Halberstam writes, "failing, losing, forgetting, unmaking, undoing, unbecoming, not knowing may in fact offer more creative, more cooperative, more surprising ways of being in the world" (2011: 2). Failure can act as an antidote to human afflictions far more detrimental to learning in the world, like certainty. As the writer Kathryn Schulz puts it, "If imagination is what enables us to conceive of and enjoy stories other than our own, and if empathy is the act of taking other people's stories seriously, certainty deadens or destroys both qualities" (2010: 165). In failing to learn to shoot a gun and kick-start my own attempts at participant observation, I can question my own presumptions about gun owners in a meaningful way. My failure to connect with gun owners through traditional anthropological methods leads me to reimagine my relationship to my research and ask more productive questions. To paraphrase Hayder Al-Mohammad, it is in failure that we may better attune ourselves to the instability inherent in the meshwork of our entangled lives.

I do not mean to romanticize the act of failure: often the imaginative takeaways that come with not succeeding are not worth the number of doors that "failure" closes. Drawing on my own experiences in fieldwork, I want to emphasize the fundamental quality of failure, and all the more negative aspects that come with it, to doing fieldwork. To revisit the opening quotation of this article, if we understand the process of learning as a somewhat treacherous path through life, we can think more critically about the political environments individuals navigate and how we/they imagine alternatives. Thinking about failure—in how people fail and how we fail trying to understand their failures—will broaden our understanding about the environments people inhabit and what it means to inhabit them in the first place.

Bradley Dunseith is a doctoral student at the University of Toronto. He received his Master's in Anthropology from the University of Ottawa.

Notes

Epigraph: The quotation is taken from a speech Tim Ingold gave at the London School of Economics on 27 April 2010 entitled, "To Learn is to Improvise a Movement along a Way of Life." The speech itself was available at the time of publication at https://www.youtube.com/watch?v=lDaaPaK-N5o.

1. Typically attributed to Matthew Arnold's *Culture and Anarchy* ([1869] 1932) which became the initial basis for distinguishing between "high" and "low" culture.
2. In other cases, the anthropologist learns later that being made to feel as if they have failed at an important task does not actually constitute failure, but is part of a community dynamic. In one classic example, Richard B. Lee gifts a cow to the Ju/ hoansi people and is then thoroughly criticized by them for the perceived shortcomings of the animal. After feeling anguish at his failed attempt to give his informants a worthy gift, Lee interprets the incident as a practice meant to maintain an egalitarian spirit within the community. "Though painful," Lee writes, "the experience gave me a deeper insight into their core system of meaning" (2011: 58).

References

Al-Mohammad, Hayder. 2013. "Ravelling/Unravelling: Being-in-the-World and Falling-out-of-the-World." In *Biosocial Becomings: Integrating Social and Biological Anthropology*, ed. Tim Ingold and Gisli Palsson, 211–28. Cambridge: Cambridge University Press.

Arnold, Matthew. [1869] 1932. *Culture and Anarchy*. London: Cambridge University Press.

Halberstam, Judith. 2011. *The Queer Art of Failure*. Durham, NC: Duke University Press.

Ingold, Tim. 2000. *The Perception of the Environment: Essays in Livelihood, Dwelling, and Skill*. London: Routledge.

———. 2011. *Being Alive: Essays on Movement, Knowledge, and Description*. New York: Routledge.

Lee, Richard B. 2011. *The Dobe Ju/'hoansi*. 4th ed. Belmont: Wadsworth.

Rowhani-Rahbar, Ali, Vivian Lyons, Joseph Simonetti, Deborah Azrael, and Mathew Miller. 2018. "Formal Firearm Training among Adults in the USA: Results of a National Survey." *Injury Prevention* 24:161–65.

Schulz, Kathryn. 2010. *Being Wrong: Adventures in the Margin of Error*. New York: HarperCollins Publishers.

Stafford, Charles. 2010. "The Punishment of Ethical Behaviour." In *Ordinary Ethics: Anthropology, Language, and Action*, ed. Michael Lambek, 187–206. New York: Fordham University Press.

Chapter 11

WONDERING WINDS

ALPINE FIRE LOOKOUTS IN THE CANADIAN ROCKY MOUNTAINS

Kristen Anne Walsh

A raw frontal wind pricked my cheeks and ruffled my hair. It was difficult to hear what the lookout observer was relaying as the wind buffeted the cabin's exterior walls and whistled through the radio tower. Was the recorder able to pick up the lookout observer's words? It certainly must be capturing the howling wind. *Perhaps this is more important*, I thought at the time. My eyes watered as the wind sneakily crept in around the edges of my sunglasses. I was suddenly feeling chilled to the bone. Looking down, goose bumps formed on my bare forearms as a telltale sign. I glanced sideways at the lookout observer; in his down vest, long sleeves, and tuque, he was prepared for these conditions—always.

Along the front ranges of the Alberta Rocky Mountains, Canada, are located a web of alpine fire lookouts that offer far-reaching views into surrounding areas—and sky! Of the 127 staffed fire lookouts in Alberta, only twenty-three consist of cabins perched atop mountains, known as alpine fire lookouts.[1] I spent the summer learning from sixteen lookout observers who work at these sites, most of whom had been doing the job for over three decades. It is a way of life attuned to winds that deeply infuse my own life as well as this written account.

Lookout observers live onsite for four to six months of the year in a simple one or two story cabin. This is rugged, remote living: cabins are exposed to the weather, supplies are delivered every three weeks, and rainwater is collected for washing. The lookout observer's primary role is to spot early smoke plumes that may signal the start of a wildfire by scanning a 25 mile radius area around their lookout with the naked eye. Lookout observers are particularly attentive to winds, given their critical implication in wildfires. The frequency of their scanning depends on wildfire danger levels and visibility (whether or not they can see out, and how far, depends on weather conditions). In this sense, the timing of their daily tasks is intimately bound up in how the wind is moving weather in or out—to the extent that many lookout observers described the weather to be their "boss" (Walsh 2016) and, as I will show in this chapter, their teacher.

The job requires excellent eyesight and a good sense of depth perception and color nuance in order to distinguish a smoke plume from ground fog, road dust, or pollen clouds that may appear as a false smoke plume or a "spook" (Walsh et al. 2018). Lookout observers use an array of instruments to make twice daily weather observations: thermometers to measure daily maximum and minimum temperatures, as well as current temperatures and relative humidity; an anemometer to measure wind speed and a windsock to measure its cardinal direction. Although collecting this weather data twice daily cultivates meteorological knowledge, their engagement with weather goes much deeper. They feel the weather through their skin and receptive vision to track lightning storms, monitor the sky, and note changes in visibility from isolated and exposed mountain tops where the air is rarely still and the conditions notoriously fast-changing. Daily living necessitates contending with a variety of winds, from gentle breezes to gales to hurricane force winds. These movements of air make themselves known differently and require a different level of engagement: hence, *winds* plural.

In my research, I explored how wind is encountered, attended to, and instills a sense of wonder among alpine fire lookout observers. In this chapter I focus on how this implied adjusting to winds and how adjusting lends to taking care amid air in motion.

Moving through Mountains

I hiked to all my interviews. The fieldwork consisted of vertical, rocky, terrain steeped in wildflowers, wildlife, and fickle mountain weather.

In the summer of 2015, I spent seven weeks hiking to lookouts; some I returned to several times, and others I lived at for a few weeks

Figure 11.1. Lookout in the distance atop an exposed mountain ridge, and popular hiking destination. Photo courtesy of Mary Sanseverino, The Mountain Legacy Project, University of Victoria.

at the end of the field season. Long hikes (10–12 miles round trip) afforded a wonderful in-between time for reflection and growing curiosity about the research at hand. The only scheduling challenges that my hiking companion, Mary, and I had to contend with were weather and wildlife-related: we were chased by thunderstorms, turned back by a grizzly bear, slowed by deep snow and slippery rock terrain. These weather and wildlife encounters required us to be agile in how we found our way to the lookout: weather does not work a traditional office schedule. As Tim Ingold (2010) aptly summarizes: weather cannot be contained. When lightning suddenly emerged, we hiked back to the car leaving our tripod and other gear containing lightning attractant metal; when fog and low-lying clouds set in, we meandered cautiously over slippery rock scree; with the sudden grizzly encounter, we turned up the volume on our singing, and upon observing its effectiveness, continued to sing throughout the summer in wildlife corridors (the off-chance of another encounter lurking in our imaginations). Yet sometimes being agile does not mean speeding or speaking up, but rather slowing down and listening. Jan Masschelein defines participant observation as a practice of waiting on things to emerge (2010: 40). One day at a lookout, we spent all day chatting and waiting for winds to blow in and lift the fog. We remained inside a cloud the whole day, surrounded in thick, grey mist. We could not see more than twenty yards so the lookout observer described the dense, tree-covered foothills that one day may lead to a mega fire, the scars from a wildfire burn from the 1930s, and the valley that was once maintained as an open landscape through Indigenous burning practices. I imagined beyond the fog, waiting for winds to unveil that which (at that moment) was unseeable.

Walking the Catwalk

The walls of a lookout cabin—or the second-story cupola observation space—are covered in windows so the lookout observer can see all the way around from inside. Yet all seasoned lookout observers know the best view is from outside the cabin, where one can escape the glare of windows that quickly strain the eyes, much like the prolonged use of binoculars. This ideal viewing place is called the "catwalk," an exterior deck that surrounds the lookout cabin. Walking the catwalk, peripheral vision kicks in. Not only are lookout observers scanning the view in front of them, they are also glancing sideways out of the corners of their eyes. Many lookout observers describe spotting a plume of smoke in such a way: when they glance a movement, color, or something "not looking or feeling right" out of the corner of their eye.[2] They also described the importance of "opening up" to the surrounding land and sky through listening and feeling—the kind of vision that arises when we stop, look, and listen—a "receptive vision" (Ingold 2000: 243). In order to heighten their ability to look for wildfire, lookout observers thus actively learn from sensing. The same can be said for learning with and from winds.

We would walk the catwalk together, pausing and taking in the weather, and remarking on the shape and movement of clouds in the sky and birds in the air. "Do you see any lenticular clouds, indicating high winds?" one lookout observer asked, before passing his afternoon weather observation over the radio. "And how about our visibility today—how many kilometers can you see clearly enough to spot a smoke [plume]?" "Can you feel the humidity on your skin—what is our relative humidity at?" Quizzing me on weather became a playful game, and word quickly got around the lookout community not to pass up the opportunity to quiz the researcher. It also further reinforced how much lookout observers use their bodies to sense the weather. I remember toward the end of my fieldwork one lookout observer said he was impressed with all I had learned and that I had a "good eye"—that is, the receptive vision required to do the job. He asked me to keep an eye on the surrounding area while he took a nap. "Just wake me up if you see a smoke [plume]," he explained. I agreed. I still remember the anxiety rising in my throat, a tightness in my chest, and a subtle pulsing behind the eyes as I took watch for twenty minutes or so, scanning the area for potential smoke plumes. The lookout observer was not really napping—he was giving me a sense of what it feels like to be responsible for an area over 3000 square miles, and the awareness of how a small smoke plume could quickly grow into a big wildfire if left undetected.

Wondering Winds

Lookout observers attune to the wind primarily through feeling and hearing, fostering relations akin to those we have with people, plants, and animals. Winds touch on practical implications of living on a mountaintop, such as whether or not one can open a door; whether the walk to the outhouse is feasible; whether helicopters can fly in with groceries and drinking water; whether a lookout observer can fall asleep in spite of all of the noise (Walsh 2016). Lookout observers learn to discern different kinds of winds: sustained or gusty; dry or humid; their force, direction, and what kind of precipitation (rain, hail, snow, fog) or air particles (haze, pollen, smoke, dust) they carry with them. For example, lookout observers can discern a dry wind from a humid one by feeling the dryness or moisture on their skin and in their eyes, or in the time it takes to dry their garments outside on the clothesline.

As the winds lookout observers described were not always present when I was there for the interview, I was left to imagine what they were like. On one occasion the cabin windows lay still as the lookout observer described the windows bouncing in winds above 50 miles per hour. How far out did they bounce, I wondered? Often and throughout my fieldwork, I was left wondering about winds that I missed. These experiences also gave me insight into how lookout observers might think and feel with winds both during their presence and absence. It struck me that wondering with winds was also a large part of their experience on the lookout—a way of sensing or knowing them—as if stretching out and into the sky.

Wonder has been subject to much philosophical inquiry and debate about how best to define it. Maxine Sheets-Johnstone describes wonder as a spontaneous state of slowness and reflection that is variably weighed by fear and longing (1999: 336). Alexsandra Kunce equates wonder with astonishment and suggests that in it we find "deeper probing" that results from listening and looking in a different way, with a willingness to renounce a formerly held position or "uproot oneself" (2012: 124). As mentioned above, lookout observers are continuously learning from the wind, and contemplating—or probing deeply—its implication in wildfire processes and life at the lookout site. A "spook," or false smoke plume, may evoke wonder about whether or not what is moving in the air is indeed a plume of smoke or something else. One lookout observer, for example, spent the good part of a day watching condensation evaporate off a rock bluff and

Figure 11.2. View from the catwalk: a frontal system moves through. Lenticular clouds and taut windsock announce strong winds. Photo by Kristen Anne Walsh.

slowly drift in the wind, wondering whether or not it was a plume of smoke. While these hours were described by her as "torturous" as an enhanced awareness needed to be maintained, the observation began in wonder, open to the possibility that what is being seen is smoke or something else. Similarly, when caught up in the drone of strong winds for two straight days, lookout observers describe different kinds of wondering: some may wonder if they will have enough food to last the coming days if the helicopter cannot land, others consider how quickly a wildfire will ignite and spread; some consider whether the pilot light will blow out in their propane fridge, or if any hikers will make it up to the lookout.

Wonder encompasses a variety of lookout observers' feelings about different winds and weather more broadly; the complexity of fear and awe due to the way continuous dry winds fan a fire and cause it to spread rapidly; the shock of a sudden upslope gust of wind, but amazement at its capacity to blow them over. Clouds of pine beetles blowing through the sky, or the "fart-like" sound produced when the roof of the utility shed ripped off, were described with both fear and astonishment. Perhaps, most of all, lookout observers were constantly marveling at the beauty of the lookout surroundings. Some were in awe at the perpetually changing view as light moved on mountains; others, at the color of sunrises and sunsets, or as a gentle wind passed through treetops and made swooshing sounds resembling ocean waves. Sources of beauty might be far away or close by: fog "dancing" in the wind over mountain ridges or wildflowers wobbling just inches off the ground and releasing scents into the air.

Between Mountains and Manuscript: Fleeting Tones, Listening, and Mapping

In one of the first conversations that I had with a lookout observer he mentioned listening for different tones on the forestry radio when lookout observers relay their morning and afternoon weather observations. Other lookout observers said they would similarly listen to the tone of each other's voices. It became apparent that as lookout observers described the speeds and intensities of frontal passages and storm winds, or the lulls of a gentle breeze cooling a warm summer's day, they were expressing and could hear from each other, tonalities of the weather. Months later, their remarks would draw my attention to tonality when listening to interview recordings. Tonality mattered to what lookout observers talked about and how they went about reporting (Walsh 2016: 25). Tonality and the inability to aptly capture its fleeting resonance—like a sudden gust of wind—would come up over and over again as I tried to transcribe the interviews. This would eventually influence why I opted out of transcribing verbatim in favor of listening multiple times to the same interviews. I wanted to hear how Lookout observers' phonetically sounded out the wind reaching 75 miles per hours and went *zzzz brrzzzzzzzz.* I was also curious about the pauses, the laughter, and the feeling behind what lookout observers were saying. In short, I wished to engage with the fullness of their words, as well as the fullness of the sounds and spaces between, the rise and fall of each human and nonhuman.

One of the ways that I did that was through a process called "ambulant listening" (Walsh 2016: 35–40): an approach that involves immersing myself in interview recordings rather than transcribing them verbatim. An emerging trend in some social sciences, and in anthropology in particular, researchers are looking for alternatives to transcribing interviews verbatim. Some researchers argue that transcripts "lack certain attributes which are characteristic of oral language production (e.g., intonation, emphasis, voice volume, changes in voice patterns and body language) that lend life to words and add meaning" (Mero-Jaffe 2011: 232). Deep listening, an attentive form of listening that requires that one be fully present in the moment (Barbezat and Bush 2014) allowed me to engage with the fullness of my recordings.

I listened to my interviews as I walked outdoors in order to enliven my research process and the lookout observers' voices. I also wanted to continue "mingling in the weather-world" (Ingold 2008: 17) as a way to stay fully immersed in my research. As I listened and walked, I would sometimes see, hear, or feel phenomena that lookout observers described in their interviews. For example, I noticed how it was very windy on a ridge top, and then ten feet below I could "hide out" from the wind, just as lookout observers described in order to escape the wind's chill and the intense noises it created. I felt the lightness of being "carried" upslope by a strong wind at my back, as one lookout observer described with great amusement. I noticed trees bent over by the sheer speed of the wind on windward slopes, as described and observed at the lookout. I continued to attend to the subject of winds as I was immersed in them. My curiosity grew. Instead of creating distance between the field and the manuscript I would eventually write, I continued to learn and apply what I was learning while I listened. This prolonged mingling would permeate my thoughts and eventually my writing.

Figure 11.3. Mind maps laid out on the living room floor. Photo by Kristen Anne Walsh.

I further engaged in mind mapping in order to visually see the content of ideas, how they flow, fit, stick out from one another, and importantly, how examples of these ideas—most often in the form of a story—illuminated lookout observers' explanations. This moved along my learning and writing. Mind maps were made based on how I listened and pieced together pathways of inquiry and understanding.

A mind map is a diagram used to visually organize information in relation to a larger topic while linking smaller connecting ideas (Hopper 2010:164). Mind maps were drawn out by hand on large sheets of 18 x 24 inch newsprint. I engaged in two rounds of mind mapping (see Walsh 2016: 40–44). I worked with color in order to group together and make distinctions between ideas and concepts. Themes that I would eventually write about most emerged when different colors would overlap: how sounds indicated certain winds, how wind is felt as pressure, how the wind is bound up in weather and views and evokes a wide range of moods and sensations depending on the circumstances.

As I began to write my thesis, I wrote almost exclusively from these mind maps. Listening and mind mapping were a large part of "writing" for me. They helped me decide what to include and what to omit. I taped all sixteen mind maps to the walls of my apartment, at different heights that were accessible either from standing or seated on the floor. Knowing from walking and listening that ideas flow well when

I am moving, I continued to weave movement into my research process. The maps covered my apartment walls for weeks. Throughout, I reflected on the ways that research permeates our lives in interesting ways when we invite it in.

On Taking Care

"The most important element to doing the job is knowing how to take care of yourself," one lookout observer explained. The words "take care," spoken with a soft, yet significant emphasis sent chills up and down my spine. I could still remember the twinkle in the lookout observer's eye, and I stopped in my tracks. I heard this on a few other occasions. Lookout observers described how weathering the mountain winds boiled down to knowing how to take care of yourself while in them. Taking care in winds meant preparing for them as best one could: storing away loose or light items (such as pails and chairs) or tying and weighing down others (such as rain barrels and wheelbarrows). Perhaps, most significantly, it meant accepting the winds as they were and learning ways to either manage or alter one's mood when required. For instance, one lookout observer indicated that it is important to know when to "change channels": sometimes taking

Figure 11.4. View from one alpine lookout, following a summer storm. Mountains are obscured in the distance by storm activity in the area. Photo by Kristen Anne Walsh.

care meant turning up the volume on the radio to drown out the rattling and howling sounds or finding a way to joke about the winds with a neighboring lookout observer.

Taking care in winds, and the mountain weather it subsequently puts in motion, seeped into research practices. I continuously sought ways to take care throughout the research process. For me, that meant first and foremost upholding good relationships with the lookout observers from whom I had learned so much. It also meant keeping things fun and pleasant as I researched my thesis topic: walking and listening in beautiful places, finding humor in the weather, taking photographs, and working with color. In a sense, taking care in research was living it fully and wholeheartedly and taking time to tinker (Mol et al. 2010) with curious thoughts.

In 2017, I returned to the Rocky Mountains to try the lookout job for a season. Although I had written and defended my thesis, the research still pulsed within and moved me to try doing it myself as a job. Learning from lookout observers opened my eyes to the sky in a whole new way: it broadened as my attention to it grew. Everywhere, I was attuned to winds and how they are bound up in larger weather processes. Throughout the season, awareness and wonder of winds, and how to take care in them, followed me: when carried upslope with gusts at my back, as cabin walls were buffeted in the first big storm, as I wore a down parka in July to protect myself from the wind's chill. I remain in wonder.

Kristen Anne Walsh graduated with a Master's in Environmental Studies at the University of Victoria in 2016. She is currently working as an environmental anthropologist in different capacities and as a research associate with the Mountain Legacy Project. Wind and fire lookouts continue to be an important part of her life.

Notes

1. Lookout towers between 20 and 120 feet tall mounted with a small observation space (known as a cupola) provide the necessary height for similar vantage points.
2. Skillful looking has been taken up in many other studies, notably Christina Grasseni (2004) with cattle breeders and Greg Downey (2007) with Brazilian martial arts. For more, see Walsh (2016: 19–20, 47–57). For an interesting account of the relationship between the eye and traveling in the mountains, see Katrin Lund (2005).

References

Barbezat, Daniel P., and Mirami Bush. 2014. *Contemplative Practices in Higher Education: Powerful Practices to Transform Teaching and Learning*. San Francisco: Wiley & Sons.

Downey, Greg. 2007. "Seeing with a 'Sideways Glance': Visuomotor 'Knowing' and the Plasticity of Perception." In *Ways of Knowing: New Approaches in the Anthropology of Experience and Learning*, ed. Mark Harris, 222–41. Oxford: Berghahn.

Grasseni, Christina. 2004. "Skilled Vision: An Apprenticeship in Breeding Aesthetics." *Social Anthropology* 12(1): 41–55.

Hopper, Carolyn H. 2010. *Practicing College Learning Strategies* (6th ed.). Boston, MA: Wadsworth.

Ingold, Tim. 2010. "Footprints through the Weather-World: Walking, Breathing, Knowing." *Journal of the Royal Anthropological institute* 16(1): S121–S139.

———. 2008. "Earth, Sky, Wind and Weather." In *Wind, Life, Health: Anthropological and Historical Perspectives*, ed. Elisabeth Hsu & Chris Low, 17–35. London: Blackwell.

———. 2000. *The Perception of the Environment: Essays in Livelihood, Dwelling and Skill*. London: Routledge.

Kunce, Alexandra. 2012. "Wonder and Anthropology." *The International Journal of Humanities*, 9: 123–36.

Lund, Katrin. 2005. "Seeing in Motion and the Touching Eye," *Etnofoor* 18(1): 27–42.

Masschelein, Jan. 2010. "E-Ducating the Gaze: The Idea of Poor Pedagogy." *Ethics and Education* 5(1): 43–53.

Mero-Jaffe, Irit. 2011. "Is That What I Said? Interview Transcript Approval by Participants: An Aspect of Ethics in Qualitative Research." *International Journal of Qualitative Methods* 10(3): 231–47.

Mol, Annemarie, Ingunn Moser, and Jeannette Pols, eds. 2010. *Care in Practice: On Tinkering in Homes, Clinics and Farms*. New York: Columbia University Press.

Sheets-Johnstone, Maxine. 1999. *The Primacy of Movement*. Philadelphia, PA: John Benjamins.

Walsh, Kristen Anne. 2016. "Blowin' in the Wind: Encountering Wind at Fire Lookouts in the Canadian Rocky Mountains." M.A. thesis. Victoria, Canada: University of Victoria.

Walsh, Kristen Anne, Eric Higgs, and Mary Sanseverino. 2018. "Weather Awareness: On the Lookout for Wildfire in the Canadian Rocky Mountains." *Mountain Research and Development* 37(4): 494–501.

Chapter 12

ETHNOGRAPHY AS BEWITCHMENT

A LITERARY STUDY OF JEANNE FAVRET-SAADA'S *DEADLY WORDS*

Bernhard Leistle

Writing Ethnography "After Method"

When teaching ethnographic writing, mostly in my capacity as academic supervisor or instructor of thesis writing seminars, I regularly confront a dilemma. On the one hand, I am convinced that there is a literary quality to ethnographic writing, as was conclusively shown by the so-called literary turn of the discipline in the 1980s (see, for example, Clifford and Marcus 1986; Marcus and Cushman 1982) and the many studies in its aftermath. On the other hand, I feel at a loss when it comes to translating the aesthetic qualities of ethnographies into a set of conventions, recipes and methods of writing. I would like to tell my students: experiment with form, narrative structure, and authorial presence; write in dialogical, polyphonic, and heteroglossic styles; try to find creative ways in which the reality of the Other can be preserved, rather than appropriated in the process of linguistic and cultural translation. I believe in the contribution of literature to fulfill what I see as the goal of anthropology: to say something about human beings that is not enclosed in any cultural world, using, however, an idiom that is necessarily culturally particular.

But when it comes to advising my students, my instructions are of a much more modest nature: describe concretely, rather than analyze abstractly, the cultural world or social scene you studied, as those living in this world experience it ("grasp the native's point of view");

provide as much ethnographic detail as possible to back up your interpretation of the cultural world ("perform a thick description"); start your chapters and weave them around narrative accounts of concrete events ("use ethnographic vignettes"); consider and make thematic your own "positionality," the personal, social, and cultural perspective from which you experience other people's experiences ("be reflexive"); imagine as your reader someone who is not necessarily a specialist, but an educated, interested person ("write comprehensively"), and so on.

I could easily extend the list and I am not saying that this is bad advice. Nor do I intend to deny that there are others who are better at identifying the rules and methods by which "good" ethnographies are written.[1] What I am saying is that while the writing advice I give to my students socializes them into the conventions of anthropology, the kind of writing I am drawn to and find more valuable anthropologically is unconventional. Or to put it in the words of the present book, there are aspects of writing ethnographies that are "after method" in the sense that they point to a realm beyond the conventional and regular.

On the following pages, I will show how a particular ethnography, Jeanne Favret-Saada's *Deadly Words: Witchcraft in the Bocage* transcends the usual conventions of ethnographic writing. I will argue that rather than by following a set of writing methods, this ethnography produces an affective hold on its readers through a unique union of content and form. The inextricable interweaving between what a text communicates informatively and how it communicates performatively is established in a realm beyond the reach of methods. The literary dimension of ethnography is situated in this realm, not only that of *Deadly Words*, but of ethnographic writing in general.

Reading *Deadly Words*

When recently reading *Deadly Words*, Jeanne Favret-Saada's ethnography of witchcraft in modern France,[2] I experienced something that surprised me: I was feeling affected by what I read. Favret-Saada's account of the aggression and symbolic violence among French peasants, how they, when confronted with a series of inexplicable misfortunes,[3] suspected their neighbors of draining their health and wealth, their "force," from them, strangely resonated with me. Especially the behavior required of the bewitched after they have identified their witch with the help of a ritual expert, the "unwitcher," gave me pause to think. The bewitched are to suspend all communication with the alleged witch, or, if this is not possible, act in what could be called a "passive-aggressive" manner: stare back at the witch when he or she looks at one, repeat the last words the witch said, if one is addressed, and so on. These behaviors reminded me of others I have encountered in the upper middle-class neighborhood of the Canadian city in which I live: sometimes people with whom I had had friendly conversations on previous occasions suddenly pretended to not recognize me (or so it seemed to me at least) when we met in the street. It also reminded me of certain situations when I myself had denied people reciprocity because I had felt that they had transgressed against me or members of my family. Reading *Deadly Words* made me aware of the "irrationality" of others, as well as my own, behavior and made me think about certain aspects of my social life in terms of witchcraft.

Perhaps I should not have been surprised by this response. Favret-Saada's book is one of those ethnographies referred to as "classics"; published in French in 1977 and in English in 1980, it was one of the first that performed a "reflective turn" toward the relationships between ethnographers and the people they encounter in the "field." During my studies in Germany in the 1990s, the book had been mentioned to me frequently, but now it seems that its glory has faded a little.[4] Be that as it may, when reading one of the "classics," one should perhaps expect that it makes an impression. On the other hand, in my experience this is not always the case, at least not on the affective level on which I responded to *Deadly Words*. For example, I had no such response when, also recently, rereading Edward Evan Evans-Pritchard's *Witchcraft, Oracle and Magic among the Azande* (1937). Surely, like most people, I admired the masterful way Evans-Pritchard made the Azande appear as magical rationalists, but my fascination remained on an intellectual level; it did not "get to me" personally. This contrast in reading experience also rules out that the topic shared by both books plays a decisive role: the effect of *Deadly Words* cannot be explained simply by the inherent uncanniness of witchcraft and magic.

While I do not want to exclude categorically the possibility that I find it easier to identify with French peasants of the 1960s than with the Azande of the 1920s, I am strongly convinced that the reason for the impact I felt when reading *Deadly Words* did not come from what was presented, but how it was presented. To state the truism explicitly: the book affects the reader because of the way it is written.

When we call an ethnography well-written, we usually mean that it contains detailed accounts of events and the persons involved in them, descriptions of behaviors and institutions that are "thick" in the sense that they allow us to decipher the meanings the described events hold for those involved in them. We also expect that this ethnographic information and its interpretation will be laid out for us in a comprehensive manner and in an accessible, perhaps even elegant style. In other words, we expect that good ethnographic writing conforms to the conventions I have addressed at the beginning of this essay.

At this point, the true marvel of *Deadly Words* begins to take shape: it contains very little of this kind of "good" ethnographic writing. In fact, it is a rather dense, difficult, at times even dry read. To be sure,it does contain a great mass of fascinating details, but these are never presented in a sequence that would create a pleasant narrative flow. Instead, the reader is suddenly confronted with condensed statements about persons or events without having the necessary context to decipher them; only gradually Favret-Saada provides this contextual information, creating a temporal experience that can be described as an "unpacking" or "unfolding" of multiple layers, rather than as linear progress. A series of cross-references within the book alerts the reader to this complex structure, but does not really provide much clarification: the perspectives from which the same event is presented at various points in the book are so divergent that it is hard for the reader to make the connection between them. A number of times, Favret-Saada even makes references beyond the realm of the book, mentioning a "second volume" or "future volumes" in which a certain topic will be treated in detail.[5] In hindsight, one can say today that these planned works either did not materialize or dealt with other matters than those projected in *Deadly Words*.[6] Instead of an author who controls the narrative and guides the reader through it step by step, the reader is faced with an unwieldy text in constant danger of spiraling out of control. This impression of "authorlessness" is strengthened by Favret-Saada's periodic admissions of lack of knowledge and resulting uncertainty about her interpretations; in such cases, she typically makes use of logical inferences, giving her account a strangely abstract, almost structuralist appearance.

I will say more about these stylistic characteristics in the next section. For now this should suffice to make understandable my astonishment that I felt affected by a text that goes to such length to create difficulties for its readers.[7] Favret-Saada's style of presentation goes against much we find in handbooks on writing, whether ethnographic or other.

One particular element needs specific mention, as it perplexed me more than any other: the way in which Favret-Saada presented her own involvement in witchcraft culture, or, as she puts it, witchcraft discourse. On the one hand, her whole ethnography and, it must be added, its nimbus in the discipline, is based on her conviction that the ethnographer cannot describe witchcraft practices from an outsider position, as an object of ethnographic knowledge. Treating witchcraft in the Bocage, which is first and foremost a form of speech, in terms of neutral information is simply inconceivable for the people practicing it. For them, the semantic meaning of words is absolutely subordinated to the performative power words possess in concrete situations. The ethnographer can, therefore, not interview people on the topic of spells, because the transmission of such knowledge would always mean a transference of magical power. From the perspective of the "native," the Bocage peasant involved in witchcraft, an ethnographer wishing to talk about spells does one of two things: either she foolishly exposes herself to the evil doings of witches or she intentionally tries to accumulate magical force for herself, to act either as an unwitcher or a witch. In this situation, as Favret-Saada notes, ethnographic distance is not an option: "In short, there is no neutral position with spoken words: in witchcraft, words wage war. Anyone talking about it is a belligerent, the ethnographer like everyone else. There is no room for uninvolved observers" (1980: 10).

In order to understand, what witchcraft is, one has to "be caught," as the peasants in the Bocage put it, become involved in the discourse of witchcraft as a participant. And, according to *Deadly Words*, Favret-Saada became involved: in the introduction, she refers to her research in the Bocage as a "memorable adventure that has marked me for my whole subsequent life" (1980: 22); she discloses her relationship to her unwitcher, Madame Flora, and calls it complicated: "For more than two years, I subjected the events of my personal life to the interpretations of this unwitcher" (1980: 18). Interspersed throughout the book, the reader finds allusions to car accidents, back pains, states of anxiety, but Favret-Saada's disclosures remain vague. She gives no detailed, explicit account of the actual events that made her believe, however temporarily and ambiguously, she was bewitched (1980: 125). It is true, that, following her style of "unpacking" dense meaning, she gradually provides more information about the all-important relationship to her unwitcher[8] but nothing that would satisfy the curiosity kindled by reading that her research was an adventure that marked her for her whole life.

It is, of course, possible to regard this allusive style as a rhetorical trick to generate interest in the reader, but the overall structure of the text quite excludes this kind of interpretation. I believe, rather, that Favret-Saada's stylistic reluctance in *Deadly Words* to provide direct, empirical, narrative evidence through what she says explicitly is in formal correspondence with what she claims conceptually regarding witchcraft in the Bocage: that it can only be "understood," if at all, from a position within the discourse. It follows from this insight that an ethnographic account of Bocage witchcraft must not treat witchcraft as an object of discourse and, hence, knowledge. Just like the ethnographer needed to take part in witchcraft herself, so the text must recreate this involvement and thus ensnare the reader in its texture. *Deadly Words* attempts to catch its readers to produce an experience of what it means to be caught. The only way to write about witchcraft "authentically" is to write a text that bewitches. I will try to show in the remainder of this chapter, how the stylistic characteristics of this complex text contribute to this overall objective. What will emerge in the process of investigation is an interweaving of form and content that is irreducibly bound to a specific project of ethnographic research and writing; *Deadly Words* is in this sense not only "after methods" itself, but also representative of a dimension of ethnography that eludes the grasp of method.

Favret-Saada is quite aware of the nexus between ethnographic text and experience addressed here. In what I regard as one of the central passages of the book, she refers to her ethnography as a "second catching":

> *Nothing is said about witchcraft which is not closely governed by the situation of utterance.* What is important, then, is less to decode what is said than to understand who is speaking and to whom. In the field, the ethnographer is himself involved in this speech process and is just one speaker among others. If he then chooses to write a scientific report on spells, it can only be done by always going back over this situation of utterance and the way he was "caught" in it; this interchange between having been "caught" and "catching" things (from a theoretical viewpoint) is precisely what must be pondered.
>
> *I wish to suggest that what is needed is a "second catching" and not a "getting uncaught"—leaving it to the rest of this book to establish this necessity. I suggest that this marks unequivocally the distance that separates me from both classical anthropology and post-structuralist thinking in France in their shared ideal of "a totally a-topical theorizing subject."* (1980: 14; italics in original)

The Intertwining of Form and Content

I am arguing that the literary form of *Deadly Words*, its style, authorial position, and composition, is determined by the content it communicates; or, perhaps better, that form and content are aspects of one phenomenon, the text. The content calls for a form in which it seeks to be expressed, and, conversely, the form is the way the content finds expression. None precedes the other, they are both sides of one and the same process. We are accustomed to think about artistic creation in terms of a marriage of form and content, less so about "science." Clifford Geertz, however, has pointed out that in ethnography, as in poetry and other arts, content and form, or as he put it, the "art of understanding" and the "art of presentation," are inseparably intertwined with each other (1988: 46n18). *Deadly Words* provides an interesting test case for exploring the aesthetic-artistic dimensions of ethnographic writing, because it holds on, as we shall see, to ideals broadly scientific, while at the same time undermining the conventional understanding of science as "neutral objectivity."

A central element of literary form is what Geertz refers to as "signature," the "establishment of an authorial presence within a text" (Geertz 1988: 10). The reader of *Deadly Words*, who has heard rumors about Favret-Saada's "personal involvement" with witchcraft, is led to expect the presence of the author/narrator as a reflective, personal subject. In this respect, the text surprises from the beginning with its very first sentence: "Take an ethnographer: she has chosen to investigate witchcraft in the Bocage of Western France" (Favret-Saada 1980: 3). This sets the tone: while we expect what John van Maanen (2011) has called a confessional tale, a detailed first person account of experiences of bewitchment, Favret-Saada addresses us directly and puts herself in the position of indeterminate third person: take an ethnographer, any ethnographer. The author/narrator makes a first appearance in the text as an exchangeable figure, an Anonymous.[9]

The book is divided into three parts, each subdivided into several chapters. The first part contains the exposition of Favret-Saada's argument about witchcraft, its characterization as discourse in which one has to become involved, to "be caught" in order to understand.[10] This process of "being caught," as indicated by the passive verb form, cannot be achieved through pursuit of participant observation or any other method. It means to be called, to be drawn into the discourse by being assigned a position and then having to respond from this position. The subject in the center of this process is not the active, reflecting, rational subject of Cartesianism, but a passive, generalized subjectivity, a subject-function, if one prefers. Favret-Saada's title for the first part of the book expresses this conception of subjectivity as assignment or call perfectly: "There Must Be a Subject"; and so does the first subchapter, titled "The Way Things Are Said." Such impersonal grammatical constructions are also found as headings of other chapters: "Someone Must Be Credulous" (Part II, chapter 4), "The Less One Talks, the Less One Is Caught" (Part II, chapter 6). Added to that are headings consisting of subjectless, participial verbal forms: "Between 'Caught' and Catching" (I/2); "Telling It All" (Part III), "Taking Over" (III/9), "Not Much Believing" (III/11). What emerges is the image of an impersonal communicative process, a discourse that, uncontrolled by any individual agent or person, "speaks itself"; it does so, however, not as the autonomous system of classic structuralism, but through assigning subjects a position from which to speak.

Another aspect of literary form bound up with signature is the relation between the presence of the author's voice and that of other voices or the question of ethnographic authority (Clifford 1988). The way in which Favret-Saada presents her material creates the impression of a multiplicity of voices, a polyphony.

Consider as an example an excerpt from *Deadly Words* that recreates a conversation between Favret-Saada and her main informants, the Babins, about the importance of avoiding their alleged witch's touch:

> *"At père Paumard's burial,"* says Jean, *"the neighbour runs to greet me: how do you explain that? He hardly greets me once a year."* This unusual handshake clenches a cow's fate: it aborts three days later. Since the neighbor does not usually greet Jean and so refuses to consider him a friend, the fact that he exceptionally greets him can only be because he means to touch him magically: and the first misfortune to occur afterwards is interpreted as a consequence (a predictable one) of his touching [*"And at the Smithy's,"* adds the wife, *"the neighbor, with eyes popping out of his head* [i.e., endowed with attributes of omnipotent magic, bulging eyes] *comes up to say hello"* [a second anomaly, since the neighbor does not usually greet him in public or does not bother to come and greet someone he considers his junior and inferior]. *Jean shakes his hand and says to himself: "that's it, there's going to be another misfortune."* [As, usual, Jean realizes too late that a handshake can only be a magic touch.] *"If only he'd touched his salt,"* she says despairingly, [blessed salt, which Josephine puts in his pocket everyday so that he has a chance to annul the consequences of his imprudent behavior]. *"The next day, he lost the wheel of the distributor [of fertilizers], and he quarreled with a man from Torcé"* [she is implying that he got drunk because he was nervous, having once again been trapped by the handshake]. Jean, who does not like to be publicly treated like an irresponsible boy, minimizes the incident, tells me that he might have lost that wheel in any case, and that *"one mustn't believe in it all, one mustn't get to the point of being credulous"* [I know . . .],[11] but he can't understand why the handshake made him nervous to the point of provoking him to fight: he is usually so calm. (1980: 114)

The voices of husband and wife switch rapidly, almost without the reader noticing it; suddenly, the wife, Josephine, takes over and recounts Jean's reacting in indirect speech, the clear separation between the positions of speaker and listener in the dialogue is blurred. The anthropologist adds her own voice to it, or more accurately, two voices: one as participant in the dialogue, when she is addressed directly by Jean, and the other, much more prominently, as commentator, providing context [marked by brackets] to aid the reader's understanding. The result is a polylogue, an interweaving of voices into a complex texture without a clearly assigned narrator/author position. The ethnographer's voice becomes one among others, enmeshed in the text, not in control of it.[12] It is worth pointing out here that the author does not relinquish control without resistance: it is possible to interpret the running commentary in brackets as an assertion of ethnographic authority and a claim to a kind of "scientific" objectivity. But this authority is not simply given but must be won in a struggle against forces of disintegration. This struggling quality is perhaps one of the most outstanding characteristics of *Deadly Words*.

Certainly, most anthropologists use quotes from their informants to preserve the "voice of the Other" and demonstrate the authenticity of their "being there" (Geertz 1988). In *Deadly Words*, however, stylistic means are employed to express something essential about the subject-matter of the text, witchcraft in the Bocage. In Favret-Saada's own words, her text represents not the attempt of "getting uncaught," but of a "second catching" (see above). Dealing with a discursive system and mode of experience that does not allow for an outsider's position, the only way to do justice to it is to recreate one's own involvement, to show how "one got caught." The text of *Deadly Words* is nothing other than this recreation.

Based on this premise, the formal and stylistic characteristics discussed up to this point become intelligible. A conventional representation of dialogue (with ordered switching between speaker and listener positions, and individually signed statements) would transform discourse into a vehicle of information, thus violating the essence of witchcraft as performative speech. The allusive way Favret-Saada refers to her own experiences of witchcraft now appears consequential: if she would present her own understanding of witchcraft in the form of an account, even that of a personal confessional, she would once again contradict her own participation in it. Witchcraft itself can only be talked about in allusions, intimations, to address it directly means to situate oneself outside of it, hence misrepresent it. Objectifying witchcraft is to miss witchcraft as an object.

The impossibility to adopt a stance of ethnographic distance to witchcraft, as described by Favret-Saada, rules out the option of an author/narrator who presents herself as in control of her text. Favret-Saada's decision to interweave her ethnographer's and personal voice with other voices, both individualized and anonymous, is an expression of this inability to establish a stable and undisputed authority. Throughout the book, the narrator emerges as uncertain of her own account of events, not in possession of all necessary information and therefore relying on conjectures and inferences.[13]

It is essential for coming to terms with this structurally complex, multivocal, and ambiguous text to recognize that the process of understanding and representing witchcraft can never come to an end, that it must be forever incomplete and ongoing. The book contains many indications in this direction: the final chapter of the first part is cryptically titled "When the Text Is Its Own Foreword." Favret-Saada seems to explain the title as a reference to the convention of "scientific ethnography" to limit all discussions of the relation between researcher and researched to the foreword or relegate them to a "methodology footnote" (van Maanen 2011: 75). "Can you still talk of science when the text is its own foreword?" she asks (Favret-Saada 1980: 26). But the title can also be read in the sense that with respect to a witchcraft discourse whose essence is, well, bewitchment, there can be no text in the usual sense, only a beginning of a text, or beginnings of texts, in other words, a foreword.

If we do not read *Deadly Words* from this perspective, then its final chapter will also be nothing but the symptom of a lack, a sign of an investigative process that has been aborted prematurely but will be completed in the future. It is possible that Favret-Saada was not fully aware that her own text, and the research she presented in it, excluded the idea of completion, for she gave its final chapter the title "Midway Speculations," suggesting that the whole distance to be traveled can somehow be measured. Read from the perspective I am proposing here, "midway speculations" adequately expresses a process of inquiry that is essentially "underway" and defies the idea of closure. It also justifies the abrupt and seemingly unmotivated last sentence of the main text: "Now we must try to understand which symbolic landmarks enable the unwitcher to wield this non-invested surplus force" (1980: 216)—a sentence that builds a bridge to nowhere.[14]

In terms of content, Favret-Saada's "midway speculations" consist in a rather abstract representation of the concept of "force" and its dynamics in the process of bewitchment and unwitching, complete with schematic diagrams featuring circles, vectors, and plus and minus signs. One of her English reviewers was disappointed by this form of conclusion, calling it a "concession to positivism" (Quayle 1982: 569). But this criticism overlooks, for one, that "positivist elements" are not restricted to a specific part of the book. Throughout *Deadly Words*, Favret-Saada makes an effort to remain "scientific," mentioning, for example, how she tried, unsuccessfully, to "cross-check" the accounts of the bewitched by talking to alleged witches. A tendency toward logical reasoning appears throughout the text, one that is highly noticeable since it is strangely at odds with the intimacy implied by the topic of witchcraft and by the emphasis on the ethnographer's involvement in it. Her peculiar use of logic finds visual expression in Favret-Saada's use of numbered or alphabetized lists to mark an argumentative sequence of logical inferences. On pages 140–146, for instance, Favret-Saada gives an account of the relationship between Jean and Josephine Babin and their "minor" witch, their relative Uncle Chicot. The account is divided into sections (a) to (h), one subsection (e) even featuring a further subdivision using numbers 1, 2, and 3. This mode of presentation suggests a logical progression, and, concomitantly, a consciousness transcending its object and an author in control of the narrative. But reading the passage, we find that the sequential arrangement does not produce a logical argument but rather reproduces the way the Babins have presented their bewitchment to the anthropologist, and, therefore, how Favret-Saada has learned what she knows about the Babins, and by implication about witchcraft in general. In other words, more than anything else, structuring the account by letters and numbers marks the progression of the involvement of the anthropologist into the witchcraft discourse.

Approaching the book as a unity of form and content, and, therefore, as an attempt at a "second catching" enables us to interpret the presence of these structuralist or logical elements in a different light. From this perspective, Favret-Saada's use of inferential logic can be regarded as a means to perform this "second catching," to create order in what first appeared incomprehensible and confused in her experience. Favret-Saada does not back up her logical method by any kind of theory; the logic she applies is the logic of common sense, the order thus invoked the order of the everyday lifeworld, defined in the words of Alfred Schütz as "that province of reality which the wide-awake and normal adult simply takes for granted in the attitude of common sense" (Schütz and Luckmann 1973: 3). This, too, makes good sense when regarded in the context of her efforts to preserve, or better, recreate the experience of witchcraft as "being caught." A more formal use of logic would transform witchcraft into an object, thereby situating writer and reader outside of its discourse, hence missing its reality. On the other hand, meaning and understanding, some kind of order, is necessary for the production of an ethnographic account. Inferences based on common sense are the most fundamental forms of logical thinking, with the closest relationship to everyday experience; they represent the form of reasoning most adequate to the task of communicating an experience that deeply affects the everyday lifeworld of those who are "caught" by it.

The abstractions, inferences, and the overall structuralist tenor of Favret-Saada's interpretations are thus not primarily motivated by any adherence to the structuralist and post-structuralist paradigms that were en vogue at the time she worked on *Deadly Words*.[15] Nor can her style simply be attributed to the French intellectual tradition, according to which, famously, "the heart has its reasons." I believe that Favret-Saada's recourse to logic and structure emerged as a consequence of the experience that her text struggles to express; in other words, logic was part of the form suggested by a particular content. It is worthwhile reminding ourselves what that original experience of witchcraft consisted of: "Persistent amnesia, dumbfoundedness, the inability to reflect when faced by the seemingly unstatable—i.e., a vague perception that something in this can't be coped with—this was my ordinary lot during the adventure" (Favret-Saada 1980: 22). Favret-Saada adds an explanatory footnote to this description: "I might just as well express it as 'can't be thought' or 'can't be said'; in talking of what 'can't be coped with', I am trying to point to an element of reality that at some point escapes the grasp of language or symbolization." (1980: 22).

The spontaneous choice of the word "cope" might be telling nevertheless, as is her broadening of its meaning in the footnote. An experience characterized by "amnesia" and "dumbfoundedness" presents a challenge to the self and threatens the order of experience itself. Logic and common sense are means to ward off this danger; they can become psychological defenses as described by George Devereux in *From Anxiety to Method in the Behavioral Sciences* (1967). I suggest that Favret-Saada's use of logic in *Deadly Words* can be understood in the context of her efforts to find and restore order in her initially confusing and anxiety-provoking experience of witchcraft. What makes her particular application of commonsense logic remarkable is that it does not fulfill the function of denying, "repressing" anxiety, but of "coping" with it, that is, "sublimating" (Devereux 1967) it. In other words, logic in *Deadly Words*, at first so surprising in a text on witchcraft, appears not as the contradiction of "magical force" and "bewitchment," but as response to them, hence as indirect admission of their reality.[16]

As I said, the logic that Favret-Saada uses to make sense of her experience is not of a high-brow, formal type, but a pedestrian, everyday logic. She lets the reader take part in her process of sense-making, and witness her many beginnings and interruptions, her groping for something to hold on to. In this halting and sometimes stumbling manner, she arrives at fascinating ethnographic insights about witchcraft in the Bocage. From the observation that witchcraft stories are inevitably told from the perspective of the bewitched, and that no one would ever admit to being a witch, she concludes that in all likelihood active witchcraft, striking the first magical blow, does not exist in the Bocage. This would mean that all actually practiced magic is defensive and performed by an unwitcher who acts as magical protector of the bewitched. If that is the case, however, if there is no aggressive witchcraft, then the person accused as witch must be, and know themselves to be, innocent. What is more, from their perspective, the behavior of the accusers, especially that of the unwitcher, must appear strange, just like that of witches. In other words, the roles of bewitched and witch are in principle reversible. This reversibility, the fact that the acts of an unwitcher can be experienced as that of a witch by someone innocently accused, constitutes a blind spot in the system of witchcraft, which, however, is necessary for the functioning of the system. Favret-Saada consequentially discovers that Jean Babin, the head of the bewitched family,[17] had indeed at an earlier point been accused of witchcraft himself. This discovery enables her to logically infer some fundamental characteristics of the witchcraft system, as well as, in a kind of dialectical movement, make sense of the behavior of her main informants:

> The way in which the Babins' case is paradigmatic is now clearer: it illustrates the typical situation where a bewitched person, "caught" in the repetition of biological misfortunes following an accusation of witchcraft, is faced with the impossibility of talking about it to any unwitcher. This impossibility seems to be part of the discourse of witchcraft itself: for I have never heard a bewitched person complain to an unwitcher of having been accused of being a witch; indeed none of the many stories I was told contain this situation, which, however, cannot be a rare one, since every time someone considers himself bewitched, he has to name a witch: so there are as many witches as there are bewitched. The problem, then, is to know how this large number of accused people deal with this imputation, since they at least know that they are innocent of possessing "books" and using them to lay charms. (Favret-Saada 1980: 186)

Over the next pages (186–89), in a truly captivating display of inductive reasoning, Favret-Saada shows how the Babins' behavior, for example, Jean Babin's reluctance to work with certain unwitchers and his ambivalent attitude toward witchcraft (the chapter is titled "Not Much Believing"), and the account they give of their bewitchment (e.g., an attack by a second witch who was vanquished by a previous unwitcher) is explicable as an effort to transform an accusation of witchcraft into a story of being bewitched. The way she arrives at this insight, however, is again not presented straightforwardly, but achieved in several movements: the reader first learns about the reversibility of the positions of bewitched and witch on pages 72–73 in the second part of the book. But the topic, crucial for the functioning of the system, is only truly elaborated much later when Favret-Saada recounts how she returned to the Babins after an absence of sixteen months to suggest to them a cure by her own unwitcher, Madame Flora. She presents excerpts from a recorded interview with Josephine Babin in the characteristic style discussed before. At one point, she comments:

> The notes I took in 1971 from a tape recording of this conversation contain the following astonishing passage, quite typical of the deafness that so often descended on me in the course of my work: *This is followed by an inaudible story, about an unwitcher—not Madame Auguste, but someone else—who accused Jean Babin of being one of his neighbour's witches. "Some people were in trouble* [bewitched], *here, in our quartier and they said my husband had done it."* . . . it seems incredible to me today that this particular passage should have been inaudible, since, later on in the recording I could hear the drone of the Babins' washing machine, but could still understand their words . . . The most likely assumption then is that I did not want to hear her account of this crucial episode—about which I did not ask a single question—because taking it into account would have meant revising my version of the Babins' story: if their troubles originally came from this accusation of witchcraft, what could they expect from an unwitcher and what exactly had they wanted from me the year before? (1980: 180)

A "Second Catching"

All that I have said about the style of *Deadly Words* is present in this unraveling of the prequel to the Babins' story: the uncertainty of the author regarding her own account, the struggle for coherence through application of common sense logic, the non-chronological "unpacking" of events.[18] Throughout the discussion, I have emphasized how the choice of these stylistic means was not determined by the author's intention to produce rhetorical effects in her readers, but motivated by the content of the text. To put it more accurately, I have tried to show how form and content are intertwined with each other as two aspects of one phenomenon, *Deadly Words* as it was written. It makes no sense in ethnographic or other kinds of writing, to speak of a preexisting content that is then translated into words; rather, writing is the performative production of content through the act of putting content in a specific, material form. Writing is "doing things with words." Favret-Saada's *Deadly Words* is unique in that it allows the reader to reflectively grasp its own process of production. The text carries, so to speak, two accounts: on the one hand, it provides the reader with information about its topic, that is, talks about witchcraft in western France. On the other hand, it gives an account of how the anthropologist acquired her knowledge, how she became involved in witchcraft, how she "got caught." This reflexivity is the only way it is possible to perform what Favret-Saada calls a "second catching": an effort not to describe one's involvement after it has come to an end, but to recreate the experience of becoming involved. Things are alluded to, hinted at, thrown in unexpectedly; at first, events confuse in their complexity and density, only gradually the subject is able to extricate itself from this confusion and to unpack layers of meanings, slowly and repetitively; but never is it able to become the master of this experience, never can it achieve objectivity as a stance of distant neutrality. This was Favret-Saada's experience of witchcraft, and this is the reader's experience of *Deadly Words*. In other words, according to what it says itself, as a unity of form and content, the text does not represent witchcraft through the information it provides about its practices, it performs witchcraft itself. *Deadly Words* has the qualities of a spell; this is the reason why it is able to produce an affective response in its readers, although, or precisely because, it goes against much of the conventional wisdom about (ethnographic) writing.

Conclusion

John van Maanen concludes his study of literary conventions in ethnographic writing with an acknowledgment of the limits of conventionality and methodology:

> ethnography is still a relatively artistic, improvised, and situated form of social research where the lasting tenets of research design, theoret-

> ical aims, canned concepts, and technical writing have yet to leave a heavy mark. In the end, this is the way I think it should be, for a persuasive and widely read ethnography will always be something of a mess, a mystery, and a miracle. (van Maanen 2011: 175)

On the preceding pages, I have tried to communicate and, hopefully re-created, some of the miraculous quality of Favret-Saada's ethnography of witchcraft in modern France. The text enchants its readers in an unexpected, unconventional way, through a paradoxical homology of form and content. The unsayable of witchcraft can only be said in indirect, inconclusive, open-ended ways—this is the stylistic principle governing *Deadly Words*, and the origin of the effect it has had and continues to have on its readers. I am still unsure how this result of my literary investigation will influence my approach to teaching writing. Probably, I will continue to teach some sort of "thick description" and "ethnographic impressionism" (van Maanen 2011). My reflections on *Deadly Words*, however, have made clearer to me that my own, or anybody's, efforts to subject ethnographic writing to a set of methodological rules must ultimately lead to frustration and disappointment. As in poetry or music, in ethnography, "method" or "technique" must be understood as an auxiliary tool, a "crutch" to reach a realm beyond its own applicability. In my opinion, that says something about the very notion of "method" itself and what it implies, the predictability and controllability of human life. What we can learn from Favret-Saada not only relates to the ethnography of witchcraft or to ethnographic writing and experience, but reflects a fundamental characteristic of human existence: its contingency and indeterminacy or, in the terms of the phenomenologist Bernhard Waldenfels (2007, 2011), its responsivity.

Coda

Looking back at the text I have written, I notice that it is less orderly, less structured than I usually wish my writing to be. It is possible that this dis-order is a result of particular circumstances and thus could have been corrected by another round of restructuring and editing. I prefer, however, to think of it as an expression of what I have just written about: that the form of a text stands in a unique relation to its content. Grappling with a dis-orderly text that struggled to express the inexpressible I have myself produced a dis-orderly text.

Bernhard Leistle is an associate professor of anthropology at Carleton University in Ottawa. His research is situated at the intersection of philosophical phenomenology, performance theory and cultural anthropology. He is the editor of *Anthropology and Alterity: Responding to the Other* (Routledge, 2017) and co-editor of *Ritual and Identity* (LIT, 2006), and has published on spirit possession and the senses in Morocco.

Notes

1. See for example John van Maanen's *Tales of the Field* (2011). Van Maanen distinguishes between "realist," "confessional," and "impressionist" styles of ethnographic writing, each following their own sets of literary conventions.
2. Jeanne Favret-Saada conducted the bulk of her fieldwork at the end of the 1960s and in the early 1970s in a region of northwestern France she calls the Bocage, a term referring to a type of landscape characterized by an alternation of woodland and fields. The Bocage is peasant country, and Favret-Saada's interlocutors were mostly farmers.
3. These misfortunes generally affect the productivity of the farm unit: animals miscarry, milk or produce decreases or gets spoiled, children or a spouse fall ill, etc.
4. My evidence for this assessment is largely anecdotal and based on the prolonged reaction time of the colleagues with whom I talked about the book. Moreover, it is true that some efforts have been made by the group of anthropologists around the journal HAU to revive discussions about Favret-Saada's work, see Favret-Saada (2012, 2015).
5. See, for example, Favret-Saada (1980: 160, 185).
6. Besides *The Anti-Witch* (2015), Favret-Saada published only one other book on witchcraft in the Bocage, *Corps pour corps: Enquête sur la sorcellerie dans le Bocage* (1981, co-authored with Josée Contreras), consisting mostly of field notes she took during her original research.
7. One of Favret-Saada's English reviewers (Quayle 1982) bemoaned the lack of an index in the English edition of the book. The French original also lacks an index, and I would prefer to regard this absence as indicative of the structural complexity of the text: it would have been a nightmare to index *Deadly Words*.
8. See for example, pages 122–23 where she describes the ambiguity of this relationship between cooperation and aggressive dominance; or the passage on pages 175–76, which starts with the promising sentence: "When, after a period of fear and uncertainty, I began an unwitching cure with Madame Flora, I immediately felt relieved" (1980: 175). But then the reader's expectations are again frustrated, as it was on previous

occasions, because we learn next to nothing about Favret-Saada's "fear and uncertainty" or the "brilliant way in which she [Madame Flora] managed her cures—including my own" (1980: 175).

9. Favret-Saada repeats the phrase on the next page, affirming its stylistic character.
10. The second and third parts of *Deadly Words* elaborate this conception. The second part, "The Realm of Secrecy," establishes the necessity of becoming involved in witchcraft by discussing a number of cases in which the anthropologist remained in the outsider position and consequentially limited in her understanding. The telling, however, is in retrospective, endowed with an insight acquired later in the research process. The third part is by far the longest section of the book, taking up more than half of the volume. In it, Favret-Saada scrutinizes the case of Jean and Josephine Babin, a married couple, childless due to the husband's impotence, who present themselves as bewitched by a neighbor. Favret-Saada takes an active role in this witchcraft crisis: first, when she is asked by the Babins to become their unwitcher, and then when she recommends her own unwitcher, Madame Flora, to them. Looking at the narrative sequence of parts, there seems to be a progressive process of discovery, with the anthropologist moving from ignorance and credulity to understanding and insight. The title of the third part "Telling It All" seems to confirm this impression. While there is some truth to such a reading and *Deadly Words* is certainly not without any conventional elements, it needs to be kept in mind that the discovering subject remains unsure of its findings, and the narrative reaches no conclusion, but ends with tentative "Midway Speculations," as the last chapter of the book announces.
11. This insertion is a shorthand version of "I know . . . but still," a phrase often used by Favret-Saada's interlocutors to express their puzzlement about what happens to them. They *know* that witchcraft and magic are "irrational" and not accepted by the wider world around them, *but still* there is something inexplicable about the occurring events that they cannot deny. The inclusion of this phrase here is yet another commentary and reference adding to the polyphonic character of the passage.
12. This does not mean to deny that the author's role is still privileged, as it is she who represents and orchestrates the text in this particular form (Clifford 1988: 54). Nor do I intend to deny that this mode of writing has a rhetorical effect on readers: doubtlessly, it draws them in, involves them in the text by refusing them an outsider's standpoint from which to observe the action from a secure and distanced stance. What I want to bring out is that this kind of involvement, or, as I call it here, bewitchment, is not the result of the application of a catalog of writing methods, but emerging from a deep resonance between ethnographic content and literary form.
13. See for example, the passages on pages 53 and 76, in which Favret-Saada speculates about the motivations and reactions of their interlocutors.

14. It fits into this reading that the main text of the book, the ethnography proper, is supplemented by a number of articles on witchcraft, previously published by the author. The last appendix finally consists in a chronology of events in the case of the Babins, one of the few concessions made to the reader in *Deadly Words*.
15. We may also remind ourselves that Favret-Saada has explicitly disavowed this adherence (see 1980: 14, quoted above).
16. Perhaps the presence of logical reasoning in anthropological accounts of witchcraft is not so surprising after all. Logic is certainly a prominent element in Evans-Pritchard's classical study, begging the question if there, too, it might fulfill a "defensive function."
17. Witchcraft in the Bocage, says Favret-Saada, is ultimately always directed at the male head of the household, even though it might first affect other members, like children or wife, or possessions, in particular animals.
18. On pages 176–77, the reader is forewarned about the coming turn of events by a footnote, in which Favret-Saada explains that she used a tape recorder "as a safeguard against my own forgetfulness. But later on we will see how illusory this safeguard was, since I was incapable, for example, of writing out part of this recorded conversation, precisely the part I didn't want to hear."

References

Clifford, James. 1988. *The Predicament of Culture: Twentieth Century Ethnography, Literature, and Art*. Cambridge, MA: Harvard University Press.

Clifford, James, and George E. Marcus, eds. 1986. *Writing Culture: The Poetics and Politics of Ethnography*. Berkeley: University of California Press.

Devereux, George. 1967. *From Anxiety to Method in the Behavioral Sciences*. New York: Humanities Press.

Evans-Pritchard, Edward Evan. 1937. *Witchcraft, Oracles, and Magic among the Azande*. Oxford: Clarendon Press.

Favret-Saada, Jeanne. 1980. *Deadly Words: Witchcraft in the Bocage*, trans. Catherine Cullen. Cambridge: Cambridge University Press.

———. 2012. "Death at your Heels: When Ethnographic Writing Propagates the Force of Witchcraft." *HAU: Journal of Ethnographic Theory* 2(1): 45–53.

———. 2015. *The Anti-Witch*, trans. Matthew Carey. Chicago: HAU Books.

Favret-Saada, Jeanne, and Josée Contreras. 1981. *Corps pour corps: Enquête sur la sorcellerie dans le Bocage*. Paris: Gallimard.

Geertz, Clifford. 1988. *Works and Lives: The Anthropologist as Author*. Stanford, CA: Stanford University Press.

Marcus, George E., and D. Cushman. 1982. "Ethnographies as Text." *Annual Review of Anthropology* 11: 25–69.

Quayle, Brendan. 1982. "Review of *Deadly Words: Witchcraft in the Bocage*, by Jeanne Favret-Saada." In *Man, New Series* 17(3): 568–70.

Schütz, Alfred, and Thomas Luckmann. 1973. *The Structures of the Life-World*, trans. Richard M. Zaner and H. Tristram Engelhardt, Jr. Evanston, IL: Northwestern University Press.

van Maanen, John. 2011. *Tales of the Field: On Writing Ethnography*. Chicago: Chicago University Press.

Waldenfels, Bernhard. 2007. *The Question of the Other*. Albany: State University of New York Press and Hong Kong: Chinese University Press.

———. 2011. *The Phenomenology of the Alien: Basic Concepts*, trans. Alexander Kozin and Tatjana Stähler. Evanston, IL: Northwestern University Press.

AFTERWORD

META-ODOS (OR THE INSCRIPTION OF FIELDWORK)

David Jaclin

This chapter is composed of two texts in dialogue with each other as they explore the relations between silence and method. Together, they propose an infra-linguistic argument to rejuvenate the practice of anthropology, a semiotic consciousness for working the field. In the main text, I broach the idea based on the experience of loss, while Everett Kehew draws from yoga in an adjacent vignette.

At home, on the road.
On the road, at home.

One always wants to be careful when dwelling on the past. Diving into previousness is no easy thing. Even more challenging is the narrating of such a past . . . So let us engage cautiously with etymology and the "kinshiping" of lexicons.

The word "method" is composed of two ancient Greek roots, μετά, *metá* (after, or beyond) and ὁδός, *hodós* (way, road, traveled path). A brief etymological probing into the life of the term "method" suggests an important idea of movement, a move on—and about—routes: a passage through, a way in, or, in a certain epistemological fashion, the acting of an action. It is no surprise that method and its historical conceptualizations are such thorny things both to design and to apply. How to conceive of things we do?

The Discourse on the Coursing of Course

Thinking the after of methods and methodology, in anthropology and elsewhere, may prove even more byzantine. What is it exactly that comes after fieldwork? In the following paragraphs, I would like to further elaborate this idea of "an *x* about *x*," particularly when it comes to moving *along* and *with* people (humans and other-than-humans).

Concerned with the production of stories, with the story about the story, with storytelling cultures, gestures, or other communicational events involving other livings, I am interested in better understanding (that is, an understanding of understandings) the multiple ways anthropologists move in and out of the world of others.

Traditionally envisioned as an exegetical activity (being able to read the world, its laws or its meanings, beyond the visible and its apparent chaos), anthropology was the (predominantly white men's) work of explaining the operating logic beyond human associations and productions. Back then, the more "exotic" and "primitive" the culture, the better. In fact, bringing back an already over-industrious West (yet not industrialized enough?) closer to an original and fantasized state of nature proved critical. Such exegesis gave rise to many of "an *x* about *x*"; the reasoning of Reason (or its absence), the progress of Progress (or lack thereof), the Human of humans (or their measurable differences), and so on.

A hundred and fifty years after France, Germany and, to a lesser extent, the Anglo-Saxon world debated ideas of cultures, civilizations, and the explanations beyond human groups' differences, contemporary anthropology does not rely on exegesis anymore (or not solely). For some of us, doing anthropology has less to do with the representation or interpretation of cultures than with the relationalities and the communicativeness between them. Along and among us all. The exegetical discipline has forked into another craft. I have difficulty pinpointing such craftship, since it proves very diverse and takes multiple forms among colleagues. What can be specified nonetheless is the increasing attention paid to different and differentiating modes of attention (as well as performativity) such craftship implies. In other words: an attention to attentions.

For me, doing anthropology has to do with the (re)working of one's sensitivities. It deals with probing rather than surveying, with challenging and engaging more-than-self attunements to a complex realm of emerging (and disappearing) events within and across novel ecologies. Doing anthropology has to do with sensing, more than with sorting, with the elaborating of a transduction rather than an elaborated incursion. Poetics and politics are still manifest, underpinning our current engagements with the world, but the collective structuration of thoughts they sustain, the metanarrative M. R. Trouillot once conceptualized, is actually on the move. The world we inhabit, the words we use, the things we do or do not do, the realities we grasp or fail to grasp, are inherently moving. Movements upon movement.

But enough with stories about words. Let me now share a few words about stories.

For more than ten years, I have been doing fieldwork in and across novel ecologies (see Jaclin 2013, 2016, 2018, 2019). Along multispecied, multisited, and multimediated lines, I set out to (diagrammatically, rather than representatively) map the booming trade of exotic animal black markets. Among the numerous goods, ideas, viruses, and people that are moving around the globe every minute, stand an incredible number of other-than-human animals—as the 2019–20 coronavirus pandemic radically demonstrated. Dead and alive, critters and their parts are being moved along illegal routes, turning such commerce into the third most important black market in the world. Animals of an animated world (or, correspondingly, the animation of an animal world).

After cruising the North American continent in a cheap camper van, searching for places where wild animals could be found (in people's yards, in sanctuaries, or in medical facilities), I intended, through an ethnographical journey, to better grasp the underground cultures of such black markets (the "demand" side, if we wish, of a strange beastness). I was interested in learning how, why, and when some humans share their life with ex-predators and engage in relationships that prove both unnatural and naturalized, destructive and creative at the same time. And this was long before Netflix's *Tiger King* frenzy . . . Those fragile ecological entanglements involve individuals of different species, institutions of different countries, environments of different geographies and histories, ideas of different cosmogonies and cultures. To me, it was like envisioning our anthropo/capitalo/plastico/Chtulu-cene futures where novel ecologies recombine previous modalities of existences. And vice versa: where emerging modalities of existences nurture novel ecologies. In other words: the emerging of an emergence.

Those emergences—such as the case of a tiger cub being heavily anesthetized, put in a sports bag, dragged across the US border, and delivered to its buyers on a sandy backroad thousands of miles away from the warmth of its mother's belly—I set out to map. As I was taught, I recorded interviews, noted conversations and situations I was observing and participating in. I even moved into the "twenty-first century" with the digital recording of places, people, and events.

But, after thirteen months of fieldwork, I lost all my data; that is, sounds, images, video clips, notes, and maps. No interviews, nor any kind of machine recordings made during the entire duration of the immersion, remained. No traces of the hundreds of files I was religiously archiving on my daily road routine. Nothing. Nothing but the white blank of an empty folder blinking on my screen. The hard drive encoding and containing all my data fell to the ground, accidentally pushed off by my brother visiting me from France, an angel jumping from the highest shelf of the room I was converting to an office in order to write my dissertation. I had no backup (I *know* . . .) and spent most of the following weeks touring as many specialized shops as possible to see if anything, really any thing, could be saved after the crash, and if the lucrative promises they made about "accidents-not-having-to-be-accidents" would actually prove real. Reality, wrote P. K. Dick, is what still remains even when you stop believing in it. At the time of our collective technological epopee, hard drives were still mainly discs, with grooves and microscopic waves. Mine had stopped communicating. An erasing over a recording.

Note that this hard drive operated an analogic encoding of digital information. I am insisting on the material qualities of the drive because, before the event, I had only a vague idea of how the actual moments of the world I was trying to record were actually inscribed, stored, and programmed to be retrieved later on a savant configuration of plastic, glass, aluminum alloy, and magnetic platters. In other words, the magic was broken, the medium failed me or, rather, I failed the Zen art of data cycle maintenance. I had forgotten two very, very important things (when it comes to any kind of method-ing). First, I forgot that using something did not necessarily equate understanding its functioning (this goes for machines as well as for ideas about technology or anthropology). Relying on something is not just a leap of faith; it is a leap into indeterminacies. And there reside the first teachings of this little catastrophe. Being and existing are two different modes, as are events and their possibilities of inscriptions. In a rather peculiar fashion, what goes for a hard drive also applies to the exotic pet black market I was investigating. The reasons why a wild animal serves a human purpose are only one part of the story. The actual existences of both a wild animal and a human could never be reduced to the utility of one to the other. We all become along and beside our utilitarian selves. Producing data is not a benign operation. Losing the data proved to be both tragic and liberating.

The experience of the concrete qualities that data manifest went along with the realization of their intrinsic reductionism (only part of what happened was recorded and could have been), their supplemental power (that recording would eventually bear the potential of both re-enacting and interpreting what would have otherwise been gone) and their value (strangely enough, data frequently turn reality into a poorer, yet simpler to grasp, image of what is). Second teaching of the loss: recording, or living, are already operations upon a complex operational realm. Recording and living are transducive movements along and upon other movements. An *x* of an *x*: they are methods.

Back to the loss of auxiliary memory apparatuses: once the mourning period was over, I faced a delicate situation: I had to decide what to do with the research. I could either let it go and throw in the towel, or decide to hold back and turn the accident into something else (which *x* over *X*?). Perhaps it could be something of a productive experience: a double experimentation of the methodological kind (what is it exactly that producing data does?) and of epistemological nature (how can we conceive of anthropology beyond the traditional practices of seeing and sorting out, of recording and interpreting?) By problematizing the absence of data, rather than solely inquiring about its presence, I ended up questioning data production altogether. At the time, as a social scientist and a developing scholar, I had to deal with a profound sense of failure, with the idea that since I had nothing to share, to show, or to use as proof, my work was non-receivable, at least not by the institution I was seeking some recognition from or by my two PhD supervisors who were pissed off, and rightly so, by my negligence—but kept supporting me nonetheless (may they be blessed by the gods of research). Nonetheless, on the other side of the epistemological academic schizophrenia, as a researcher, I thought I had to get past the tragic, move on from the empathy all my colleagues were kindly manifesting and think about accidents in general and about inscriptions in particular.

I had to start reflecting (more) seriously on our anthropogenic capacity to (1) record an event that otherwise would have been lost to its haecceity; and (2) to allow, via both a technical and a cultural apparatus, the re-enactment of such an event later in time, by different people, in different places. What was that mo(ve)ment, exactly? And why did rendering present the absence (or the gone) prove so critical?

When something happens, it is never just one thing that happens, but several inscribing processes that are unleashed (from cellular reproduction/mutation to social networks' viralities, both running analogically and digitally). But inscribing implies at least two moments, two movements. First is the action of recording what would otherwise have left only a few traces or even no trace at all. Second is the potential for this recording to be mobilized (or actualized) in the future, eventually by someone else, allowing that person to re-enact fragments of the past. I mentioned that about etymology already, but think of any kind of *écriture*: in the context of studying, recording often proves cardinal. No recording, no study. To record is, we tend to think, to provide proof of being (where the existing proves the being). But the picture you take, the voice you capture, the words you draw at night in your logbook can also be regarded as existential (where the being fosters the existing). That is, as a movement drawing upon other movements—a danced method, if you prefer.

Rewind. Following classical ethnographical practices, I was engaged in rendering nonhuman existences into human-formalized language, transcoding and translating realities from distinct worlds, that is, from disparate *umwelts*, maybe irreconcilable ones. And then, the material I thought would help me do so, well, vanished. It returned to silence, it had nothing else to say, except this silence. In many ways, it resembled the silence of all those animals I was interested in. What I was left with was the deep impression and the profound transformation inflicted by those humanimal encounterings, on my body and sensibilities.

But would that be of interest to anyone? Would that be useful to better grasp the underground realities of some troubled ecologies? Could that be valuable to someone interested in engaging with human and other-than-human contemporary relational entanglements? Would that be of any help to address deep and complex issues of environmental change, relational power beyond the human, or, more simply, questions about the ways multispecies stories are actually told, or could even be otherwise told?

No, it would not be of interest to academia. At least, not in that form. That is, not under its current problematization/formalization. What could be of interest, though, is to think again, to rethink, differently—and by necessity in my case—the relationship between language, life forms, and power dynamics in emerging ecologies. That is, to think about the conditions of possibility for knowledge to be produced and the various expressions such knowledge production can take. At that time, my intuition was that, with regard to my own research, life forms per se were less accountable than the actual movements that gave life to those forms. More than form, it was the forming I was really interested in mapping out. The mapping of a mapping, the forming of new and emerging ecologies, the (re)forming of ideas, the (de)forming of a loss.

Losing (which, in my case, was also the loosening of) my data was a forceful way to realize the incompressible affective dimensions of any experience: dimensions of in-formation and in-scription.

I am writing all this because I want to draw anthropological attention to the etymology of method. More to the point, I am interested in re-intensifying an old word with ancient/new possible meanings, and to build on those possibilities to think through any kind of practice involving "paying attention to," especially paying attention to shared mo(ve)ment. It is not only interesting to note (in a book about the after of method) that *meta*/μετά already bears an idea of beyondness (the after that makes an after), but also that *odos*/ὁδός actually refers to the action of moving along some traces. Here, one can wonder about the distinction (and not just of an etymological order, but also of an epistemological nature) between the object and the subject. Because I try not to separate movement between object and subject, between the path and the passenger, but rather try to think of their coupling (and the emerging situations such relations inevitably create), I pay particular attention to the action of going through and passing by.

Breathe.

Mobilizing both an empirical experience (the loss of all my research data) and an etymological argument (the meta of odos), I wanted to draw one's ethnographical attentiveness to the importance of inscription. If doing anthropological research implies the inscription of experience, then we should be particularly attentive (and provide special care) to the plurality of modes that any inscribing movement actually implies: the mechanical modes we know well (writing/reading/multimedia recordings), but also the organic ones we less often consider (moving/inferring/transducing/becoming more-than-one).

A direct implication of such ideas is the necessity to reassess the supposed permeability between fieldwork and the rest, between going there and coming back, hitting the road and returning home. The road is always there, with its potential for transcription taking place along various modes, intensities and regimes, concomitantly or disparately. Together and apart.

At home, on the road. On the road, at home.

Vignette 8
Inner Experience and Ethnographic Yoga
Everett Kehew

In 1943, his city under Nazi occupation, Parisian writer Georges Bataille set to work on *L'expérience intérieure*, an attempt to write his "voyage to the end of the possible of man" ([1943] 1988: 7). His project aimed to valorize in-and-of-itself the ecstatic, rapturous sensation brought about by the questioning of all authority external to his inner experience. The authorities that he sets against are primarily theological and philosophical: he opposes God as "a dead object and the thing of the theologian" ([1943] 1988: 4) to "the movement which carries us to the more obscure apprehension of the unknown" ([1943] 1988: 5) and the feeling of "emptiness of intelligent questions" ([1943] 1988: 8) and their answers to "the place of bewilderment, of nonsense" ([1943] 1988: 3). Determined points of linguistic meaning and authority are to Bataille only obstructions to the explosive power of experience itself, which "attains in the end the fusion of object and subject, being as subject non-knowledge, as object the unknown" ([1943] 1988: 9). This fusion is a place of unbridled communication that surpasses the linguistic, objectified limits of the possible that are imposed on inner experience by external forces. Inner experience itself neither begins nor ends at a determined, positive basis that can then be conveyed textually. "One must grasp the meaning from the inside . . . One must live experience" ([1943] 1988: 8).

If a "voyage to the end of the possible of man" sounds like some angst-y, Nietzschean melodrama that disgruntled grad students read instead of working on "serious" things like their thesis, it is because it is and that is why I read it. So what does it have to do with methods?

My research is about yoga and as I read up on the wide-ranging, interdisciplinary field of Yoga Studies a pattern emerged: in Yoga Studies, undertaken by anthropologists, philologists, philosophers, and others, and in various South-Asian textual traditions not centered in Western academia, the study of yoga usually anchors itself in textual or discursive analysis, often while hinting at the importance of personal practice. Clearly, it is important to describe and think critically about how yoga manifests textually, discursively, and symbolically, and to problematize it based on insights thus gathered, but it seemed to me that any ethnographic project derived from these methods would fail to appreciate yoga's non-linguistic, non-symbolic dimensions. It would remain an ethnography of an objectified yoga and fail to accede to anthropology with yoga, that is, in "correspondence" with yoga in a mutually transformative process of education (Ingold 2017: 23).

There are plenty of techniques available for "doing" yoga and reading is generally not considered to be one of them. To refer to a text that has been reinvigorated as a canonical cornerstone of "classical" yoga (Singleton 2008: 77), *The Yoga Sutras of Patanjali*, "conceptualization is based on linguistic knowledge, not contact with real things" (Hartranft 2003: 97). Anthropologist Joseph Alter, in his book on yoga in modern Indian, explains that "as a way of knowing . . . yoga is regarded by many people as inherently self-explanatory . . . It is not something that needs to be understood as such since it is the means by which to understand what is beyond normal consciousness" (Alter 2004: 34). He distinguishes yoga as science from the science of yoga, that is, the non-yogic study of yoga. This poses a challenge for the would-be yogic anthropologist: How to valorize yoga as a way of knowing in itself and not simply an ensemble of discourses and performative practices? How to push beyond the description of yoga and practice yoga as science? To condense in a way that brings us back around to where this essay began: how to valorize the epistemological authority of inner experience in anthropology?

Bataille foregrounds two methods to unmoor oneself from linguistic modes of inquiry and to silence inner grasps at signification. First, the "mastery of our innermost movements, which in the long run we can acquire, is well known: it is yoga" ([1943] 1988: 15). He uses the example of *pranayama*, yogic breath control. The breath he considers an object prone to "slippage" in the sense that as an object of attention, the breath leads one inward to inner experience. He uses the word "silence" as analogy, since it is simultaneously a word and the negation of words and slips thus from linguistic registers to intensive, non-linguistic interiority. "Silence is a word that is not a word and breath an object that is not an object" ([1943] 1988: 16).

On the whole, however, Bataille is disparaging of yoga and of "hindus" whose travails are invalidated in his eyes by their concern for salvation and their lack of capacity for expression ([1943] 1988: 18). I suppose he would rather they write books about teenagers pissing on each other like he did (see *L'histoire de l'oeil*, if you must). "Mais je sais peu de choses, au fond, de l'Inde" ([1943] 1954: 30).

His demeaning and ethnocentric critique of yoga is much less interesting than the second method he proposes, and which he himself aspires to: mastery of language. Writing is for Bataille an exercise in frustration, of "making ourselves familiar, cruelly so, with a helpless foolishness" ([1943] 1988: 15). Inner experience being that which exceeds the constraints of linguistic determination, it perpetually overflows its seizure in writing. He frames writing as a losing battle against the "law of language" ([1943] 1988: 14), under which anything that cannot be expressed linguistically is divested of authority by that which can. Inner experience is subordinated to the positive authority of language and remains as such until the writer contests the ability of language to circumscribe the possible. By trying to inscribe non-linguistic inner experience in writing, the limits of language expose themselves and attention is brought to the wide-open vistas lurking behind meaning. He valorizes writing not for its ability to capture and communicate the subtle realms of experience in words—it is not up to the task—but for its capacity to induce states of realization of inner experience in the writer. The "intensity of the states builds quite quickly and from that moment they absorb—even enrapture" ([1943] 1988: 15).

Anthropology is bound to textual production and all of the complications that entails. Bataille's assessment of the limits of language could resonate with anyone struggling with the translation of field experience into ethnographic accounts, since there are whole dimensions of experience that no quantity or style of writing could positively capture. Talking about the limits of language is sort of banal by itself, but the method proposed by Bataille is a helpful invitation to embrace writing as productive and not descriptive of experience. Writing that aims to correspond with its research subject or to go to the extreme of "communication" in Bataille's sense of the word, is like ethnographic yoga: a means of knowing from the inside. It is, after all, this inner experience, deeper than the thickest description you can muster, that breathes life into the practice of anthropology.

David Jaclin is Associate Professor in Anthropology at the University of Ottawa, where he also runs the HumAnimaLab (HAL). His work engages with issues pertaining to wildlife trafficking, green criminology, and global conservation initiatives, and crosses the fields of media and cultural theory, anthropology, animal studies, and philosophy. Author of *Beastness School* (2010), his second book, *La laisse du tigre: F(r)ictions humanimales en Amérique du Nord*, has just released, while *Poacher's Moon*, his first experimental documentary (with Jeremie Brugidou) started screening. As part of the Coral Triangle Expedition, he created (with Peter Nelson and Kishav Singh) an interactive kinetic installation depicting relationships between pathways of turtle migration and pathways of the exotic animal trade, presented at the Run Run Shaw Creative Media Center, Hong Kong (2017).

Everett Kehew is an MA candidate in Anthropology at the University of Ottawa. His current research is focused on the intersections of science and postural yoga in the milieu of North American yoga studios. Broadly, he is interested in the body, affect theory, and the politics of physical culture movements.

References

Alter, Joseph. 2004. *Yoga in Modern India.* Princeton, NJ: Princeton University Press.

Bataille, Georges. [1943] 1954. *L'expérience intérieure.* Paris: Éditions Gallimard.

——. [1943] 1988. *Inner Experience*, trans. by Leslie Anne Boldt. Albany: State University of New York Press.

Hartranft, Chip. 2003. *The Yoga Sutras of Patanjali.* Boston: Shambhala.

Ingold, Tim. 2017. "Anthropology contra Ethnography." *HAU: Journal of Ethnographic Theory* 7(1): 21–26.

Jaclin, David. 2013. "In the Eye of The Tiger: An Anthropological Journey into Jungle Backyards." *Social Science Information* 52(2): 257–271.

———. 2016. "Poached lives, traded forms: Engaging with animal trafficking around the globe." *Social Science Information* 55(3): 400–426.

———. 2018. "Becoming Mammoth: The Domestic Animal, Its Synthetic Futures and the Pursuit of Multispecies F(r)ictions." In *Animals and Animality in the Literary Field*, ed. Bruce Boehrer, Molly Hand, and Brian Massumi, 301–18. Cambridge: Cambridge University Press.

———. 2019. *La laisse du tigre : F(r)ictions humanimales en Amérique du Nord.* Ottowa: Presses de l'Université d'Ottawa.

Singleton, Mark. 2008. "The Classical Reveries of Modern Yoga: Patanjali and Constructive Orientalism." In *Yoga in the Modern World: Contemporary Perspectives*, ed. Mark Singleton and Jean Byrne, 77–99. New York: Routledge.

Trouillot, Michel-Rolph. 1991. "Anthropology and the Savage Slot: The Poetics and Politics of Otherness." In *Recapturing Anthropology*, ed. Richard G. Fox, 17–44. New Mexico: School of American Research Press.

EPILOGUE

Julie Laplante

Throughout this volume we argue for grounded, sonorous, aerial, watery, vegetal, pointed, and situated ways of doing research that stem from contexts in flux, tracing creative lines through and along their potentials. It is a call to work closely with and from what is going on, taking chance encounters as generative forces in the (re)search process, learning how to steer them, continuing to do so in writing. We offer a counterbalance to a dominant trend to follow a pre-designed research model—essentially a practice of collecting data that turns the living into stale objects to test the model—currently considered the scientific gold standard, meant to be the best method "out there." This has become dogmatic and systematic, is reproduced blindly (literally, double-blind), and is close to imposing a distant bureaucratic or administrative procedure. Fixed in time and anachronistic, it is paradoxically more likely to be out of sync with what is unfolding. To the contrary, the "after" methods described here emerge from contexts in tandem with theory, getting caught just enough in one and the other to learn and compose from what the world is expressing, in sometimes nearly inexpressible ways.

We have organized the contributions to the volume in accordance with their emphasis on sensing, moving, and imagining as some of the rhythms taking place during the process of research. Across and converging along these three lines are other overlapping ones, creating a meshwork. Listening is another motion that emerges, in the broad sense of paying attention to what is yet to come, whether it be done through recording, discerning, waiting on things, or to be invited. Presence and absence also emerge thematically throughout the contributions as they deal with distance or proximity, yet also in terms of intensities and silence, speeds and slowness as well as in terms of becoming more or less caught or bewitched. Finally, healing appears in a number of ways, whether it be transformative, shamanic, martial, clinical, or back-to-the-roots movements, personal or collective, territorial or aerial. In a sense weathering or inscribing ourselves in worldly human and more-than-human processes is a kind of healing. The evoked "methods" per se are those of filming, recording, interviewing, listening, searching the archive, drawing, walking, mapping, (web) surfing, participant observation, all of which are done through sensing, moving, and imagining understood as occurring on a plane of immanence in a world in flux and thus always exceeding the execution of a technique. Whether it be more specifically in shooting ranges, homes, forests, mountains, rituals, on roads, trails, or in classroom settings, all the accounts come from experience or in co-responsivity to content, context, or topic, making rhizome or coupling with winds, falcons, plants, water, people, reindeer, novelists, philosophers, or other anthropologists. Overall, we point toward doing "slow anthropology" to which we might want to hold on to as a principle for the discipline; to allow things of interest to emerge unforcefully, waiting for the right timing, sometimes in an untimely or un-tuned manner to create a counterpoint. Our search after method aims to maximize possibilities of doing meaningful research, steering in ways that add value and offer new compositions that will never exhaust themselves.

How does this matter? Considering the amount of research done in the positivistic objective manner that excessively favors decomposition—whether it be too much striation, grids, or information—we have to consider that we take part in this process. Taking the world apart or out of context in research breaks it up in worldly practices. While it is not to say that one kind of research is better than another, since both can be done in beneficial and fortuitous ways, it is at least to say that we should attend to the process of doing research while it is happening since it inevitably takes part in making up the world it wants to know. It appears of utmost importance to do research in co-constructive, subtle, and meaningful ways, supposing it will make such corresponding worlds through its process and beyond. Hence the need for powerful anthropologies attuned to ways in which the world unfolds and might unfold differently, perhaps more carefully and joyfully, augmenting desires and efforts to persevere in existence, or in other words, creating space for life to proliferate.

Julie Laplante is Professor in Anthropology at the University of Ottawa. She works in phenomenological approaches in anthropology with interests in indigenous and humanitarian medicine, attuning to bodily, clinical, sensorial, and sonorous abilities in healing with plants or molecules. Her fieldwork in the Brazilian Amazon and at two edges of the Indian Ocean (South Africa, Java Indonesia) has more recently moved to Cameroon. She produced the anthropological film *Jamu Stories* (2015) and is the author of *Pouvoir guérir* (2004) and *Healing Roots* (2015, 2018).

INDEX

www.ingramcontent.com/pod-product-compliance
Lightning Source LLC
Chambersburg PA
CBHW070914030426
42336CB00014BA/2416
* 9 7 8 1 7 8 9 2 0 9 3 8 9 *